Significant Events and the People Who Shaped Them

Volume 3: *Indian Removal to the Antislavery Movement (1825-1852)*

Indian Removal
Black Hawk, John Ross, Winfield Scott

Industrialization
Samuel Slater, Eli Whitney, Harriet Hanson Robinson

Women and Reform
Sarah Grimké and Angelina Grimké Weld, Susan B. Anthony, Amelia Jenks Bloomer

Plantation System
James Henry Hammond, Harriet A. Jacobs, Mary Boykin Chesnut

Slave Resistance
Denmark Vesey, Nat Turner, John Quincy Adams

Antislavery Movement
David Walker, William Lloyd Garrison, Frederick Douglass, Sojourner Truth, Harriet Beecher Stowe

Volume 4: *Westward Movement to the Civil War (1829-1865)*

Westward Movement
Christopher "Kit" Carson, Marcus Whitman and Narcissa Prentiss Whitman, John Augustus Sutter

Mexican War
José Antonio Navarro, Sam Houston, Zachary Taylor, John Charles Frémont and Jessie Ann Benton Frémont

Transcendental and Romantic Movements
Henry David Thoreau, Margaret Fuller, Nathaniel Hawthorne

Pre-Civil War Controversies
Stephen A. Douglas, Dred Scott, John Brown

Civil War
Abraham Lincoln, Robert E. Lee, William Tecumseh Sherman, Martin Robinson Delany, Anna Ella Carroll, Mathew B. Brady, Walt Whitman

(Continued on inside back cover)

PROFILES IN AMERICAN HISTORY

Immigration to Women's Rights and Roles

1873
The Comstock Law bars written discussion of birth control.

1889
Jane Addams founds Hull House as a refuge for the downtrodden in Chicago.

1892
The Chinese Exclusion Act bars Chinese immigrants to the United States for ten years. It is extended in 1902 for an additional ten years.

1906
Sinclair Lewis's *Jungle* stirs President Theodore Roosevelt to investigate the meat-packing industry.

1908
Henry Ford revolutionizes the automobile industry and American transportation by unveiling the Model T.

1909
Herbert Croly's *Promise of America* heralds the progressive era. The National Association for the Advancement of Colored People is founded.

1914
World War I begins in Europe.

1916
Margaret Sanger opens the first birth control clinic in America.

1917
The United States enters World War I.

1919
John L. Lewis becomes head of the United Mine Workers. The "Red Scare" upsets American society as some look to the Russian Revolution as a model.

1921
Congress sets immigration quotas drastically reducing the number of immigrants to the United States.

1925
Tennessee tries and convicts Thomas Scopes for daring to teach about evolution.

1927
Italian immigrants Nicola Sacco and Bartolomeo Vanzetti are executed for a 1921 murder after a lengthy battle in the courts.

1929
A stock market crash marks the beginning of the Great Depression.

1935
John L. Lewis founds the Congress of Industrial Organizations.

PROFILES IN AMERICAN HISTORY

Significant Events and the People Who Shaped Them

Immigration to Women's Rights and Roles

JOYCE MOSS

and

GEORGE WILSON

AN IMPRINT OF GALE RESEARCH INC.
AN INTERNATIONAL THOMSON PUBLISHING COMPANY

PROFILES IN AMERICAN HISTORY:

Significant Events and the People Who Shaped Them

VOLUME 6: IMMIGRATION TO WOMEN'S RIGHTS AND ROLES

Joyce Moss and George Wilson

Staff
Carol DeKane Nagel, *U•X•L Developmental Editor*
Thomas L. Romig, *U•X•L Publisher*

Christine Nasso, *Acquisitions Editor*

Shanna P. Heilveil, *Production Assistant*
Evi Seoud, *Assistant Production Manager*
Mary Beth Trimper, *Production Director*

Mary Krzewinski, *Cover and Page Designer*
Cynthia Baldwin, *Art Director*
Arthur Chartow, *Technical Design Services Manager*

The Graphix Group, *Typesetting*

Moss, Joyce, 1951-
Profiles in American history : significant events and the people who shaped them / Joyce Moss and George Wilson.
p. cm.
Includes bibliographical references and index.
Contents: 6. Immigration to Women's Rights and Roles
ISBN 0-8103-9207-0 (set) : $225.00. — ISBN 0-8103-9213-5 (v. 6) : $29.95
1. United States—History—Juvenile literature. 2. United States—Biography—Juvenile literature.
I. Wilson, George, 1920–. II. Title.
E178.M897 1994 920.073
973—dc20
94-6677
CIP

∞™ This book is printed on acid-free paper that meets the minimum requirements of American National Standard for Information Sciences—Permanence Paper for Printed Library Materials, ANSI Z39.48-1984.

Printed in the United States of America

Published simultaneously in the United Kingdom by Gale Research International Limited
(An affiliated company of Gale Research Inc.)

I(T)P™
The trademark ITP is used under license.

Contents

Reader's Guide

The many noteworthy individuals who shaped U.S. history from the exploration of the continent to the present day cannot all be profiled in one eight-volume work. But those whose stories are told in *Profiles in American History* meet one or more of the following criteria. The individuals:

- Directly affected the outcome of a major event in U.S. history
- Represent viewpoints or groups involved in that event
- Exemplify a role played by common citizens in that event
- Highlight an aspect of that event not covered in other entries

Format

Volumes of *Profiles in American History* are arranged by chapter. Each chapter focuses on one particular event and opens with an overview and detailed time line of the event that places it in historical context. Following are biographical profiles of two to seven diverse individuals who played active roles in the event.

Each biographical profile is divided into four sections:

- **Personal Background** provides details that predate and anticipate the individual's involvement in the event
- **Participation** describes the role played by the individual in the event and its impact on his or her life
- **Aftermath** discusses effects of the individual's actions and subsequent relevant events in his or her life
- **For More Information** provides sources for further reading on the individual

Additionally, sidebars containing interesting details about the events and individuals profiled, ranging from numbers of war casualties to famous quotes to family trees, are sprinkled throughout the text.

Additional Features

Maps are provided to assist readers in traveling back through time to an America arranged differently from today. Portraits and illustrations of individuals and events as well as excerpts from primary source materials are also included to help bring history to life. Sources of all quoted material are cited parenthetically within the text, and complete bibliographic information is listed at the end of the entry. A full bibliography of scholarly sources consulted in preparing the volume appears in the book's back matter.

Cross references are made in the entries, directing readers to other entries in the volume that elaborate on individuals connected in some way to the person under scrutiny. In addition, a comprehensive subject index provides easy access to people and events mentioned throughout the volume.

Comments and Suggestions

We welcome your comments on this work as well as your suggestions for individuals to be featured in future editions of *Profiles in American History.* Please write: Editors, *Profiles in American History,* U·X·L, 835 Penobscot Bldg., Detroit, Michigan 48226-4094; call toll-free: 1-800-877-4253; or fax: 313-961-6348.

Preface

"There is properly no History; only Biography," wrote great American poet and scholar Ralph Waldo Emerson. *Profiles in American History* explores U.S. history through biography. Beginning with the first contact between Native Americans and Vikings and continuing to the present day, this series offers a unique alternative to traditional texts by emphasizing the roles played by individuals, including many women and minorities, in historical events.

Profiles in American History presents the human story of American events, not the exclusively European or African or Indian or Asian story. The guiding principle in compiling this series has been to achieve balance not only in gender and ethnic background but in viewpoint. Thus the circumstances surrounding an historical event are told from individuals holding opposing views, and even opposing positions. Slaves and slave owners, business tycoons and workers, advocates of peace and proponents of war all are heard. American authors whose works reflect the times—from Walt Whitman to John Steinbeck—are also featured.

The biographical profiles are arranged in groups, clustered around one major event in American history. Yet each individual profile is complete in itself. It is the interplay of these profiles—the juxtaposition of alternative views and experiences within a grouping—that broadens the readers' perspective on the event as a whole and on the participants' roles in particular. It is what makes it possible for *Profiles in American History* to impart a larger, human understanding of events in American history.

Acknowledgments

For their guidance on the choice of events and personalities, the editors are grateful to:

Jonathan Betz-Zall, Children's Librarian, Sno-Isle Regional Library System, Washington

Janet Sarratt, Library Media Specialist, John E. Ewing Junior High School, Gaffney, South Carolina

Michael Salman, Assistant Professor of American History, University of California at Los Angeles

Appreciation is extended to Professor Salman for his careful review of chapter overviews and his guidance on key sources of information about the personalities and events.

For insights into specific personalities, the editors are grateful to Robert Sumpter, History Department Chairman at Mira Costa High School, Manhattan Beach, California.

Deep appreciation is extended to the writers who compiled data and contributed the biographies for this volume of *Profiles in American History:*

Diane Ahrens
Lisa Gabbert
Erika Heet
Dana Huebler
Lawrence K. Orr
Colin Wells

The editors also thank artist Robert Bates for his research and rendering of the maps and Carol Nagel at U•X•L for her careful copy editing.

Introduction

The identity of the United States was largely shaped by events of the late 1800s to the 1920s. Immigration soared at this time, and many feared the new ethnic populations threatened American culture and government as they knew it. Business leaders and middle-class reformers tried vigorously to bring order to the rapidly growing society. The federal government joined them in the effort, with the United States Congress, for example, passing laws to curb immigration.

The era saw more cooperation between government and industry as Americans manufactured materials for use in World War I and then became involved in the war themselves. While the war cemented the power of the federal government at home and abroad, it also revealed tensions in American society. Women were not yet entitled to vote and the U.S. military was segregated, yet America was entering a war, said President Woodrow Wilson, to make the world safe for democracy.

Millions of immigrants were drawn to America by its freedom as well as by the great array of jobs offered in mines, on railroads and sugar plantations, and in factories. A rising number of workers settled in cities, where they endured miserable conditions because there were no living or working standards. Middle-class activists took it upon themselves to rescue the unfortunate masses, while muckrakers—journalists, lawyers, social workers—exposed unjust business practices of the time.

The nation was filled with ideas and remedies for society's ills. Industry, led by a few powerful individuals, ran mostly unchecked and took great advantage of its workers. One of the proposed solutions to business run amok was to follow the socialist notion of government ownership of business and industry. The socialists, though a minority, were greatly feared as a threat to freedom (capitalism) in America. The nation was thus thrown into a "Red Scare," its citizens tending to see reds, or communists, everywhere. Positively, the idea that the national government should exercise strong control in society's working and living conditions began to gain ground.

Also at the turn of the twentieth century the national government emerged as a strong, independent player in world affairs. Though reluctant to enter into global warfare, Wilson nevertheless led the nation into World War I. Aside from supplying materials and a fighting force during the war, America laid the groundwork for the peace talks at its end.

U.S. industry both affected and was affected by the war. The nation's factories produced deadly new weapons and desperately needed goods for the Allied forces. Less obviously, the war changed the makeup of the industrial workforce. Emptied of men who were off at war, factories drew into their ranks women and African Americans. The lure of jobs, in fact, encouraged an ethnic shift in location as thousands of African Americans migrated from southern farms to northern cities.

The factories also produced new consumer items such as the automobile, using new methods such as the moving assembly line. Lowering the cost of goods to a price that was affordable to many, these methods changed life dramatically in America. They also led industry to rely more than in the past on unskilled workers. Soon the labor movement, at first limited to skilled craftsmen, changed and grew as unskilled workers, at great risk, organized into industry-wide unions.

City folk began to acquire some of the new conveniences produced by industry while country folk often did without, which aggravated tensions in American society. One such tension was a dispute over whether the scientific rather than Biblical theory of creation could be taught in American schools. The controversy led to the Scopes Trial, a court case heard in rural Tennessee that was turned into a symbol of the urban overpowering the rural way of life in the early 1900s.

Despite the clashes, society experienced great advances during this period. The rich outpouring of the art, literature, and music of the Harlem Renaissance was enthusiastically received by a number of whites as well as blacks. Americans themselves were beginning to acknowledge and value the different ethnic groups that were coming to make up their nation.

There were more male than female artists at the time, and more men than women in industry. Yet the number of females in the workforce did increase, and women made great political and personal gains during this era. After decades of struggle, women won both the right to plan the size of their families through birth control and the right to vote with the passage of the Nineteenth Amendment.

The turn of the twentieth century was an age of upheaval. It saw major changes in America's ethnic make-up, in city and country life, in school and art, and in the strength of the national government at home and abroad.

Picture Credits

The photographs and illustrations appearing in *Profiles in American History: Significant Events and the People Who Shaped Them,* Volume 6: *Immigration to Women's Rights and Roles* were received from the following sources:

On the cover: **Courtesy of the Department of Special Collections, University Research Library, University of California at Los Angeles:** Margaret Sanger; **courtesy of the Library of Congress:** Marcus Garvey, Clarence Darrow.

Courtesy of the Library of Congress: pages 4, 23, 25, 33, 52, 65, 71, 77, 90, 107, 109, 115, 123, 137, 143, 150, 173, 176, 183, 185, 189, 197, 204, 213, 244, 245, 248, 251, 258, 265, 269; **courtesy of the *International Examiner:*** page 7; **courtesy of the National Archives:** page 17; ***Jewish Daily Forward:*** page 29; **courtesy the Department of Special Collections, University Research Library, University of California at Los Angeles:** pages 51, 89, 181, 233, 255, 264; **courtesy of the *New Republic:*** page 55; **courtesy of David Sinclair:** page 80; **William H. Walker Collection, Department of Rare Books and Prints, Mudd Library, Princeton University Libraries:** page 117; **UPI/Bettmann:** page 160; **courtesy of the United States Information Agency:** pages 167, 223; **AP/Wide World Photos:** page 218; **courtesy of the Jane Belo Estate:** page 239.

Immigration

1860

Chinese immigration to U.S. begins to increase; about 264,000 appear on the West Coast by end of century.

1870s–1880s

Mobs burn Chinese homes in San Francisco, California, and kill Chinese workers in cities of the West.

1873

Chinese immigrant **Chin Gee-hee** moves to Seattle, Washington.

1880

Origin of most U.S. immigrants changes from northern and western Europe to southern and eastern Europe.

1882

Chinese Exclusion Act bans entrance of Chinese into the U.S. for ten years. **Abraham Cahan** moves to the U.S. from eastern Europe.

1892

Chinese Exclusion Act is extended for ten years. Japanese immigrate to Hawaii and California.

1899–1914

About 280,000 Mexicans migrate to the U.S.

1900–1910

About 5.8 million immigrants arrive from eastern and southern Europe.

1902

Chinese Exclusion Act is renewed. Cahan becomes editor of *Jewish Daily Forward.*

1907

U.S. government makes gentleman's agreement with Japan to stop its workers from immigrating to the U.S.

1910

40 percent of New York's population is foreign born.

1921

Nicola Sacco and **Bartolomeo Vanzetti** are arrested, convicted, and sentenced to death for theft and murder.

1921

Congress sets a quota on immigrants based on their nation of origin.

1924

Congress passes National Origins Act, lowering quota on total number of immigrants to 164,667 per year.

1927

Congress again lowers quota on immigrants to 150,000 per year. Sacco and Vanzetti die in the electric chair.

IMMIGRATION

Before 1880 three-fourths of America's immigrants came from northern and western Europe. They emigrated mostly from the British Isles, Germany, and Scandinavia, the Irish and the Germans becoming the largest groups of newcomers. But the Europeans were not the only immigrant populations, and in some regions they were not the most important. Around the mid-1800s, the California gold strike and the building of railroads attracted Chinese immigrants. Mexicans too crossed the border to work the mines and build railroads.

All these early immigrants would be dwarfed by the great tide of immigration that began in the 1880s. Called the "new immigrants," the post-1880 wave came from southern and eastern Europe. Largest among the new immigrant groups were the Italian Catholics and Eastern European Jews.

The immigrants came from Italy, Russia, Greece, and other lands for various reasons: to escape famine, disease, or religious massacres. The typical immigrant, a young, single man with few skills, intended to find a job, work for a few years, then, having earned enough money, return to his homeland. (About 40 percent of those who immigrated to America from 1900 to 1910 would in fact return to their native lands.) There were exceptions. Few Jews—who had long suffered persecution because of religious and other dif-

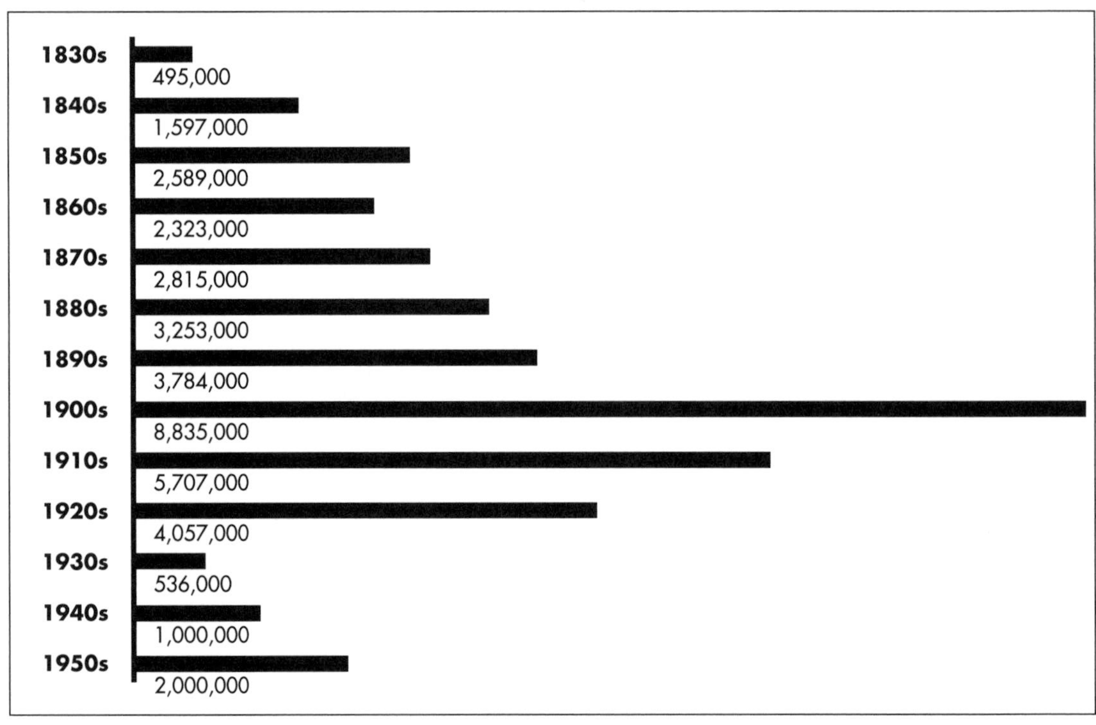

▲ **Immigration to the United States by decade, 1830-1950**

ferences—planned to return. And some immigrants voyaged back and forth repeatedly.

A job-placement system developed among the Italian immigrants. Labor agents, called *padrones,* would greet young males when their ships docked on the East Coast and, for a price, send them wherever industry needed a large supply of labor. In similar fashion, Chinese merchant companies on the West Coast found jobs for Chinese laborers. Under **Chin Gee-hee,** an immigrant himself, the Wah Chong Company became the largest Chinese labor agent in the Pacific Northwest.

Roughly 264,000 Chinese immigrated to the United States between 1860 and 1900, forming a large minority in the West. From railroad construction to mining and factory work, they were hired to perform the most dangerous and dirtiest jobs. Other Americans, both native-born and immigrant, cast the Chinese as scapegoats during hard times. When depression struck in the 1870s, for example, and whites had trouble finding jobs, they blamed the Chinese. Venting their anger, mobs burned Chinese homes and killed Chinese workers in San Francisco, Seattle, and elsewhere.

Congress swung into action the next decade, passing the Chinese Exclusion Act of 1882. The act, which banned Chinese immigrants from the United States for ten years, became the first of many ethnic barriers written into law. The ban on the Chinese was extended in 1892 for another ten years, then extended and lengthened in 1902. It was followed, in 1907, by the Gentlemen's Agreement to exclude Japanese workers. According to this agreement, the Japanese already in the United States would be treated well if Japan stopped permitting its workers to leave for America.

Meanwhile, Italians continued to immigrate in droves. From 1900 to 1910, about 5.8 million immigrants arrived from southern and eastern Europe. About 3 million were Italians and 2 million were Jews. Immigrants flocked to cities, forming with their children about 75 percent of the population in New York, Chicago, and Boston. They began at the bottom of the ladder, working in mining, construction, and similar fields. There were some ethnic patterns. Jews often worked in the garment industry; Poles, in the steel industry. **Bartolomeo Vanzetti,** an Italian pastry chef, bounced from one hard-labor job to the next, bumping into anti-Italian prejudice. Like other immigrants, Vanzetti eventually found his way into an ethnic neighborhood in Plymouth, Massachusetts. Here, among other Italian Americans, he found the acceptance for which he had thirsted in the larger society. Immigrants were preoccupied at first with making enough to survive, but slowly they built ethnic neighborhoods with features such as synagogues or churches and Italian or Yiddish newspapers.

The larger population held images of the different immigrant groups. Americans thought of Italians as gangsters, for example, an undeserved stereotype since the vast majority were hard-working immigrants. A victim, in his mind, of the prejudice against Italians, Vanzetti was later, along with

▲ **Aboard an immigrant ship**

Nicola Sacco, accused of theft and murder and then executed on flimsy evidence. Whether or not Sacco or Vanzetti was in fact guilty has remained unclear to the present day.

While ethnic neighborhoods seemed to be one solid unit, they actually included separate subsections. The Lower East Side of New York City, for example, was a Jewish immigrant district with subsections for Hungarian Jews, Russian Jews, Romanian Jews, and more. Fleeing Lithuania in 1882, the year the Chinese were first excluded, **Abraham Cahan** settled in the Lower East Side. He became a factory worker, writer, and finally editor of the *Forward,* a Yiddish newspaper that went far in helping Jewish newcomers adjust to life in America.

All three immigrants—Chin, Vanzetti, and Cahan—set out to earn a decent living in America. There was, however, an added goal for Vanzetti and Cahan. Each had his own idea of how government should operate that contradicted the type of democracy then practiced in America. Vanzetti, like a minority of others in his time, favored anarchy, or the absence of any structured form of government. Cahan at first supported socialism, public ownership of the industries. The spread of such ideas by "foreigners," felt long-time Americans, threatened the well-being of the country. And the continuing stream of immigrants threatened their own job security. Developments in industry had greatly transformed the work force so that there was less and less need for skilled labor. An unskilled, non-English-speaking immigrant could operate a machine and willingly did so for a lower salary than most old-time Americans. To crush the threat to their jobs, Americans moved to limit immigration.

The first law that set a quota was the Immigration Act of 1921, which looked at the total number of newcomers from a European country in 1910 and said it would now allow 3 percent of that number to immigrate to America. So if 300,000 newcomers had arrived from Italy in 1910, America would open its borders to 3,000 Italians in 1922. The result was a huge drop in the total number of immigrants to around 310,000 in 1922. New laws further reduced the total to 165,000 in 1924, then to 150,000 in 1927. Though there would be changes and exceptions through the years, America would continue to limit immigration by placing a quota on other countries until 1965.

Chin Gee-hee

1844-1929

Personal Background

Toishan. Chin Gee-hee was born in 1844 in Toishan, a region in southeastern China inhabited mostly by peasants. During the mid- to late 1800s, a series of natural and social disasters hit the region, driving peasants from their homeland in search of better opportunities.

By the beginning of the 1800s, China had closed all its ports except for Canton in the Toishan region in protest to the British importing of opium. Britain objected and wars, known as the "Opium Wars," began. After China lost the Opium Wars of 1839-42, Western powers reduced the country to a semicolonial state with British-occupied Hong Kong as a trade center. China's traditional farms, which grew food for the peasants to eat, gave way to large farms that sold crops for money. This transformation led many peasants to lose their smaller farms. Massive social unrest in the form of three rebellions killed tens of thousands of people. Earthquakes, typhoons, famine, drought, and epidemics between 1851 and 1908 left those still alive poverty stricken. The citizens of Toishan, because of their location near the ports of Macao and Hong Kong, had been exposed to Western contact and ideas. When the need for cheap labor arose in the American West, many individuals from Toishan left their land to work.

▲ Chin Gee-hee

Event: Chinese immigration and exclusion.

Role: Chin Gee-hee immigrated to the United States from China as a boy. He worked as a laborer in the American West, surviving the racial tensions of his era to build a successful business in Seattle, Washington.

Coolie labor. Economic developments in America and Africa led to the rise of the Coolie trade, a system of virtual slave labor that flourished in China in the mid-1800s. The discovery of gold and the construction of the American transcontinental railroad required massive amounts of cheap labor. With the abolition of black slavery in 1863, America looked toward China to provide the labor. Chinese recruiters, called *crimps,* often used dishonest methods to find workers. They deceived, kidnapped, even drugged peasants and forced them to work in foreign lands. Unwilling peasants were tied up by their thumbs or plunged into cold water until they agreed to leave.

Coolie, meaning "hired servant," was used to describe the Chinese unskilled laborer. The conditions of coolie status were so harsh that peasants had to pass a medical examination before they signed a contract. Once a coolie signed a labor contract, the "credit ticket" system was enforced. Chinese coolie dealers paid the coolie's passage to the new country, and the peasant, forced to work under extremely harsh conditions, paid back the money at an extraordinarily high interest rate. Additionally, the voyage itself was grim. The coolies traveled on crowded cargo ships, where lack of food, water, fresh air, and medical supplies often led to the death of the Chinese voyagers.

Opportunity. Chin Gee-hee grew up in a poor family in Luk Chuen, in the Toishan region. One day, as he walked to the market to sell the soy sauce his father made, a group of boys playing games accidentally knocked him over, breaking the clay pots containing his family's wares. Chin could do nothing except pick up the broken pieces of pottery. A man named Uncle Hung observed Chin's misfortune and recognized that for a poor Toishan family the spilled soy sauce and broken pots were a great loss. Uncle Hung had been a coolie and returned to China from America with some money. He planned to sail once again for America and invited Chin to accompany him. Chin accepted Uncle Hung's offer.

News of gold in California reached Hong Kong as early as 1848. America soon became known as a place to get rich quickly, and San Francisco was affectionately titled "Gold Mountain." Tired of the difficult life in Toishan, many people viewed America as a place offering new opportunities.

Ocean vessel advertisements claiming a surplus of Californian gold helped fuel the Chinese dream of riches. Transportation was expensive, however. Some families pooled their money to send one member to America to work. In return, this member sent back money to the family still in China. Poorer people borrowed money and paid it back at very high interest rates. Uncle Hung's offer made it easier for Chin to reach America because Chin would not owe money to outsiders. Together they survived the difficult three-month journey to San Francisco, docking sometime in the late 1850s or early 1860s.

Participation: Chinese Immigration and Exclusion

Work—jobs and conditions. The expansion of the American West required vast amounts of manpower. Settlers generally welcomed the Chinese because they worked at distasteful and difficult jobs. In some areas of the West there were few women; Chinese men filled in gaps of frontier society by taking undesirable positions in "feminine" work areas of the time, such as the kitchen and laundry. John McDougal, the governor of California in 1851, stated in a message to Congress that the Chinese were "one of the most worthy classes of our newly adopted citizens—to whom the climate and the character of these lands are particularly suited" (Coolidge, pp. 22-23).

The Chinese filled various positions in frontier society. The railroads alone hired 15,000 Chinese workers during the 1860s to tie rail in a mad race to finish the transcontinental project. They worked under harsh and unfair conditions. Chinese workers blasted rock, cleared trees, laid tracks, and worked with pick and shovel. They even worked through the winter of 1866 in snow tunnels, which sometimes collapsed and killed the workers. Chinese men also worked by themselves in abandoned mines or under contract, performing backbreaking labor without mechanization. Yet the Chinese laborers were paid only $.84 a day, while the white workers earned $1.75. Chin worked briefly in the California gold mines, then, by 1862, operated a laundry at a lumber company in Port Gamble, Washington.

Chin eventually earned enough money to buy a wife from China. In those days, Chinese women were scarce in America. American women and Chinese men did not generally associate with each other, so in order to marry, a Chinese man had to bring over a woman from China. Chin and his wife had their first baby, a son, in 1875, and a daughter a few years later.

Domestic agencies were formed in the United States to direct the Chinese immigrants, and most immigrants found jobs through these agencies. These companies, called *hui-kans,* organized around geographical boundaries in China. *Hui-kans* acted as a form of government, resolving conflicts, providing aid and social services, maintaining order, and imposing fees. Eventually, these companies grew quite powerful. During the 1860s, six major San Francisco–based Chinese companies claimed to control all Chinese labor on the Pacific Coast.

Wah Chong Company. Chin moved to Seattle from Port Gamble in 1873. He laid rail for the Central Pacific Company, excavating rock and driving railroad spikes into the ground. Eventually, Chin realized that he could earn more money by working with a Chinese company than as a laborer. He joined the Wah Chong Company, founded by Chun Hock, one of the most important Chinese merchant shops of its time. The company, among other things, sold imported Chinese goods to people in the United States. Also, like many other merchant companies, it was heavily involved in contracting Chinese labor. Wah Chong found Chinese men in need of work and brought them to employers who requested workers, and for this service took a portion of the worker's paycheck.

The company contracted labor to Northwest lumber camps, canneries, coal mines, and fishing industries. The company was responsible for the labor involved in grading many Seattle streets. As the broker, Chin sought out labor contracts from companies and recruited new immigrants just off the boats to fill them. He paid the laborers and took a percentage of their earnings. The Wah Chong Company also functioned like a *hui-kan,* providing such services to its workers as a mailing address, translation services, and the location of eating and sleeping quarters. Under Chin, the Wah Chong Company became the largest labor contractor in the Pacific Northwest area.

Growing tensions. During the early years of immigration, white settlers tolerated the Chinese but treated them as inferior. During the 1860s, Chinese immigrants were not allowed to vote or testify against a white person in court and were forced to pay special taxes. During the 1870s, racial prejudice increased. When the railroad was finished in 1869, thousands of Chinese looked for work elsewhere. Then the boom economy slowed and jobs grew scarcer; white settlers saw the Chinese as a threat to their economic security. Settlers viewed the immigrants as a "Yellow Peril," foreseeing future throngs of Chinese people who would arrive to grab the remainder of the country's shrinking riches.

Many factors contributed to racial tensions of the day. White workers resented the Chinese because they accepted cheaper wages, and employers fueled these feelings by hiring them to save money. Employers also occasionally hired the Chinese to break strikes. They would give the Chinese temporary jobs while they bargained with the white workers over working conditions and salary.

Many Chinese intended to return to China and therefore did not adopt Western ways. They kept their own cultural identity by resisting white religion and staying with traditional styles of community. For example, Chinese culture promotes interdependence among people. When a person needs help, the family or other community members provide support. In return, the person gives later earnings back to the providers. In many ways, this system of values clashed with the one practiced on the individual-oriented frontier of the American West.

Exclusion. Congress passed a series of anti-Chinese legislative acts beginning in the mid-1870s. In 1879 the number of vessels arriving from China was limited. In 1880 a treaty was signed with China allowing the United States to legally restrict immigration. In 1882 Congress passed the most significant legislation, the Chinese Exclusion Act, which banned the immigration of Chinese laborers for ten years. Signed by President Chester A. Arthur, the act marked a change in U.S. policy from one of open, unrestricted immigration to a closed system. This act affected Asians for a long time. Using the Exclusion Act as a foundation, many new laws were passed in order to keep Asians out of the country for the next sixty years. Restrictive immigration policies against Asians were not reversed until the Immigration Act of 1965. Furthermore, anti-Chinese sentiment led to the deportation of many of those already in America.

The 1880s and riots. During the 1880s, violent anti-Chinese sentiment led to a series of riots. White workers forced employers to fire their Chinese workers and hire white ones instead. The demand spread to Port Madison, Washington Territory, in December 1875. In 1877, in the Port Gamble lumber mill, employers had to replace Chinese workers with whites due to local hostility. The most significant event occurred on September 5, 1885, in Rock Springs, Wyoming. Twenty-eight Chinese were murdered in a mining area, with eleven burned and several dismembered. The event, known as the Wyoming Massacre, sparked racial violence across the West.

That same day, eleven Chinese were murdered at a farm in the Puget Sound, Washington, area. Two days later, in Washington, D.C., a national workers organization was formed called the Knights of Labor. Its members were openly anti-Chinese. On September 11, 1885, in Newcastle, Washington, one Chinese was kidnapped and burned and the sleeping quarters of thirty-seven others were destroyed. That same month, the Port Townsend mill fired all Chinese workers. In a statement of violent opposition to Chinese workers, Dan Cronin issued a warning in the *Seattle Post-Intelligencer* of September 22, 1885. Cronin, a member of the Knights of Labor, assured readers that if the Chinese were not removed there would be riot and bloodshed. He and other workers in Seattle did not intend, he said, to see their wives and children starve.

On September 18, government officials met in Seattle. They issued a warning to all Chinese in the Washington area to leave their homes by November 1. Chin, however, along with other businessmen in the area, ignored the order and continued to conduct business by advertising cheap labor on short notice. On November 3, 1885, a group of 500 men gathered in the Chinese section of Tacoma and rounded up the inhabitants. They forced the Chinese to marched eight miles to the train station. The Chinese waited twenty-four hours for a train to Portland, Oregon. Two people died of exposure, and three days later the Chinese houses and businesses of the area were burned to the ground.

When news of Tacoma's events reached Seattle, Chin, now a noted leader in the Chinese community, wired the Chinese consulate for help. Through his business dealings, he knew several important people in the community, including its mayor. Chin met with the mayor several times during the following months. Little was achieved, however. On February 7, 1886, committees entered the homes of Chinese people at daybreak, rounding up Chin and the remaining Chinese people in the community for deportation. About 100 Chinese boarded the *Queen of the Pacific,* but were saved for a few days by a habeas corpus. (A habeas corpus states that nobody can be imprisoned or deported until they come before a court of law.) The Chinese on board, including Chin and his family, were told they could return to their quarters until another ship arrived. As the Chinese, escorted by armed militia, walked down the wharf, a mob attacked the group, crying, "Kill them! Put them in the bay! Drown them!" A riot ensued, leaving several people dead and wounded. During the riot, Chin and his family were kidnapped by the mob and then rescued by a government force. President Grover Cleveland declared a state of emergency in Seattle and sent federal troops to quell the riots. The Fourteenth Infantry stayed in the city from February 10 to February 22, 1886, when marital law was lifted. In the end, the majority of the Chinese population left or were deported, although the community allowed Chin and a few other wealthy and respected merchants to remain.

Aftermath

Railroad baron. By the late 1880s, racial tensions slowly ebbed because the Chinese population was small and Washington Territory was applying for statehood. Chin, with support from his business contacts, remained in Seattle throughout the riots. In 1888 he opened his own business, the Quong Tuck Company. This company paralleled the Wah Chong company, engaging in both general merchandising and labor contracting. After a city fire burned his building in 1889, Chin rebuilt it. His new structure became the first brick building in Seattle.

Chin made several trips back to China. Transportation in Toishan was poor. People walked or rode in sedan chairs and transported materials in handcarts. These conditions inspired Chin, who had gained much railroad experience in America, to build a railroad in Toishan. In 1904 Chin left the Quong Tuck Company to his son and son-in-law and returned to China to begin this project. Affected by the growing nationalist movement in China and by prejudice in America, Chin determined to build the railroad without any foreign loans, investors, or engineers. This feat gained enormous support from both the local people and the Toishanese abroad. Preparing for the venture, Chin returned to the United States several times to raise money from the Chinese community in America for the Sunning Railroad Company.

Many problems plagued the Sunning Railroad during its construction between 1906 and 1920. Chin fought the Chinese government for more than a year to obtain the permit for his rail. He battled local clan chiefs, who prevented the railroad from passing through their territories. Also, the Sunning Railroad depended on imported raw materials, such as coal, to keep it running. These problems led to such financial difficulties for Chin that he eventually asked for foreign money to keep the railroad running.

Yet the Sunning Railroad ultimately contributed to the development of Toishan. Towns along the route prospered, houses and highways were constructed, and industry grew. The rail also influenced class structure by forming the first core of modern industrial workers in the region.

Despite the Sunning's technical difficulties, Chin remained optimistic. In letters to friends in Seattle, he wrote that he pictured a rail leading all the way to Europe and dreamed of a free Chinese port. He was decorated with an honorary peacock feather by the Emperor of China and was recognized both in China and in the United States as a community leader. Chin realized the immigrant dream of wealth and success, even contributing to the growth of his native land. The railroad, however, fell into disrepair after Chin died. In 1939 it was finally dismantled to hinder the Japanese invasion of China.

All his life, Chin remained true to his Chinese upbringing. For example, in the Chinese tradition, Chin had six wives. This helped assure him of a son to carry on the family name. When his daughter-in-law did not produce a male child, he forced his son to abandon his wife and daughter and return to China. Chin died in 1929, his critics faulting him for leaving his poor granddaughter without an inheritance.

For More Information

Chin, Art. *Golden Tassels: A History of the Chinese in Washington, 1857-1977.* Seattle: Chin, 1977.

Coolidge, Mary. *Chinese Immigration.* New York: H. Holt & Company, 1909.

McCunn, Ruthanne Lum. *Chinese American Portraits: Personal Histories, 1828-1988.* San Francisco: Chronicle Books, 1988.

Bartolomeo Vanzetti

1888-1927

Personal Background

Birth in Italy. The oldest of Giovan Battista and Giovanna Nivello Vanzetti's five children, Bartolomeo Vanzetti was born in Villafalletto, Italy, on June 11, 1888. A rural community surrounded by mountains and olive groves, Villafalletto provided a wealth of outdoor adventures. Young Bartolomeo, who quickly developed a love of nature, spent most of his early years playing in the woods and working on the family farm. He liked also to garden, bird-watch, and play the guitar—hobbies his mother, to whom Bartolomeo was extremely close, encouraged.

Education. As well as loving music, Vanzetti was a born leader and often mimicked the Catholic priests in his church, leading his friends in singing Mass. Though a bright boy, Bartolomeo was only sent to school for three years because his father did not believe in formal education. The boy taught himself to read and write and gained most of his education through observation.

Helping out his father from the time he was a small child, Bartolomeo also taught himself to be a good worker. He did everything from farm labor to bartending in his father's café. Because of his strong work ethic and ability to learn on his own, up until the age of thirteen it looked as if Bartolomeo would follow in his father's footsteps and take over the family businesses. But in 1901, Giovan

▲ **Bartolomeo Vanzetti and Nicola Sacco**

Event: Italian immigration; Sacco and Vanzetti case.
Role: A strong advocate of workers' rights, Bartolomeo Vanzetti came to America from Italy seeking freedom and opportunity but instead found persecution and discrimination as the United States turned strongly anti-immigrant in the face of World War I and the Red Scare. Vanzetti was ultimately executed along with fellow Italian immigrant Nicola Sacco for a crime he did not commit.

Vanzetti sent his son away to learn a trade. The move changed Bartolomeo's life and attitude toward business and capitalism forever.

Apprenticeship. When Bartolomeo turned thirteen, his father apprenticed him to a baker in a distant city to learn to be a pastry chef. Bartolomeo was sent to Cuneo, away from his family and friends, and put to work fifteen hours a day, seven days a week. He worked in a hot, unventilated kitchen on his feet all day without a break and, despite this abrupt end to his carefree childhood, never complained. Bartolomeo wrote home to his parents shortly after his arrival in Cuneo that he was content and in good health: "I am happy and I like staying here" (Feuerlicht, p. 16). Yet it was apparent that none of these claims were true. By December he wrote to his parents: "I wish terribly to see you, and am saddened by the thought that so much time still separates us" (Feuerlicht, p. 17). He felt lonely, spending his first Christmas away from home.

But despite being overworked and homesick, Bartolomeo kept up his breakneck work pace for nearly five years out of respect for his father. Finally, however, the harsh working conditions took their toll not only on Bartolomeo's emotions but also on his health, and he was sent home in 1907 with a severe lung ailment called pleurisy.

Now nineteen, "Bartolo," as he was known to his friends, lay bedridden at home for three months battling his illness. He had by this time become quite resentful toward his father for sending him away and denying him an education. While confined to his bed, Bartolomeo began to read and further educate himself, as he had done as a child, choosing history and literature as his two favorite topics of study. His mother, as she had done with his gardening and music, encouraged him in his efforts while she nursed him back to health.

Changing philosophies. As Bartolomeo read, he not only gained knowledge of the outside world and various political philosophies but also began to question and change his religious beliefs. When he recovered enough to get out of bed, he began to associate with the town scholars and further question the ideals his parents had taught him. He said that though his mother was responsible for "all that is good in me ... even my parents, in spite of their love and goodwill, they teach me many wrong ideas, false principles, and a false divinity" (Avrich, p. 18).

Bartolomeo had experienced firsthand some very negative aspects of capitalism, or the economic system of private ownership of goods and businesses, as it was then commonly practiced: unbearable working conditions, long work hours, and poor pay for the workers—while the business owners prospered. Because of his experience, he was beginning to turn against the system and toward believing in the right of workers to earn a decent living and be treated fairly. Bartolomeo thought it was a crime to profit from the labor of others and embraced the social idea of his day that the distribution of goods and services should be according to need, not greed. By the end of 1907, he knew that he would not be able to take over his father's business interests. But, despite his change of heart, Bartolomeo did not voice his feelings to his family. Out of respect, he kept his new ideas to himself until his mother died.

Death. Vanzetti's mother died of cancer shortly after his own recovery. He had spent nearly three months at his mother's bedside, caring for her as she had cared for him, and it was in his arms that she died. Her death was devastating to Vanzetti. He considered that when he buried his mother, he buried part of himself, and he never found another woman to fill her place in his heart.

Immigration. With his mother gone, his strong resentment toward his father, and his firm opposition to taking over the family businesses, Vanzetti felt there was nothing left for him in Italy. Catching the immigration fever, he began to think that perhaps in America "freedom of the mind and ideas" was possible, and he decided to find out (Avrich, p. 19). Though his father was opposed to the move and offered him a well-paying job if he stayed, Vanzetti left Italy and sailed for New York two days before his twentieth birthday in June 1908.

Participation: Sacco and Vanzetti Case

Vanzetti. Vanzetti's image of America soon changed. He arrived in New York City not knowing a soul and had a difficult time finding work and housing. In the big city where job competition was fierce, discrimination—especially against dark-skinned Italian immigrants—was common, and Vanzetti could only get work as a hard laborer, not as a pastry chef, which would have paid much better.

In addition, Vanzetti was often fired from his jobs for defending workers' rights. He began to find out that perhaps "freedom of the mind and ideas" was not possible in America, and he started to think that:

> Here public justice is based on force and brutality, and woe betide the stranger *and particularly the Italian who uses energetic methods to defend his rights;* for him there are the clubs of the police, the prisons and the penal codes. (Feuerlicht, p. 21)

Vanzetti had no idea how prophetic and true that statement actually was. In less than twenty years, he, an Italian, would be executed for, he believed, energetically asserting his rights.

From 1908 to 1913, Vanzetti bounced from job to job and town to town around New England, trying to find decent work. He became a loner and often was forced to sleep in doorways, lining his clothing with newspaper in order to keep warm. Few people were willing to help a foreigner in his position, and he was insulted and looked down upon for being an Italian immigrant, a menial worker, and speaking little English. In most cities, he said, he was treated like "a 'Dago' [dog] to be worked to death." In 1913 Vanzetti moved to Plymouth, Massachusetts, and got a job with the Plymouth Cordage Company, where he hoped to find better working conditions (Avrich, p. 34).

Finds community. For a time, Vanzetti did enjoy better working conditions, but more important, he found living conditions vastly improved. In Plymouth, he discovered the first sense of community he had felt since his Villafalletto childhood.

The original landing site of the Pilgrims, Plymouth had a sizable Italian population, most of whom worked for the Cordage Company. Vanzetti, who understood English but did not speak it very well, could now speak to people in his native Italian. He was, furthermore, among fellow immigrants who did not discriminate against him. Once again, Vanzetti emerged as the leader he had been since a child.

He moved into a boardinghouse with the Alfonsina Brini family, and they became like a second family to him. There Vanzetti pursued all his old pastimes: gardening, playing guitar, and studying. He took English classes and began reading Karl Marx and other socialist and anarchist philosophers' books. Alfonsina Brini, who worked with Vanzetti, was himself an anarchist who believed in the concept of no government and a completely equal society. Voluntary organizations, the thought was, would give enough order to society. Though a very idealistic concept, anarchism was becoming quite popular among the workers in Vanzetti's community. It was appealing to Vanzetti too, and he soon found himself not only attending anarchist meetings with Brini but leading them. An idealist himself, Vanzetti defined anarchy as equality in ownership, rights, and duties among human beings, and he genuinely believed that it was possible in the United States.

First strike. After hearing of other workers around the country striking for better working conditions such as the eight-hour workday and better wages, Vanzetti helped lead a strike to end the fifteen-hour workday at the Plymouth Cordage Company. He picketed, raised money for defense of jailed strikers, and spoke at rallies, but the strike ended with a deal he thought was unfair, and he refused to accept it. As a result, he was labeled an undesirable worker by his former employers and, once again, had great difficulty finding work.

About this time, 1917, America was beginning to send troops to fight in World War I. Like most anarchists, Vanzetti felt that war was a crime against humanity and especially unfair to the poor who had to risk their lives for a government that did little to help them. When the United States began to draft its citizens *and* immigrants to fight overseas, anarchists advocated moving to Mexico until the draft was over. To the unemployed and discouraged Vanzetti, the move sounded like a good idea, so he left.

Mexico. Vanzetti did not consider the move to Mexico a cowardly act, but it was perceived that way. In Vanzetti's trial three years later, his dodging of the draft made jurors and many Americans think less of Vanzetti. One of the headlines in the *Boston Post* read: "Went to Mexico to Escape War Service, He States—Proud of Having Been a Slacker" (Joughin, p. 52).

Mexico proved to be fateful for another reason as well. There, Vanzetti met Nicola Sacco, a fellow Italian anarchist whose name in three years would forever be linked to his.

Sacco. Ferdinando "Nicola" Sacco had emigrated from Italy the same year as Vanzetti but had faired much better in the United States. He found steady employment in shoe factories, married, and had a child. Like Vanzetti, Sacco settled in an Italian community in Massachusetts and took a great interest in the plight of the worker. He participated in many strikes, raised money for the anarchist cause, and attended its meetings.

Having so much in common, Sacco and Vanzetti became friends after they met in Mexico. When the Immigration Act was passed in late 1917, barring non-U.S. citizens from being drafted, Sacco and Vanzetti returned together to their family and friends in the Massachusetts area and became more active than ever in the anarchist movement. The peasant workers' takeover of the government in Russia had just succeeded, and Sacco and Vanzetti felt a similar workers' revolution could occur in the United States. Both of them wrote articles for anarchist newspapers, spoke at rallies, participated in protests and strikes, and raised money for the cause. In addition, they purchased guns and may have associated with a few anarchists who were bombing government officials.

"Red Scare." In response to the communist revolution in the Soviet Union and to increasingly violent radical activity in the United States, the American government began to crack down on revolutionaries. The Russian Revolution had sparked a general panic known as the "Red Scare"—"red" because of the color of the Soviet (Communist) flag—and U.S. authorities began arresting and deporting radicals—those who favored great changes in government. Especially suspect were those with any association to Russian communism, like the anarchists. Congress passed tough laws, such as the Sedition Act, which banned any public statements against the U.S. government.

Salsedo's death and panic. Since anarchists wanted to totally eliminate government, they became a prime target of authorities, and it wasn't long before Sacco and Vanzetti's friends were arrested. When Andrea Salsedo, a member of the same anarchist

▲ **Vanzetti, second from left, at the time of his trial**

organization as Sacco and Vanzetti, was arrested in 1919 and suspiciously died after falling from the roof of his nine-story prison, Sacco and Vanzetti became afraid for their lives. Reading in the newspaper that Salsedo had given authorities the names of his fellow anarchists before his death, Sacco and Vanzetti decided they should get rid of their weapons and anarchist literature before authorities arrived to arrest them. Sacco and Vanzetti might have also been hiding explosives, but the facts are that they were found only with two guns, twenty-three rounds of ammunition, and anarchist literature.

Fate. Sacco and Vanzetti met on the evening of May 5, 1920, and took the train to Bridgewater, Connecticut, where they were to borrow a friend's car. They were then to load the car with their anarchist literature and take it to the country to be destroyed. Sacco was planning to leave for Italy two days later with his family, and Vanzetti was at least going to move from the area. However, Sacco and Vanzetti never got the car or made it to the country. Instead, they were arrested when they arrived at their friend's garage.

It was a case of being in the wrong place at the wrong time. Sacco and Vanzetti had asked to borrow a car that was suspected to be the getaway vehicle in an unsolved crime of theft and murder that had taken place six months earlier. By asking for the car, Sacco and Vanzetti became suspects, and detectives searched them. When they found that each possessed weapons and anarchist literature, police became convinced they had found the men guilty of a crime that had been committed in December 1919. Though both had alibis for the night in question and earnestly denied any participation in the crime, Sacco and Vanzetti were arrested for the murder of a shoe factory guard and theft of the factory payroll and were sent to jail.

The case. Prosecuting attorneys did not find any trace of the money Sacco and Vanzetti had allegedly taken and could not establish that the men were in town on the night the crimes were committed. Also, there were only a handful of highly questionable witnesses who changed their testimony repeatedly. Yet, with public sentiment strongly against Sacco and Vanzetti, they were easily convicted. There was a strong anti-immigrant feeling in America at the time, especially against Italians who were considered to be "the vagrants, paupers, and ... outcasts of Europe" and were associated with organized crime (Feuerlicht, p. 52). In addition, because they could speak little English, were anarchists, and had "deserted" America during the war, the men were ravaged by the American press and pronounced guilty before the trial even began. They were officially convicted in 1921 and sentenced to death.

From 1921 to 1927, Sacco and Vanzetti remained in prison appealing their conviction and trying to convince authorities—and the public—of their innocence. But in appeal after appeal they were struck down. Not even when a man named Celestino Madeiros con-

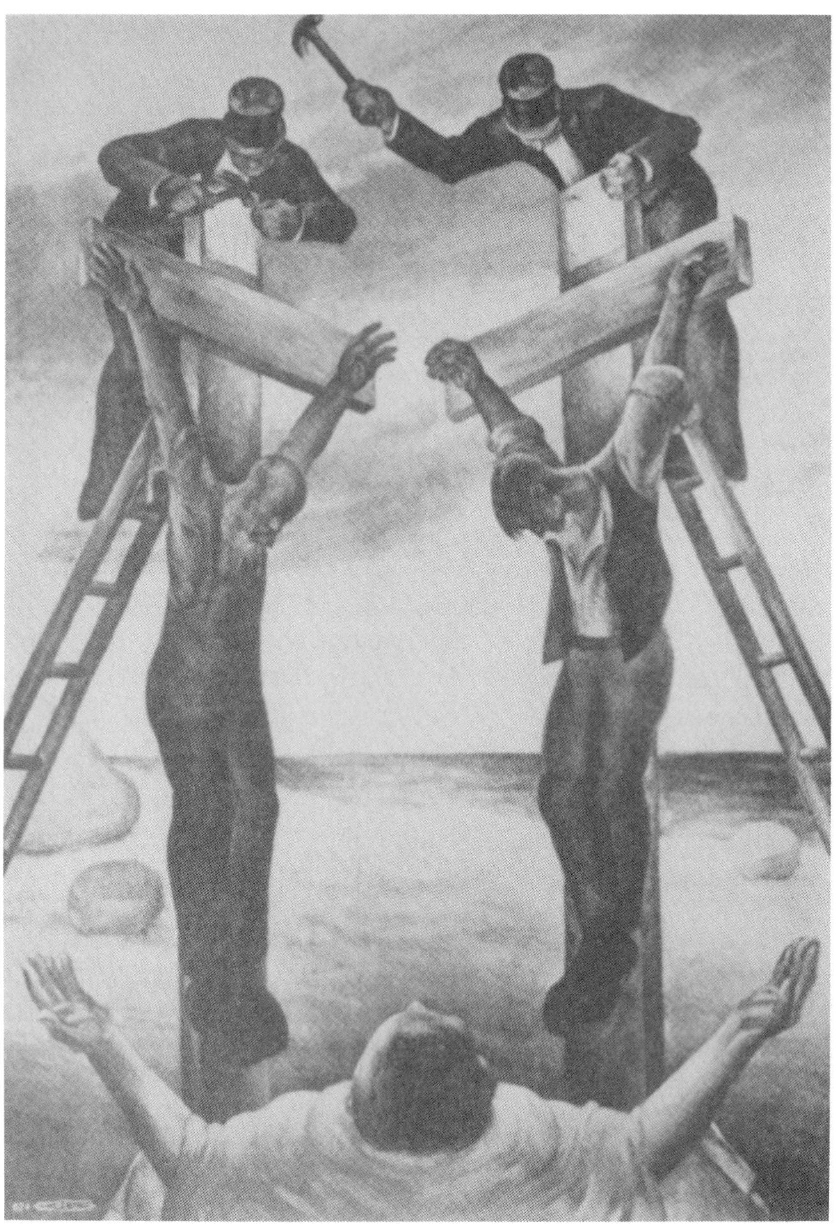

▲ An artist's rendering of Sacco and Vanzetti's execution

fessed to the crime were Sacco and Vanzetti freed. Instead their sentence was carried out. The two died by electrocution on August 23, 1927.

Aftermath

The judgment. Up until the end, Sacco and Vanzetti maintained their innocence and asserted that the only thing they were guilty of was being Italian anarchists in America. In one of his last statements, Vanzetti said:

> I would not wish to a dog or to a snake ... what I have had to suffer for things that I am not guilty of. But my conviction is that I have suffered for things I am guilty of. I am suffering because I am a radical, and indeed I am a radical; I have suffered because I am Italian, and indeed I am an Italian. (Vanzetti in Joughin and Morgan, p. 500)

Though there were relatively few supporters who came to Sacco and Vanzetti's defense during the 1920s, most historians and politicians today agree that their deaths were a terrible miscarriage of justice. In 1977 Massachusetts governor Michael Dukakis declared August 23 to be Sacco and Vanzetti Memorial Day. He stated that "any stigma and disgrace should be forever removed from their names" and called upon Americans to:

> Reflect upon these tragic events, and draw from their historic lessons the resolve to prevent the forces of intolerance, fear and hatred from ever again uniting to overcome rationality, wisdom, and fairness to which our legal system aspires. (Dukakis in Joughin, p. 6)

A tragic chapter in U.S. history, the Sacco and Vanzetti case has come to stand for the type of racial big-

A Few Supporters

Though there weren't many who supported Sacco and Vanzetti while they were alive, there was a vocal minority who not only led a mass protest down the streets of Boston, Massachusetts, after their electrocution but wrote in support of the two men for years. Among them, poet Arthur Davison Fickes wrote "Prayer in Massachusetts," which summarizes the outrage felt over the horrible injustice that occurred. The first few lines follow:

> Upon this soil may no tree ever grow.
> In this land may no lips ever again
> Speak the word justice, now that all men
> know
> Those lips have long boasted in vain.

(Fickes in Joughin and Morgan, p. 387)

otry and breach of human rights the United States Constitution is supposed to protect against. Though Sacco and Vanzetti paid for freedom of expression with their lives, their legacy is serving to protect others from the same type of racial and political persecution that cannot exist in a free society.

For More Information

Avrich, Paul. *The Anarchist Background.* Princeton, New Jersey: Princeton University Press, 1991.

Feuerlicht, Roberta Strauss. *Justice Crucified.* New York: McGraw-Hill, 1977.

Joughin, Louis, ed. *Sacco-Vanzetti: Developments and Reconsiderations.* Boston: Trustees of the Public Library, 1982.

Joughin, Louis, and Edmund M. Morgan. *Legacy of Sacco and Vanzetti.* Chicago: Quadrangle, 1948.

Abraham Cahan

1860-1951

Personal Background

Abraham Cahan was born on July 6, 1860, in Podberezy, Lithuania, at that time a part of Russia. When he was nearly six he moved to the bigger city of Vilnius (considered by Jews to be the Jerusalem or spiritual capital of Lithuania), where he grew up working in the tavern and liquor store his parents and relatives operated.

Close-knit Jewish community. The Cahans lived in an apartment situated directly behind the tavern, amid one of Vilnius's many busy courtyards. "Jermunski's courtyard," as it was called, was filled with peddlers and surrounded by apartments and cafes. The residents were mostly Jewish and provided a nurturing environment in which young Abraham, an only child until his teens, found companionship and learned everything from Sabbath traditions to how to pour beer.

Education and religion. From age six to fourteen, Abraham worked in the tavern and attended *cheder,* or Jewish school. As the grandson of a rabbi and only son of Jewish schoolteachers, Abraham felt a special obligation to excel in religious studies, which he did. Devoting most of his time to learning Yiddish, the language of Jews in eastern Europe, and Hebrew, the ancient language of the Jewish religion and of Jews in the Middle East, he knew very little of the Russian language. Likewise, his studies of Jewish culture and traditions left little time for Russian history.

▲ **Abraham Cahan**

Event: Jewish immigration.
Role: An influential novelist and newspaperman, Abraham Cahan wrote about the Russian Jewish immigrant experience, particularly life in the crowded ghettos and sweatshops of New York's garment district. His work would contribute significantly to the Jewish labor movement and social welfare reform of the 1920s and 1930s.

Learns community sacrifice. Like most Jewish residents of Vilnius, the Cahans were very tied to the community. Poor or wealthy, the families banded together and made sacrifices as necessary. Cahan's family, for example, often did without the traditional Sabbath meal of gefilte fish, puddings, and other favorites, substituting a cheaper meal of challah bread and herring. They then contributed the savings to a community fund so that all Jewish families in their neighborhood could eat equally on the Sabbath. These childhood experiences not only provided Cahan with a lifelong sense of obligation to his fellow Russian Jews, but the practice of shared sacrifice cemented his belief in socialism, or the political and economic system where the means of production and distribution of wealth (farms, factories, stores) are collectively owned by all the workers in a society.

Discovers books. A second strong influence on Cahan's development was books. At the age of fourteen, he discovered the Vilnius Public Library and began studying there five hours a day. Thrilled by the beauty of language, Cahan at this point became especially interested in literature, science, and Russian history.

Public school and socialism. At the same time, Cahan enrolled himself in public school and for the first time stopped attending Jewish school. In public school, as well as through his independent study at the library, he mastered Russian and began making money by filling out government forms in Russian for some of his Jewish classmates who could not write the language. He soon earned a reputation as one of the smartest students in Vilnius.

By age fifteen, Cahan became more independent. The previous winter, his parents had had another son, Isaac, and no longer held such a strong influence over the older boy. He began to explore the world around him and consider what he would do in the future. Cahan soon developed an interest in politics and, in particular, socialism. He began associating with the city's intellectuals in a town square called "The Goosery," and it was here that he was provided with his first socialist pamphlet, "Haemet" or "Truth." In it, the socialist called for a radical change in the political and economic systems, where classes and poverty would be wiped out. The concept appealed to Cahan's sense of community sharing.

The underground (government-banned) pamphlet and Goosery conversations had a strong impact on the restless teenager and marked a major turning point in his life. He decided to become a teacher so he could spread the socialist revolution.

Revolution and higher education. In 1877, at age seventeen, Cahan cheerfully entered the Vilnius Teacher Training Institute. However, the school quickly proved to be very confining, and within the first few months Cahan wanted to drop out.

Run by the government, the institute supported the dictatorial rule of the czar and discriminated against Jews. Among fifty-three students and twelve teachers, there were only two Jewish instructors and a handful of Jewish students. Yiddish was a forbidden language in the classroom. Furthermore, according to Cahan, the teachers were like robots who promoted only government interests and never explained what they taught:

> In the classroom the teacher was the representative of the imperial government.... The teachers were not concerned. Most of them simply required that the material be memorized.... The order of the day was: "Do not dare to think! Do as everyone does! Stick to the beaten path!" (Cahan in Stein, p. 112)

Rebel Student

Abraham Cahan challenged his teacher's authority at the Vilnius Teacher Training Institute. One day, when Cahan failed to repeat a poetry assignment exactly as it had been given, Cahan's teacher began shouting at him to sit down. Cahan, heart thumping and forehead sweating, refused and shot back at his teacher, "You are picking on me!" He was immediately sent to detention and was locked in a bathroom for three days. This made him feel far more supportive of the socialist movement: "as I paced my 'cell' I realized that I was being punished for telling ... the truth. And the revolutionaries were also being punished for telling the truth. I was imprisoned in a bathing room. They were exiled to Siberia. They were hanged for telling the truth about a despotic government." (Cahan in Stein, pp. 126, 141)

Because he would have been drafted into the czar's army if he dropped out, Cahan was forced to continue at the school. He meanwhile stepped up his efforts to support the underground movement, which was now highly active, plotting to kill Czar Alexander II, whom they viewed as the leader of a heartless government. By 1881 Cahan had met Vladimir Sokolov, one of the main leaders of the socialist movement and key organizer of the assassination plot. Cahan began working directly with Sokolov, attending meetings at his home and distributing socialist pamphlets around the city.

Persecution and flight. Late that winter, just before Cahan was to graduate, the underground assassination plot was successful and Czar Alexander II was killed on March 1, 1881. Cahan's life was immediately thrown into chaos as anyone suspected of ties to the plot was forced into hiding. Cahan, however, was able to elude authorities, graduate, and move to the country, where he assumed his first teaching position. Soon after, his name was linked to Sokolov and officials came to search his home, looking for underground pamphlets.

Meanwhile, there was mass hysteria on the streets of Russia, and the goals of the assassins were not being achieved. They had expected to incite a peasant uprising. Instead, the peasants turned their anger on the Jews who seemed to be leaders of the disturbances. Several were arrested for the assassination, and suddenly all Jews became the target of attack. A government-supported policy of "pogroms," or mass killings and tortures of Jews, ensued. Thousands of innocent families were forced to flee the country for safety. The pogroms touched off a massive wave of Jewish immigration to the Americas and Palestine.

Cahan realized he too would have to flee the country for safety. Through his underground connections, he was able to get a false passport and sneak out of the country. Without being able to say good-bye to family or friends, Cahan boarded a ship for America. He was leaving his homeland forever.

Participation: Jewish Immigrant Experience

Cahan arrived in Philadelphia in June 1882. From there he was sent to Castle Garden in New York City to be processed as an immigrant, along with thousands of fellow Russian Jewish refugees. Once in New York, he arranged to move into a boardinghouse in the Jewish section of the city, the Lower East Side. Though an educated man with a teaching certificate, Cahan learned upon arrival that immigrants could get employment only as factory workers or peddlers, and he found a job at a cigar factory for $3 to $4 a week.

▲ **An immigrant home industry**

Lower East Side. As Cahan described in his novels *Yekl* and *The Rise of David Levinsky,* the Lower East Side of the 1880s was a Jewish ghetto. One of the most crowded areas in the world, it was populated by approximately 150,000 Jews who had emigrated mainly from Russia and Germany. The area was for the most part a garment manufacturing district, but it also swarmed with street peddlers and Yiddish-speaking immigrants like Cahan, newcomers who were called "greenhorns." Most of the residents worked and lived in sweatshops, which were set up in crowded tenement buildings that lined the streets. Yet, in Cahan's words, there was a freshness in the air:

> The scurry and hustle of the people were not merely overwhelmingly greater, both in volume and intensity, than in my native town. It was of another sort. The swing and step of the pedestrians, the voices and manner of the street peddlers, and a hundred and one other things seemed to testify to far more self-confidence and energy, to larger ambitions and wider scopes, than did the appearance of the crowds in my birthplace. (Cahan, *The Rise of David Levinsky,* p. 93)

Cahan noticed not only the physical differences between America and Lithuania but the differences in philosophy and politics. On his first day touring the East Side, he visited a newsstand and purchased a copy of a socialist newspaper—one that he would have been thrown in jail for owning in Lithuania. Cahan was impressed by the freedom of expression allowed in America and began to think that perhaps some of his socialist ideas could be expressed and achieved here.

American socialism. Cahan at the same time felt a "crushing longing" for his homeland and its Old World traditions (Sanders, p. 241). Though surrounded by Russian Jews, he missed his family, his ties to the revolution, and the sense of community he experienced in Vilnius. In order to overcome his loneliness, Cahan began attending meetings of Jewish Social Democrats with some people from work. At his first "Propaganda Verein" meeting, after listening to various speakers conduct the meeting in German and Russian, Cahan addressed the group and urged that they conduct sessions in Yiddish and increase their ties to the Jewish revolutionaries in Russia. He said to his fellow immigrants, "We are now in a country that is relatively free ... but we must not forget the great struggle for freedom that we left behind in our old home" (Cahan in Sanders, p. 62). Cahan's motion was greeted with thunderous applause, and the leadership requested he give a speech the following week in Yiddish on the state of the Russian workers' revolution, which he did. Invited back repeatedly, Cahan started making friends and a name for himself among the city's socialist Jews.

English educator. But, while the socialist meetings provided comradery and a political outlet, they were not enough for Cahan.

As he became wrapped up in his new life as a factory worker, he saw the great need for labor reform and felt there was a spiritual void in the Jewish community that needed to be filled. Though information was available on both the American system of government and labor laws, all of it was written in English, which few of the immigrants could read. Cahan also felt there was little to bind the Russian Jewish community together, and that his fellow immigrants needed to strengthen ties to their homeland and maintain certain traditions. As an educator, Cahan thought he could accomplish these goals through writing for the East Side community, but first he himself had to learn English.

Just as he had done with Russian, Cahan taught himself English and learned about the growing labor movement and the U.S. system of government. He then taught English to his coworkers at the cigar factory and founded the first Jewish Labor Lyceum, a discussion society for Jewish workers on the concepts of organized labor and government procedure. Cahan later helped organize the first Jewish Garment Workers Union.

The writer. Meanwhile, Cahan started writing articles for publication in both English and Yiddish dailies. He wrote on a wide range of subjects, from the establishment of labor unions to the hardships that face immigrants in America. Cahan's articles were well received by immigrants and natives alike, and it was not long before he was offered a job as an editor for a Yiddish daily. From 1883 to 1902, Cahan worked for several publications. In 1885 he married Anna Bronstein, also a Russian Jewish immigrant.

Forward. In 1902 Cahan became editor-in-chief of the socialist *Jewish Daily Forward,* and under his guidance the paper's circulation rose from 6,000 to 200,000. Written in Yiddish for a specifically Russian Jewish audience, the *Forward* had a major impact on the community, and it was with this newspaper that Cahan made his most significant contribution as a writer.

Cahan, who wrote in a very conversational style, sought through the *Forward* to educate his readership and instill in them a sense of pride in themselves. While the general public discriminated against most immigrants—especially greenhorns—because they did not speak English and were generally laborers, Cahan praised their accomplishments. For many immigrants, this was the first—and only—public praise of this kind they ever received. One of his columns read:

> On Second Avenue at around eight o'clock every morning, one can see hundreds of Jewish boys from fourteen to eighteen ... walking with books under their arms.... These are Jewish college boys, children of immigrants.... The Jew undergoes privation, spills blood, to educate his child. We know of a poor Jewish worker's family in which the father earns barely eight dollars a week and the mother is ill. But when the boy wanted to go to work, his parents absolutely refused to let him.... There are hundreds of examples like this. (Cahan in Sanders, p. 260)

Cahan also invented the "Bintel Brief" column in the *Forward* that encouraged direct community involvement in the newspaper. In it, he printed letters from Lower East Side residents that not only made fascinating reading but provided concrete examples of the immigrant struggle and labor abuses. In advertising for submissions, he told his readers that under their tenement roofs were the stories of real life, the stuff of which great literature could be made. Cahan encouraged his readers to write, scribble, or tell their stories any way they could because the world needed to hear them. Through his efforts, he succeeded not only in giving voice to a silent population but in alerting many Americans as to the plight of the immigrant worker.

Excerpt from *A Bintel Brief*—1908

My dearest friends of the *Forward*,
I have been jobless for six months now. I have eaten the last shirt on my back and now there is nothing left for me but to end my life.... I am an ironworker. I can work a milling machine and a drill press. I can also drive horses and train colts. In Russia I served in the cavalry, and there I once hit my superior. For that I was sent to prison.... If I had known it would be so bitter for me here, I wouldn't have come....

Answer: The writer of this letter is told to go first to the Crisis Conference at 133 Eldridge Street, New York, and they will not let him starve. And further we ask our readers to let us know if someone can create a job for this unemployed man. (Metzker, pp. 76-77)

Aftermath

Cahan's achievements. In addition to editing the *Forward* until his death at age ninety-one, Cahan wrote several novels, short stories, and a five-volume autobiography. He most often wrote about the immigrant experience, and in the vernacular, or the language of the people.

His first novel, *Yekl,* for instance, portrays a young Jew arriving in New York. When another character, Jake, speaks to Yekl about the importance of learning to speak English, his conversation illustrates Cahan's realistic style:

> When I was in Boston ... I knew a *feller,* so he was *perticly* friend of [particularly friendly with] John Shullivan's. He is a Christian, that feller is, and yet the two of us lived like brothers. May I be unable to move from this spot if we did not. How, then, would you have it? Like here, in New York, where Jews are a *lot* of *Greenhorns* and can not speak a word of English? Over there every Jew speaks English like a stream. (Cahan, *Yekl,* p. 3)

Through the years, Cahan continued to call for labor and social welfare reform but after the communist revolution in Russia in 1917, his ideas changed. Cahan's experiences in America and his belief in freedom of expression turned him strongly against communism, which he saw as another form of dictatorship. He became convinced that human rights were better protected in a democracy, in which everyone had a voice.

Cahan's ideas and activities not only had a deep impact on Russian Jewish immigrants during his lifetime but also shed a bright light on the struggle of the immigrants. Revealing their physical and spiritual hardships, Cahan helped the world to better understand their plight and the Russian Jewish community to understand and take pride in itself. He helped millions join American society and at the same time hold on to their own cultural identity. His efforts had a long-lasting effect on the conditions of life for Russian Jews in the United States.

For More Information

Cahan, Abraham. *The Rise of David Levinsky.* New York: Harper & Row, 1917.

Cahan, Abraham. *Yekl: A Tale of the New York Ghetto.* New York: D. Appleton and Company, 1896.

Metzker, Isaac, ed. *A Bintel Brief: Sixty Years of Letters from the Lower East Side to the "Jewish Daily Forward."* Garden City, New York: Doubleday, 1971.

Sanders, Ronald. *The Downtown Jews.* New York: Dover Publications, Ltd., 1969.

Stein, Leon. *The Education of Abraham Cahan.* Philadelphia: The Jewish Publication Society of America, 1969.

Social Welfare

1886

Stanton Coit and Charles B. Stover establish the first American settlement house, the Neighborhood Guild, in New York City.

1889

Jane Addams founds Hull House to help immigrant families adapt to city life in America.

1890

Photographer Jacob Riis publishes *How the Other Half Lives,* which pictures life in New York city slums.

1893

S. S. McClure publishes first issue of *McClure's Magazine.*

1899

Professor John Dewey redirects education in America.

1902

Ida Tarbell begins "A History of Standard Oil Company," a series of articles for *McClure's.*

1904

Theodore Roosevelt is elected president.

1906

Upton Sinclair's *The Jungle* is published. Congress passes Meat Packing Act as well as Pure Food and Drug Act.

1908

Louis Brandeis wins Supreme Court case *Muller* v. *Oregon* on limiting the workday for Oregon women.

1909

Herbert Croly publishes *The Promise of America.* Addams becomes president of the National Conference of Charities and Corrections.

1914

Croly begins magazine the *New Republic.*

1915

Addams is awarded the Nobel Peace Prize.

SOCIAL WELFARE

Great efforts were made around the turn of the twentieth century to improve living and working conditions in America. Members of these groups concerned with society's advancing—or progressing—toward a better life for all Americans belonged to what came to be known as the Progressive Movement. A patchwork of interest groups with various goals investigated and exposed to the public such problems as unsafe factories, filthy tenement housing, and impure foods.

More women than men became active in the movement, though both played leading roles. Progressives were typically young, white, and middle class. Often they pressed their own middle-class values on lower-class immigrants who crowded into the cities. A book by writer and photographer Jacob Riis, *How the Other Half Lives,* documented the overcrowding, filth, and hopelessness of New York City slums. Other reformers set out to pass tenement-house laws and standards. All these reformers made assumptions about how the immigrant lived and what changes were needed to improve his or her life. They assumed, for example, that clutter was bad, when in fact an immigrant family might prefer a cluttered room. The reformers, then, were trying to reshape society according to their own ideas of good and bad rather than making room for different ideas. But all in all their efforts brought about improvements in health, safety, and other conditions.

Some reformers exposed problems; others tried to solve them. One solution was the settlement house, a social service center that aimed to help immigrant families, especially women, adapt to city living in the United States. In 1880 **Jane Addams** opened Hull House in Chicago for this purpose. Aside from living quarters, it offered classes in cooking, health care, English, and more, as well as nursery care.

Reporters of the day exposed corrupt practices in business and politics. Objecting to their methods, President Theodore Roosevelt labeled them "muckrakers." They seemed intent on raking up the muck or dirt in society and government—an honorable enough activity—but Roosevelt complained that they were interfering with his own attempts to improve American society. He believed that life in the Industrial Age had grown so complicated that the president needed greater decision-making power. He himself was a Progressive, but the movement's reformers had different opinions about how to go about improving society. Roosevelt echoed the views of **Herbert Croly,** a thinker who greatly influenced America with his book *The Promise of America* and magazine, the *New Republic.*

In contrast to Croly, the lawyer **Louis Brandeis** cautioned against government growing too big. And he warned also about "bigness" in industry and labor. Bigness, he felt, was dangerous to the survival of liberty in America. Yet Brandeis, too, was a progressive. Progressives were a statistics-minded group. They gathered facts about an issue, then shared them in novels and articles. Brandeis would generally collect information and then organize it into a legal brief, or argument.

A Brandeis brief on women workers changed courtroom arguments in American law. For the first time, attention was paid not only to legal reasoning but also to social and economic evidence that took into account the health of society as a whole. He used this technique to win a case brought before the Supreme Court, *Muller* v. *Oregon,* concerning a ten-hour limit on the workday for women. The Supreme Court ruled in favor of Brandeis and upheld the right of Oregon to regulate the workday for women, which then encouraged other states to pass similar laws.

In the early 1900s, new methods of printing and photography led to the birth of low-cost magazines, such as *McClure's Magazine,* which printed articles by muckrakers that revealed some disgraceful practices in society and had sensational news value. Lincoln Steffens exposed crooked political leaders in *McClure's,* while **Ida Tarbell**'s articles were targeted at John D. Rockefeller and his Standard Oil Company. A novel by **Upton Sinclair** inspired new regulations in the meat-packing industry. *The Jungle* exposed stomach-turning practices in meatpacking houses that raised a public outcry for stricter rules. Roosevelt, who could no longer enjoy a sausage at breakfast after reading the book, ordered a study of the meatpacking industry, then used this study to pressure Congress into passing the Meat Inspection Act of 1906. The act required federal inspection and sanitary conditions in companies that sold meat in interstate commerce.

The Progressive Movement was mostly conducted by white Americans who intended to achieve reforms for less fortunate white Americans. Seldom were blacks included in the schemes of the reformers. Jane Addams did help found a settlement house that served a black neighborhood in Chicago, and Ray Stannard Baker wrote about the plight of blacks in *Following the Color Line.* There was on the whole, however, little concern among the Progressives about racial inequality and the problems it could prompt. Nor did they foresee the growth of the city ghetto. Living in a nation with a growing lower class, largely of white immigrants, they instead raised other basic questions. What responsibility does society have to care for the poor? And how much control should government have over society? Through books, magazines, court cases, laws, and settlement houses, reformers of the day tooks steps to answer these questions.

Jane Addams

1860-1935

Personal Background

Named Laura Jane Addams, Jane Addams was born on September 6, 1860, in Cedarville, Illinois, to John and Sarah Addams. John, a miller of Quaker descent, served on the Illinois State Senate as a Whig and helped found the Republican party before Jane's birth. One of his closest friends was Abraham Lincoln, who called him "My Dear Double-D'ed Addams" (Tims, p. 19). Sarah Addams was a hard-working mother of eight children who ran the household very efficiently while her husband tended to the mill. When Jane was only two, both Sarah and her unborn ninth child died from the effort of helping to deliver a friend's baby. Sarah had used up all her energy to save her friend and the friend's new baby, a heroic act that Jane would never forget. Thereafter, Jane was raised by servants, her siblings, and her father, who taught her the Quaker values of honesty and charity.

The ugly duckling. Born frail and sickly, Jane had a curvature of the spine that caused her to carry her head slightly to one side throughout her life. During childhood, she called herself "the ugly duckling," although one of her school friends described her as "a little girl with very pretty, light brown hair" (Tims, p. 9). Her physical ailments would only worsen as she grew older. She would have a kidney removed, be stricken with bouts of bronchitis, and generally suffer from one ailment or another over the years.

▲ **Jane Addams**

Event: The settlement house.
Role: Jane Addams founded Hull House, a settlement home for women, students, orphan children, and immigrants. She also fought for various social causes throughout her life, becoming one of the first social workers in the United States.

Though physically frail, Jane had a capable mind. She was an eager reader who picked out books from her father's well-stocked library. She gladly received five cents from her father for every book she finished. She even kept a journal in which she wrote her favorite book passages, personal thoughts, and observations.

The shape of things to come. Although Jane herself was not poor, her first sight of poverty had a tremendous impact on her life. After noticing the "horrid little houses" (Tims, p. 20) in Freeport, Illinois, she decided she wanted to live in a big house among, not away from, the poor. She wanted to help people, too. At age six, Jane began having dreams that were to determine her actions in later life. She recalled:

> I dreamed night after night that everyone in the world was dead except myself, and that upon me rested the responsibility of making a wagon-wheel.... I fully realized that the affairs of the world could not be resumed until at least one wheel should be made and something started. (Addams in Tims, p. 20)

The vision made her feel that she had a responsibility to all people, giving her the determination to help as many as she could.

When her father remarried, Jane was eight years old. Her stepmother had a son from whom Jane became inseparable for nine years. It even appeared that Jane and George Haldeman, her stepbrother, would marry and settle down with their parents' blessing. However, as Jane began focusing on social issues and planning to attend college, she became disenchanted with George for mocking her social concern. His one influence on her was his interest in medicine, which Jane quickly shared. It was a subject she considered studying.

Success in college. After a feud with her father over which women's college to attend—Smith or Rockford—Addams enrolled at Rockford, in Alabama, in 1877 at the age of seventeen. She studied Latin, Greek, philosophy, literature, and history, and her social life was not lacking; she even turned down a marriage proposal from a class president from Beloit College. She was elected president of her own class in 1881 and graduated as a valedictorian the same year, before her twenty-first birthday. She declared, in her graduation speech, "We stand united today in a belief in beauty, genius and courage, and that these expressed through truest womanhood can yet transform the world" (Addams in Tims, p. 25).

Depression. Immediately following her graduation, a cheerful Addams accompanied her father and stepmother on a trip to Lake Superior. While surveying land, her father suddenly fell extremely ill. He was rushed to nearby Green Bay, Wisconsin, where his appendix burst and he died two days later. He was fifty-nine, while Jane was not yet twenty-one. Several days later, she wrote to her friend Ellen Starr, "The greatest sorrow that can ever come to me has passed, and I hope it is only a question of time until I get my moral purposes straightened" (Addams in Tims, p. 27).

The same summer offered more tragedy. The half-brother of Addams' closest friend, Flora Guiteau, was Charles Julius Guiteau, the man who assassinated President James Garfield. Although mentally disturbed, Guiteau received the death sentence. Addams went into hiding with Flora to protect her from the public spectacle of her brother's hanging and the wrath of angry neighbors.

With the coming of fall, Addams enrolled at the Women's Medical College, but this did not seem to help her state of depression. During the first few weeks she wrote, "I am growing more sullen and less sympathetic every day" (Davis, p. 27). Severe health problems pulled her out of school seven months later. She spent a good deal of the next two years recuperating from spinal surgery.

New inspiration. In order to lift Addams out of depression, her stepmother took her to Europe in 1883. Not until she reached the poverty-stricken city of London, England, did Addams show signs of improvement. She began writing more about her surroundings, noticing "myriads of hands, empty, pathetic, nerveless and workworn, showing white in the uncertain light of the street, and clutching forward for food which was already unfit to eat" (Addams in Tims, p. 31). Her spirits were rising rapidly, and her passion for the welfare of other people was reemerging.

During a second trip to Europe at the age of twenty-seven, this passion translated itself into a plan. While watching a bull-fight in Madrid, Spain, Addams was inspired. Long after her friends grew disgusted and left, Addams stayed, transfixed by the spectacle. She

▲ Hull House

later realized that she "had seen the slaughter through the romantic haze" and recognized her own "failure to perceive the reality of the bull-fight" (Tims, p. 37). Addams then related the incident to the way she had been living her life, idly dreaming and not turning those dreams into reality. She decided that day upon a plan.

Participation: The Settlement House

The search for a home. Further inspired by observing the workings of England's Toynbee Hall, a home for young male Oxford students, Addams returned to the United States with a vision. She would create and live in a settlement home for young female students in Chicago, Illinois, a poverty-stricken, rapidly growing city located near her home. The house had to provide more than living quarters. It had to be a cooperative dwelling in which the seeds for reform would be planted through lectures, meetings, and clubs centered around social education.

Addams began her search for a large home in the slums of Chicago in the fall of 1889. She recruited her friend Ellen Starr to help look for the perfect home, and at the end of a long day of searching they somewhat by accident discovered a house on the corners of Halsted and Polk streets. Addams was immediately impressed with the vacant structure, later remembering it as "a fine old house ... supported by wooden pillars of exceptionally pure Corinthian design and proportion" (Tims, p. 43). She contacted the owner, Helen Culver, and explained her plans for the house. Culver was so excited by the idea that she allowed Addams to lease the home for free until 1920.

The dream house as a reality. Built by real estate dealer Charles J. Hull thirty years earlier, the old house had become known as Hull House. It was complete with offices on the ground floor and boarding rooms on the second floor, but the rundown building needed some repairs. Addams and Starr moved in on September 18, 1889, and set to work on turning Hull House into a home.

Hull House took boarders almost immediately, and within weeks of the opening, all of the upstairs rooms were full of female students, a waiting list was growing, and a kindergarten was established by a wealthy Chicago woman. The neighborhood children, mostly immigrants and orphans who had spent a good deal of time on the streets, flocked to Hull House where they were received with open arms by Addams herself.

Hull House expands. The instant success of Hull House was overwhelming, even to Addams. In the first year, 50,000 people were served by the settlement house. In the second, an average of 2,000 people a week, most of them seen personally by Addams, descended upon Hull House. The female-only household soon turned into one of the first mixed public settlements in the country. Within the first few years, volunteers helped establish an art gallery, a working women's union, a gym, a library, a college extension program, a coffeehouse, and a public kitchen with affordable meals for immigrants, women, and laborers. Immigrants could learn English and study world literature in the college courses as well as learn about their rights as workers in America in the many labor union meetings held there. On one occasion, Addams and her friend and fellow Hull House member Julia Lathrop even delivered a young woman's baby in one of the upstairs rooms.

Hull House seemed to be fulfilling more objectives and attracting more people than its frail founder could ever imagine. The first objectives of the settlement house were:

> to provide a center for a higher civic and social life; to institute and maintain educational and philanthropic [humane] enterprises; and to investigate and improve the conditions in the industrial districts of Chicago. (Tims, p. 49)

Successfully meeting these objectives in the first few years, Hull House also became involved in outside affairs. "Even in the very first years of Hull House," Addams wrote, "we began to discover that our activities were gradually extending from the settlement to a participation in city and national undertakings" (Tims, p. 52). Hull House became a leader in a wide range of reform movements in Chicago and the nation, from factory inspection to the eight-hour workday for women to housing regulations. Chicago's first public playground was started by Hull House in 1893.

Tolstoy and labor. In 1896, at the age of thirty-six, Addams was invited to meet with the author Leo Tolstoy in his European home. Tolstoy was a Russian noble who championed the cause of the Russian poor and working class. Their meeting was brief and filled with mutual admiration as they primarily discussed the importance of the recognition of labor. Addams came away from the visit with a renewed respect for physical work at any level. Upon returning to Hull House, she began baking bread for two hours each day (in addition to her other duties) to make sure that physical labor was a part of her daily life. Tolstoy, in turn, presented half of the proceeds from his book *Resurrection* to Hull House.

In another tribute to labor, she went out every morning and helped the neighborhood children shovel inches of garbage off the streets. Several of the young male volunteers decided they no longer wanted to shovel garbage and would rather practice military-style drills. The quick-thinking Addams offered to let them use sewer spades in place of bayonets. Accepting her offer, the boys were able to perform their drills and keep the sewers clean.

Chicago's mayor appointed Addams "garbage inspector" of the district surrounding Hull House.

The swings of fame. Addams's popularity skyrocketed. By 1912 she had became the symbol for social justice in the United States. One of her listeners, Doctor Maude Roydan, remarked: "In America in 1912 I learned that it was unsafe to mention Jane Addams in public speech unless you were prepared for an interruption, because the mere reference to her provoked such a storm of applause" (Tims, p. 132). Besides Hull House, Addams worked for a host of social and political groups, including the National Women's Trade Union League and the National Association for the Advancement of Colored People (NAACP), in which she served as a board member for decades. In the election of 1912, she became an outspoken champion for women gaining the right to vote, the aim of the National American Woman Suffrage Association.

Addams's fame took a downturn in 1914 when she publicly opposed World War I. In keeping with her Quaker upbringing, she condemned the use of any form of violence, whether physical, spiritual, or economic. Addams was widely criticized for stating in a speech that "the war was an old men's game inflicted on the young" and that "no soldier could go into a bayonet charge until he was made half-drunk" (Tims, pp. 98–99). The general reaction to her comments was unfavorable, as was public opinion, as described by Roydan: "How well I remember, when I spoke in America in 1922 and 1923, the silence that greeted the name of Jane Addams! The few faithful who tried to applaud only made the silence more depressing" (Tims, p. 132).

Some Evening Clubs and Classes Held at Hull House—January 1895

Gymnastics (women)
Beginning Latin
English and Letter Writing
Gymnastics (men)
Social Science Club
Geometry
Italo-American Club
Young Citizens
Mandolin Club
Jolly Boys' Club

Singing
Arithmetic
Parliamentary Law
Chemistry
Italian Class
Dancing Class
Club Lectures
Cloak Makers' Union (women)
Physics
Italian Reception

Despite public opinion, Addams refused to change her stances and continued to work for peace. She became chairperson for the International Committee of Women for Peace and toured fourteen countries in the middle of the war with the sole purpose of pleading for a peaceful end to the fighting. In 1919, when the battles finally did cease, the fifty-nine-year-old Addams joined the Red Cross on tour through the war's destructive path and offered her assistance to the wounded. In spite of such efforts, the general public's dislike of her continued well into the next decade.

Addams Criticizes Schools

Addams considered schools the chief agency for preserving and extending American culture, but she thought they were failing at the task. The problem, she criticized, was that they had become too detached from experience. In fact, her purpose in forming a settlement house was to apply knowledge to life. "The settlement stands for application as opposed to research," she wrote. (Adams in Lasch, p. 187)

The greatest prize. Not everyone dismissed Addams, however. She had the consistent support of the people at Hull House, which was still a great success. Her popularity finally returned in 1931 when, at the age of seventy, she received the Nobel Peace Prize for her lifetime accomplishments. Receiving $16,000 in prize money, she donated it all to the Women's International League. Addams shared the prize with the well-known educational reformer Doctor Nicholas Murray Butler.

Aftermath

Writings. Throughout her life, Addams documented practically everything she did. The social worker included her experiences in ten books, one of which was the well-received autobiographical *Twenty Years at Hull House*.

She traveled as much as her frail body would allow and enjoyed some of the finer things in life, such as staying in elegant hotels, being waited on, eating in good restaurants, and being entertained by famous and important people. Her travels at one point took her to Arizona, where her friend Ida Tarbell, the author who exposed misdealings of the Standard Oil Company, was teaching a class in biography (see **Ida Tarbell**). Self-critical, she wrote in a letter, "it seems that biography is an Art. I certainly discovered that autobiography was an Art that I did not possess" (Linn, p. 385).

Vote for Roosevelt, Jane Addams Urges the Women of California

CHICAGO, Nov. 4.—The Tribune, Los Angeles, Cal.: I venture to send an appeal to the enfranchised women of America to vote for the Progressive party because the platform embodies the very humanitarian measures social workers have been advocating for many years and for which they always have found women ready to help.

We have seen the bitter war of working girls for regulated hours, for a minimum wage and for protection against industrial diseases and accidents. The Progressive party submits a well-considered program fitted to such industrial needs, with candidates of experience and courage who are able to secure this legislation and later to enforce it.

JANE ADDAMS.

▲ **Addams asked American women to show their support for the Progressives in the 1912 presidential election**

Besides books, Addams wrote more than 400 articles with titles like "Why Women Should Vote." Her energy seemed boundless. She impressed women's leader Carrie Chapman Catt as someone who had tremendous ability to stick to a project until she made it a success, and then to keep on sticking to the success.

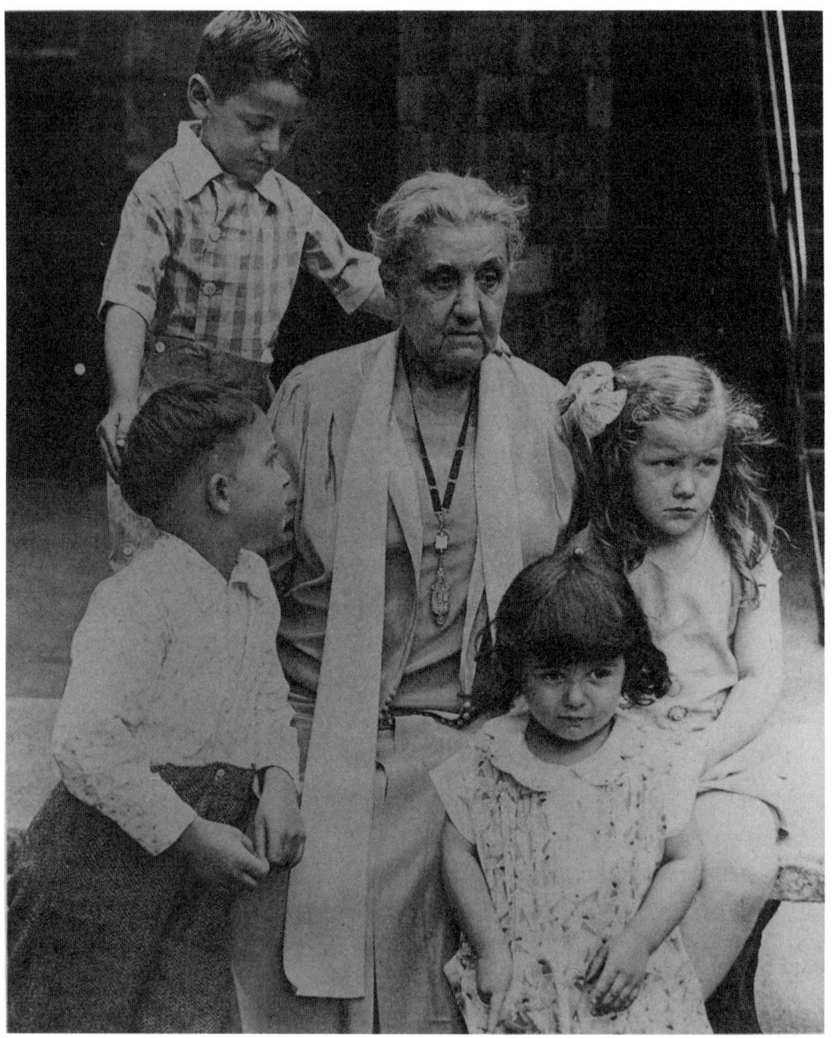

▲ **Addams with young visitors at the fortieth anniversary of Hull House, May 9, 1930**

Mary Smith. Although Addams never married, she had close friends. Among them was a lifetime companion, Mary Smith, with whom she shared everything, including a house they purchased together in the later years of their lives. Addams and Smith became inseparable—they traveled and worked together as often as possible. When business would pull one away from the other, they wrote loving letters to ease the pain of separation. Addams compared their relationship to a marriage, once writing to Smith, "You must know, dear, how I long for you all the time ... there is reason in the habit of married folks keeping together" (Davis, p. 88). Smith returned the feeling in a letter which read, "I'm given to turning sentimental at this season, as you know, and I feel quite a rush of emotion when I think of you" (Davis, p. 89).

Perhaps the most difficult blow, aside from the death of her father, was the death of Smith in 1934. "I suppose I could have willed my heart to stop beating," Addams wrote, "but the thought of what she had been to me for so long kept me from being cowardly" (Addams in Tims, p. 144).

Addams Campaigns

By 1911 there were thirty-seven settlements like Hull House in Chicago. They joined forces to promote reform in the city. In the 1912 election, a number of settlement workers supported a new political party whose candidate for president was Theodore Roosevelt. The platform of the Progressive Party called for improvement in housing, unemployment insurance, the vote for women, and other popular settlement goals. Giving a series of campaign speeches and writing essays on behalf of the new party, Addams was regarded as the leading Progressive in the country.

Final days. Addams's health declined rapidly after Smith's death, and the Women's International League, sensing her growing weakness, held a large celebration in Chicago in her honor. Ten days later, on May 21, 1935, she died of cancer at the age of seventy-four. A large funeral was held at Hull House, in which thousands of fans, including friends and strangers of all ages and nationalities, paid their final respects. Much was written about her following her death. Most telling perhaps was the simple comment that "those who have known her say that she was not only good, but great" (Davis, p. 291).

For More Information

Davis, Allen F. *American Heroine: The Life and Legend of Jane Addams.* New York: Oxford University Press, 1973.

Lasch, Christopher, ed. *The Social Thought of Jane Addams.* Indianapolis: Bobbs-Merrill Company, 1965.

Linn, James Weber. *Jane Addams: A Biography.* New York: D. Appleton-Century Company, 1935.

Tims, Margaret. *Jane Addams of Hull House: A Centenary Study.* New York: The Macmillan Company, 1961.

Herbert Croly

1869-1930

Personal Background

The Crolys. Herbert's mother, Jane Cunningham Croly, was a very popular and financially successful writer and editor. Using the pen name Jenny June, in her nine books and magazine work she instructed women on such topics as etiquette as well as discussed more challenging "women's" issues. His father, David Croly, was an Irishman full of ideas for improving society. A fine speaker and writer, Herbert's father rose through the ranks to become editor of two of America's most popular periodicals before losing his job as editor in chief of the *New York Daily Graphic* because of his rebellious spirit. He was an abolitionist and a member of Auguste Comte's Religion of Humanity, a creed that substituted for the worship of the Christian God the worship of the Great Being, or all the good in humanity past, present, and future.

Early life. Herbert was born into this well-spoken and well-read household of New York City on January 23, 1869. He turned to books at an early age, and he seldom spoke—and then only at a whisper. The future adviser to presidents would always be painfully shy.

Herbert's mother was careful with her time. She allowed three morning hours each day to family chores and talking with her son. After that period, she seldom had time for him. She would pick up

▲ **Herbert Croly**

Event: Defining the role of government in social welfare.

Role: A journalist, Herbert Croly managed the *New Republic,* a magazine of opinion, and wrote books that raised questions about government and society in his readers' minds. His views influenced presidents in the first quarter of the twentieth century.

her pen and write into the night until past eleven—sometimes even until one or two o'clock in the morning.

Shortly after birth, Herbert was christened into his father's Religion of Humanity. Although the son eventually abandoned this religion and adopted Christianity, the christening marked the beginning of a lifelong friendship. It was Herbert's father who could always find the time to discuss ideas with his son.

Education. Herbert's parents took a keen interest in their son's education. As soon as he was able, Herbert was sent to J. H. Morse's English, Classical, and Mathematical School for Boys. By the time he was fifteen years old, it was apparent that Herbert would attend college. He registered at City College of New York to prepare for entering the more demanding Harvard University. Two years later, Herbert packed his bags, moved to Cambridge, Massachusetts, and set out to enroll at Harvard. Although well prepared and from an educated home, Croly immediately failed the Harvard entrance examinations. He was allowed to enroll as a "special student" until he passed the examinations. Croly was to attend classes at Harvard off and on for the next fourteen years but would leave before he graduated. In fact, it would not be until 1897 that he would be allowed to enroll as a regular student, and then only as a sophomore.

Edmund Wilson's Description of Visiting Croly

Edmund Wilson, a professor at Columbia University, once described visiting Croly: "If the visitor were himself at all difficult, he would be likely to find the conversations subsiding [deteriorating] into a discontinuous series of remarks ... to which Croly would utter responses more and more fragmentary and more and more imperfectly audible. In time the conversation would stop altogether; the air would became taut with panic while Croly sat absolutely motionless, his eyes dropped on his hands ... clasped in his lap, his face ... hostile and morose." (Forcey, p. 6.)

Editor. Meanwhile, Croly followed the example his parents set in their writing and editing careers. Leaving college in 1888, he took a job as editor of the *Real Estate Record and Guide,* a magazine to help real estate dealers keep up with the rapid changes in New York. He moved to edit the new *Architectural Record* three years later, in 1891. Eighteen ninety-one was an important year for Croly, personally and professionally. The new job allowed for a wider range of writing topics, and he married Louise Emory. The daughter of a moderately wealthy family, Louise was twenty-six, and he was twenty-three at the time. They would have no children, and they would live happily together until death separated them.

Perhaps supported by his wife's family or perhaps by his mother (his father had died in 1889), Croly decided to return to Harvard in 1892. This time the student remained in classes for a year, minus a week or two. He was forced to drop out because of a nervous breakdown.

To recover, Croly and his wife traveled for three years to Cornish, New Hampshire, and then to Europe, Cambridge, and back to Cornish. Cornish would become a haven for the Crolys throughout their lives.

Return to Harvard. Back in Harvard in 1895, Croly stayed long enough to be admitted in 1897 as a sophomore. His classes at Harvard introduced him to such great intellectuals as the psychologist William James and the educational philosopher John Dewey. The Harvard experiences convinced him to give up his father's godless religion and adopt Christianity, keeping those elements of humanity from the former religion as were acceptable to his new religion. His Harvard studies taught him to look for answers to society's problems in history and in natural evolution. In 1899 Croly left Harvard altogether and returned to his old job as editor of the *Architectural Record.*

Jefferson or Hamilton? Croly's head was spinning with ideas, however, and while he edited the *Architectural Record,* he was thinking of a new republic. For most of its history, America had followed the ideas of Presidents Jefferson and Andrew Jackson, ideas that favored strong rights of individuals and states but weaker rights for the federal government. Croly studied Jefferson's ideas and also the opposing views of Alexander Hamilton, who had preferred a strong and organized federal government. Croly observed the changes in America at the end of the 1800s toward a strongly industrialized society. He felt the growth of large business needed to be guided and favored movement toward a Hamiltonian-style government.

Participation: The Role of Government in Social Welfare

Book author. By 1905 Croly's ideas had become too strong to ignore. He demoted himself to an associate editor position at the *Record* and worked part-time in order to write about his political notions. For four years prior to this move, he had faithfully devoted four hours a day to writing his own ideas. By 1909 he had written a 450-page book, *The Promise of America.*

In *The Promise of America,* Croly outlines his view of history. The years, he felt, between the Revolutionary War and the Civil War had been dominated by a pioneering spirit. Land was abundant, and the nation so large that the people approached it as a land of opportunity. But by the end of the Civil War, the old land frontiers had disappeared, and along with them a need for "pioneers." Consequently the people of the United States had begun to search for ways to put their country and their own lives in order. With the weak central government of Jefferson and Jackson, protecting individual interests was difficult as the country grew.

The debate over how strong the federal government should be had gone on throughout the 1800s and had been dominated by those who favored a weak government. In the atmosphere of the industrial growth that followed the Civil War, powerful business directors had led the nation, often to the detriment of their own laborers. But there was, Croly argued, a promise in American life of economic well-being and of the possibility of a better society. Croly's book called for a stronger central government but a government of the people, not of the elite. In addition, he argued for more presidential powers so that the nation could respond to the inevitable changes.

In the early 1900s, society seemed to be operating reasonably well. Farmers were earning more than ever. Industrial leaders were taking advantage of nearly complete freedom to build great banks and collections of industries called trusts. At the same time, labor union organizers, such as Samuel Gompers, were organizing workers into larger groups able to demand more of the profits. As industries grew, a flood of powerless immigrants came to America hoping for jobs. The result was a growing poverty and abuse in contrast to the growing industrial wealth. A new selfishness arose in this age of opportunities.

Croly's ideas about progress. It was a fitting time for Croly to propose a new direction for the country. He felt that the changes in industry and labor were part of the natural evolution of society and would continue. The nation needed to recognize that changes would continue and prepare to use them for the national good. What was needed, he argued in his book, was a strong central government directed by a president with much more authority. This president needed to be on a path that would always look out for the national welfare and be prepared to guide industry and labor for the national good. Changes would bring problems, and it was the government's obligation to solve these problems. Good citizens needed to dedicate their actions to unselfish purposes. They should forgo the pursuit of personal wealth if that limited the national freedom and happiness.

Progressive Party. Just as Croly published his book, a new political party emerged that was based on the idea of a strong government to ensure the national welfare. Its candidate for president in 1904 was Theodore Roosevelt, who was running for reelection. His Progressive Party called for basic standards of safety in industry, a department of labor, and educational services for immigrants. Roosevelt had been a strong president, and his ideas in 1904 appealed to Croly. Croly did not agree, however, with Roosevelt's idea that the industrial trusts should be broken up. They were, Croly felt, part of the natural evolution of industry. The trusts needed to be regulated but not destroyed.

Influencing the nation. Although only 7,500 copies of *The Promise of America* were ever sold, it reached the intellectual elite who would guide the country on its new way. The book became a popular topic among political leaders such as Henry Stimson, who became secretary of war; Ray Stannard Baker, editor of the popular *McClure's Magazine;* Senator Henry Cabot Lodge; and Learned Hand, whom some believed to be the greatest of America's legal minds. Former president Roosevelt was impressed and invited Croly to his home at Oyster Bay, New York.

The Promise added to the debate about the scope of government in guarding the welfare of the people. Croly's ideas about a powerful and benevolent government later guided politicians who sought ways to shield the American people from the Great Depression of the 1930s and helped Franklin Delano Roosevelt gain unusual powers as president. He used this influence to involve the national government in many forms of social welfare.

His own magazine. Perhaps Croly's most important readers were not attracted by *The Promise of America* but by his writing in the *Architectural Record.* China had just been forced by threats on Peking to open its doors to foreign commerce, and the United States had taken a leadership role in preserving all other nations' rights to trade there. Croly was convinced that China would become a major power because of its natural wealth and that there would be quarrels among the nations to do business there. He anticipated trouble in China and proposed that the United States greatly increase the fighting power of its Pacific navy.

Croly as Writer

A slow writer, Croly had trouble expressing himself as clearly or briefly as he or others would have liked. He wrestled to communicate the powerful ideas in his mind.

A wealthy American couple, Willard and Dorothy Straight, had just returned from China with the same impressions and agreed with Croly's argument in the *Record.* The Straights and Crolys consequently met and became good friends, and when Croly wanted a better vehicle for getting his ideas across to the people of America, the Straights stepped in. They agreed to finance a new magazine that would publish carefully thought-out articles about current issues and report the ideas of the Progressive Party. The new magazine, the *New Republic,* published its first edition on the day that World War I began in Europe, November 7, 1914.

Aftermath

The *New Republic.* Croly's first step in producing the magazine was to hire the strongest writers about change whom he could find. Walter Weyl and Walter Lippmann had already become well known as champions of a form of society called socialism—a form of government in which the people controlled the industries. Felix Frankfurter would later become a Supreme Court judge. These and other "editors" of the *New Republic* wrote 25,000 words for each issue about a wide range of topics. The magazine would remain in Croly's total control and fiercely independent of outside forces for many years.

Croly had supported Theodore Roosevelt in his bid for a second term as president and in his formation of the Progressive Party.

But when, in 1914, Roosevelt took issue with the direction of the government and verbally attacked President Woodrow Wilson, the *New Republic* opposed the action. Wilson became the new hope of the magazine's editors.

World War I. The *New Republic* at first pressed for the United States to stay out of World War I and was even powerful enough to delay the country's entry into the war when that became necessary. The demands of the magazine influenced Germany to promise not to interfere with neutral ships at sea. For six or seven months, Germany kept this promise and America's entry into the war was postponed. However, when conditions worsened and the country joined the battle against Germany, Croly and his staff supported the war effort and pressed for more arms for the struggle.

Woodrow Wilson. Woodrow Wilson remained the favorite of the editors, mostly because he had entered the war with the idea not of winning a victory over Germany but of forcing a peaceful and agreeable settlement. Wilson felt that the German people should not be punished for the war, and the *New Republic* agreed. But when the war was over and the allied countries gathered to design a peace treaty, President Wilson was pressed into compromises with the European allies who wanted to severely punish Germany. In the end, Wilson agreed to a harsh peace that resulted in carving central Europe and the Middle East into new and sometimes unnatural countries. The editors of the *New Republic* abandoned their support of Wilson.

Decline. After World War I, Croly was very pessimistic about ever changing the politics and economics of America. He continued to produce the *New Republic,* but the magazine lost more and more of its influence. Only one of its editors, Lippmann, remained optimistic. Until the Great Depression, he continued to advocate changes that would improve the fate of the laborer. He eventually left his position at the *New Republic* to write independently and to counsel with presidents. However, not even Lippmann's ideas withstood the depression that began with a stock market crash in 1929. Lippmann afterward became known as a conservative who opposed the great power of government and, in his view, its interference in the lives of Americans.

As early as 1922, Croly indicated that he was prepared to give up the fight for Americans, placing their own interest behind a higher commitment to nationalism and care for humanity. He wrote to the lawyer Learned Hand:

> I have had a rather forlorn feeling of recent years that the N[ew] R[epublic] was making a difference between me and the friendship of some of the people I most loved, and it made me wish to give up the *New Republic.* (Croly in Forcey, p. 291)

Nevertheless, the *New Republic* continued to voice its opinions in the ongoing debate over the role of government in society. In the late 1920s, a new champion of progressive politics used articles from the *New Republic* to show how the older progressive ideas had gone wrong.

The *New Republic* and Herbert Hoover. There was a brief period in the 1920s when it appeared that Croly's magazine would regain some of its glory during his lifetime. The magazine took a strong position in support of Herbert Hoover for the presidency. But Hoover lost the Republican nomination. The magazine, which had been a leader in progressive ideas, was at this point passed up by rapid changes in the country. Croly, a man so shy that he could not speak except among his best friends, had stirred up thoughts about the role of government and had influenced the direction of change in the nation. But by the time of the depression, he had fallen behind political thought of the day.

Death. In 1928, a year before the stock market collapse that would trigger the Great Depression and consequent great increases in the power of the federal government, Croly suffered a massive stroke. He struggled hard but never recovered his strength. On May 17, 1930, Croly died. For nearly a quarter of a century, he had been the spokesman for a new, unselfish way of life for Americans. A writer for the *New Republic* reflected on his importance as a man and an American:

> I suppose he most often must have asked himself, as all journalists are forced to do, what would be left of this seemingly impermanent work. In his case I have no doubt about the answer. He gave us what is, I think, the most inspiring spectacle that a man can

give his fellows—the spectacle of a mind of unusual power and still rarer integrity, struggling to apply its high standards and ideals to the daily world. (Stettner, p. 171)

For More Information

Forcey, Charles. *The Crossroads of Liberalism.* New York: Oxford University Press, 1961.

Levy, David W. *Herbert Croly of the New Republic.* Princeton, New Jersey: Princeton University Press, 1985.

Stettner, Edward A. *Shaping Modern Liberalism: Herbert Croly and Progressive Thought.* Lawrence, Kansas: University Press of Kansas, 1993.

Louis Brandeis

1856-1941

Personal Background

The Brandeis family in Europe. The Brandeis family had long lived in Prague, Bohemia, in the present-day Czech Republic. However, peasant rebellions beginning in Prussia spread over Europe during the 1840s and made conditions more difficult for Jews—who had a long history of persecution because of religious and other differences. Jews in Bohemia, as elsewhere in Europe, were already targets of government repression. Already they were restricted by the government in the types of businesses they could start and the land they could own; the new government after the 1848 rebellion promised to be more punishing. The Brandeis family, along with the Wehles and Dembitzes, other merchants in Prague, considered moving to America.

Adolph Brandeis had recently graduated from the Technical School in Prague. He was chosen to go to America and investigate farming possibilities there. Adolph arrived in New York in the fall of 1848. By January of the next year, he wrote his family, "I already love our new country so much that I rejoice when I can sing its praises" (Paper, p. 8). However, reported Adolph, farming was not a good idea. Instead the three families should try a grocery business. On April 8, 1949, the twenty members of the Dembitz, Wehle, and Brandeis families set sail from Hamburg, Germany. The Wehles and Brandeises soon settled in Madison, Indiana. There G. and M.

▲ **Louis Brandeis**

Event: Protecting American workers.
Role: Although his own law business made him a millionaire, Supreme Court Justice Louis Brandeis battled what he called "bigness" in industry, labor, and government. His championing of workers earned him a reputation as a "people's lawyer."

Wehle, Brandeis, and Company began to sell groceries and to manufacture starch.

Within a few years, Adolph and another partner, Charles Crawford, were operating a flour mill, a tobacco factory, a farm, and their own steam freighter called the *Fanny Brandeis.*

Life in America. Early in their stay in Madison, Adolph reunited with his fiancée Frederika, and the two married. Madison was not growing quickly enough for the young family trying to build a business. After two years, Adolph and Frederika moved to Louisville, Kentucky. Their son, Louis David Brandeis, was born there November 13, 1856.

The move to Louisville proved profitable. Louis's youngest years were spent in a house staffed with servants. The Brandeis family was wealthy enough to take several vacation trips to Niagara Falls, Canada, and Newport, Rhode Island.

Education. Louis grew to be tall and slender. He had inherited his father's deep blue eyes and straight black hair as well as his deep interest in learning. Attending the Louisville public schools, Louis excelled in all his studies. In 1872 he received a gold medal from the Louisville University of the Public Schools.

After the Civil War, the grocery's Southern customers were unable to pay their bills, and the business suffered. Adolph was certain that conditions could only worsen. He decided to sell his company and take the family on vacation, in hopes that the situation would improve in a year or two. The family set out in 1872 for a tour of Europe.

Sixteen-year-old Louis decided that he wanted to continue his education at the Gymnasium in Vienna, Austria, but failed the entrance examination. It would be one of his few academic defeats. After tagging along with his father and older brother through the mountains of Switzerland, the physically weak Louis decided again to pursue more formal education. He arranged with his father to travel to Dresden, Germany, and try to enter the famous Annen-Realschule there. A friend would introduce him to the director of the school. However, just as they were about to make the trip, Adolph became ill. Louis made the trip himself in 1873, only to find that his friend was not there to introduce him to the school. Louis Brandeis introduced himself.

The head of the school refused to admit Brandeis. He had no recommendations, no birth certificate to prove who he was, and no record of vaccinations, and he had not taken the entrance examination. Brandeis argued that since he was there, it was proof enough that he had been born and marks on his arm would show that he had the necessary vaccinations. But there was still the matter of the exam. The director suggested that he spend the few remaining weeks in the semester visiting classes. Brandeis agreed, and he did so well in the classes he visited that there was no more mention of the entrance examination. The next semester he enrolled as a full-time student. Although he disliked the discipline at Dresden, he did well in his studies.

Studies law. Brandeis's uncle, Louis Dembitz, was a successful lawyer in Louisville and was also active in politics. He had worked for the election of Abraham Lincoln, even though Kentucky was a slave state housing more than 200,000 slaves. Apparently Brandeis looked up to this uncle and wanted to be like him. He changed his middle name from David to Dembitz and decided to become a lawyer.

The family returned from Europe in 1875, and Brandeis soon set off to Cambridge, Massachusetts, to law school. In 1869 Charles Eliot had become president of Harvard University and had set out to make it a stronger institution. Harvard had had a floundering law school since 1817. Eliot persuaded a New York lawyer, Christopher Columbus Langdell, to become its dean and to develop a strong legal training program there. College graduates began to enroll in the school. Though Brandeis had no college training, he easily passed the entrance examinations at the age of nineteen.

The case study method at Harvard Law School required students to study real cases and to analyze them. Brandeis found that he loved analyzing the data and presenting arguments. His arguments, always founded on facts, impressed fellow students, who would later remember that he had "the keenest and most subtle mind of all" (Paper, p. 14). Physically, however, Brandeis had never been strong. The school doctor instructed him to exercise regularly, and Brandeis established a daily physical routine that he would continue throughout his life. By 1877, however, his eyesight had grown so weak that he could not read for his classes. Friends read the lessons to him, and he continued to excel in his studies.

Some of the Activities of Louis Brandeis

1910 Chaired the arbitration board in the New York garment workers' strike.

1911 Helped the Interstate Commerce Commission investigate railroad rates.

1914 Represented the people of California in a trial over the eight-hour workday.

1914 Wrote a book, *Other People's Money and How the Bankers Use It.*

1914-15 Chaired a provisional committee for Zionist affairs.

Beginning lawyer. When Brandeis graduated from Harvard at the top of his class, there were several offers of employment. His family wanted him to establish a practice in Louisville. Brandeis, however, chose to begin his law practice in St. Louis, Missouri. Within a year, he had become disappointed with the western city. Besides, his old friend from Harvard, Samuel Warren, was a member of the Boston aristocracy and wanted Brandeis to join him in a new law firm there. In 1879 the two friends established the firm of Warren & Brandeis. Their partnership was soon so successful that Warren and Brandeis began to take associate attorneys into the firm.

In time, Brandeis established a set routine that included taking an exercise period each day, quitting work precisely at five o'clock, and spending the month of August on vacation each year. He had found that he could do more in eleven months with a break than he could by working steadily for twelve months.

Personal life. Brandeis, an outdoorsman, traveled back to Louisville on vacations. His family had grown to include two sisters and a brother. Brandeis would visit with family members in Louisville, spending hours on horseback with his father, in conversation with his mother, or on walks with his brother.

Tragedy and fortune. In 1890 tragedy struck the family. Brandeis's sister Fanny committed suicide following the death of an infant son. Brandeis rushed home to be with his family. There he met a slim, dark-haired twenty-four-year-old second cousin named Alice Goldmark. They married in a civil ceremony in 1891 and had two daughters, Susan and Elizabeth. A private man, Brandeis revealed little about his family life to outsiders.

A people's lawyer. Brandeis began to be recognized as a champion of the people and as a careful attorney at court. He always knew more about the facts of any case than his opponents. He started attracting national attention when the owner of *Collier's Magazine* hired him at $5,000 a month to represent the magazine and one of its writers in a case involving the secretary of the interior, the director of land management, and even the president of the United States, William Howard Taft. Brandeis's persistent investigation revealed some violations of the law concerning land grants to a coal company in Alaska. Federal officials were involved in illegal grants, and the president seemed to have been involved in covering up the misdealings.

Brandeis won the case but, as was often true later in life, lost the major battle. Congress soon changed the laws to make land grants in Alaska more liberal, and Taft was soundly beaten in his attempt for a second term, but was returned to Washington, D.C., a few years later as the chief justice of the Supreme Court. In 1916 Brandeis would be appointed to that same court.

Brandeis vs. Croly

Unlike Herbert Croly, Brandeis did not believe that trusts, or supercorporations, were manageable by government. Even if they were, he felt, the agency regulating them would grow so big that problems would repeat themselves. The main danger was that such an organization was impossible to really control. Croly, on the other hand, felt that large corporations were an advancement in society and that it would be taking a step backward to break them up. He believed that bigness was bound to occur and could be well regulated by the national government.

Participation: Protecting the Working Class

Brandeis's reputation was now established, and he began to receive calls from all over the country. Many of the cases that he took involved fighting against bigness or trying to improve conditions for the working people. He fought against bringing the Boston subway system under the control of a large New England firm, feeling that a large organization would not respond to the needs of local commuters. He also took part in debates over the effect such companies as United States Steel would have on workers and on business competition. These companies were growing larger by combining small companies into one large management called a trust.

Brandeis involved himself in causes in which he firmly believed. He was not shy in voicing his opinion on political issues of his time, from financial affairs, such as rising tariffs, to international affairs, such as the growing movement to create a separate Jewish nation (Zionism). His activities were varied and far reaching but always thoroughly carried out. His challenging of the insurance industry illustrates the careful work and follow-through that earned Brandeis fame.

"Industrial" life insurance. Many workers tried to put aside money from their meager wages to help their families in case they died from one of the many diseases of the day or from the growing number of industrial accidents. One way to save was to buy life insurance. A worker made regular payments to an insurance company, which in turn invested the money and took some of the earnings, then returned the rest to the family of the person holding the insurance when that person died. Most workers in the early 1900s, however, were paid in small amounts each week. They could not afford to pay several dollars every three or six months for insurance.

In order to sell life insurance, the companies devised a way to pay for it in small payments. In 1905 more than 20,000 insurance agents were spread over the country selling "industrial" life insurance to industrial workers. Industrial accidents were becoming a major cause of death, so workers toiling long hours at poor pay were easy prey to agents who promised them insurance for small fees. Premiums were as little as fifty cents a week and could be paid directly to a visiting agent. It was as easy to have insurance as to buy a magazine. But there was a problem with the system. A worker paying fifty cents a week from age twenty-one to age sixty-one could expect to leave his family as much as $820 under the insurance policy. However, if the insurance company chose to reinvest that fifty cents in a savings bank, the company could collect, at the end of the forty years, $2,265. In fact, the insurance companies were growing rich by investing in properties much more rewarding than the savings banks.

Equitable Life. The high cost of industrial insurance and the mismanagement of insurance companies became news when reporters investigated the Equitable Life Insurance Company. The vice president, for instance, had been spending company money for

▲ Brandeis

personal uses—a private gardener and entertainment. To stop such practices, Boston citizens formed the New England Policy-Holders' Protective Committee and asked Brandeis to represent them. He agreed, provided that he receive no fee. He wanted to be free to do whatever his conscience directed.

To escape the bad publicity, the vice president decided to sell his stock in the company to Thomas Ryan, a powerful stockbroker. The sale gave Ryan a majority of the stock, and he controlled the company. The policyholders rebelled, calling for the company to reorganize so that they would have a voice in the company's management. Brandeis's approach to the problem was typical of the thoroughness with which he attacked any of his many commitments.

Gathering information. Brandeis began by gathering as much information as possible. The information led him to suspect that insurance companies could benefit by adopting the management styles of banks. He found that insurance companies were spending unusual amounts of money to gain favor with politicians. New York Life, for example, had contributed $48,702.50 to the presidential campaign of Theodore Roosevelt. In October 1905, Brandeis revealed his information to the Boston Commercial Club in a speech titled "Life Insurance: The Abuses and Remedies." In the speech, he showed that banks were earning seventeen times more than insurance companies while spending less. In fact, insurance companies were using their profits to buy control of the more efficient banks. Brandeis began to believe that banks could sell insurance more effectively than the insurance companies. He prepared a plan for savings banks to issue insurance policies. The efficiency of the banks would allow for greater profits at lower premium rates.

Going public. Then Brandeis began a speaking campaign to convey his idea to the people. He persuaded the governor of Massachusetts to appoint a committee to investigate insurance. Brandeis next wrote an article to be published by *Collier's Magazine,* at that time run by an old friend, Norman Hapgood. This article stirred even the interest of President Theodore Roosevelt.

Political action. Brandeis prepared a detailed plan for the more efficient sale of life insurance. He then persuaded the Massachusetts legislature to propose laws allowing the banks to carry out the plan. When the laws came before the legislature, he made sure the action was well publicized. His publicity brought large and sympathetic crowds to the hearings. Brandeis enlisted impressive leaders in business, religion, and politics to speak to the legislative committees. His work in "marching along" approval of the legislation ended in an insurance reform law in Massachusetts. He now had legislation but knew that few people would take advantage of the new insurance unless it was sold to them. Brandeis then turned his attention to this job.

Persuading the public. The legislation had called for the appointment of a board to regulate insurance companies—a General Insurance Guaranty Fund. Brandeis recommended seven possible trustees whom he felt would provide good leadership and regional balance. When this board appointed an accountant to prepare rates and policy forms, Brandeis sent him recommendations. Brandeis then set out to convince the public. He spent the next several years publicizing the benefits of the new insurance and its regulation. Through his hard work, insurance reform began in Massachusetts and spread throughout the country.

It was this solid investigation and complete follow-through that made Brandeis a successful champion of the people. But his most well-known efforts were in defense of women workers.

Women's working hours. In 1903 the state of Oregon established a law providing a maximum workday of ten hours for women. The manager of Curt Muller's Grand Laundry in Portland promptly broke the rule and was fined $10. He appealed to the Supreme Court of Oregon and then to the Supreme Court of the United States. Brandeis was called on to defend the Oregon law. Although his argument might be frowned upon today, it was considered supportive of women for its time. Brandeis presented it with enough facts and enough personal testimony that Justice David Brewer, speaking for the court, declared, "We are of the opinion that it cannot be adjudged that the act in question is in conflict with the Constitution" (Strum, p. 115). Brandeis based his case on these points:

1. In structure and function, women are different from men and, therefore, weaker.
2. Women are, because of this weakness, affected more than men by the strain of industrial work.
3. The evil of overwork has a disastrous effect on childbirth.
4. To protect women and their children, special laws are needed to control the working hours of women.

This argument won over the Supreme Court, even though it was challenged by claims based on the Fourteenth Amendment. Under that law, Brandeis's opponents declared, women restricted in their work hours were being deprived of a basic liberty to control their own contractual agreements. In preparing for the trial, Brandeis had written a two-page argument, accompanied by fifteen pages of old laws to show that similar legislation had never been thought unconstitutional and ninety-five pages titled "The World's Experience upon Which the Legislation Limiting the Hours of Labor for Women Is Based." Brandeis's method of arguing cases from a mass of supporting information was an original approach at the time.

Minimum wage for women. In 1913 Brandeis was again called to Oregon, this time to defend a minimum wage law for women against the charge that it was unconstitutional. The case reached the United States Supreme Court at the end of 1914, with Brandeis there to make his argument:

> No proposition in economics is better established than that low wages are not cheap wages. On the contrary, the best in wage is the cheapest.... Why should the proposition be doubted, that wages insufficient to sustain a worker properly are uneconomical? Does anybody doubt that the only way you can get work out of a horse is to feed the horse properly? Does anyone doubt that the only way you can get hens to lay is to feed them properly? Regarding cows we know now that even proper feeding is not enough, or proper material living conditions.... Experience has taught us that harsh language addressed to a cow impairs her usefulness. Are women less sensitive than beasts in these respects? (Brandeis in Mason, p. 252)

The court was unusually impressed by Brandeis's moving words. Reacting to the argument, Judge William Hitz wrote, "I have just heard Mr. Brandeis make one of the greatest arguments I ever listened to" (Mason, p. 253).

Aftermath

Brandeis continued to participate in public affairs at all levels. He became an advisor to presidents on such ideas as tariffs and Zionism. He continued to be an activist even after President Woodrow Wilson appointed him to the Supreme Court in 1916.

Supreme Court justice. As a Supreme Court justice from 1916 to 1939, Brandeis continually spoke out against bigness—opposing big unions as strenuously as big business. He continued to demonstrate exceptional ability to get at the facts by persuading witnesses before the court. Brandeis had a way of looking at witnesses and talking with them that persuaded each witness of his integrity and his genuine interest in their ideas.

Meanwhile, off the bench, Brandeis gave political advice to whomever he felt could benefit from it. Woodrow Wilson felt the need for his advice on the matter of creating a separate Jewish state after World War I. He knew that Brandeis would consider it a violation of the separation of branches of government if he were to be summoned to the White House. President Wilson called on him at his home instead.

Brandeis died of a heart attack on October 5, 1941, mourned by his fellow justices and almost equally by his enemies, who recognized his fairness and integrity. He had spent his life in courts championing the people's rights.

The Curse of Bigness

Brandeis connected bigness to the loss of liberty. At United States Steel Corporation, for example, men worked seven days a week for twelve hours or more a day in poorly lit, crowded, unsafe factories. Such conditions, argued Brandeis, would not be possible unless management silenced every worker who might dare protest. "You cannot have true American citizenship," added Brandeis, "you cannot preserve political liberty, you cannot secure American standards of living unless some degree of industrial liberty accompanies it. And the United States Steel Corporation and those other trusts have stabbed industrial liberty in the back." (Brandeis in Paper, p. 170)

For More Information

Brandeis, Louis D. *The Curse of Bigness.* Edited by Osmond K. Fraenkel. New York: The Viking Press, 1934.

Mason, Alpheus Thomas. *Brandeis: A Free Man's Life.* New York: The Viking Press, 1946.

Paper, Lewis J. *Brandeis: An Intimate Biography of One of America's Truly Great Supreme Court Justices.* Englewood Cliffs, New Jersey: Prentice-Hall, 1983.

Strum, Philippa. *Louis D. Brandeis: Justice for the People.* Cambridge, Massachusetts: Harvard University Press, 1984.

Upton Sinclair

1878-1968

Personal Background

Family. Upton Sinclair was born on September 20, 1878, in Baltimore, Maryland, the only son of Upton Sinclair, Sr., and Priscilla Harden Sinclair. His childhood was unusually miserable in spite of the fact that he came from a long line of Southern aristocrats. His great-grandfather was a hero in the War of 1812, and the Sinclair name was known and respected throughout the South. The Civil War, however, left the Sinclairs without money or property, and Upton, Sr., found himself unable to adjust to the changes forced by the war.

Charming and good-looking, Upton, Sr., found work as a salesman of such items as whiskey and men's hats and clothing. He drank up most of his earnings from the whiskey sales, making it increasingly difficult for him to work. As a result, the family lived mostly in poverty, moving often from boardinghouse to boardinghouse when they could not come up with the rent. Sinclair later wrote of living in one-room apartments and sleeping with his parents in the same bed. At night they often awoke to do battle with bedbugs that infested the rundown boardinghouses:

> One adventure recurred; the gaslight would be turned on in the middle of the night, and I would start up, rubbing my eyes, and join in the exciting chase of bedbugs. They came out in the dark,

▲ **Upton Sinclair**

Event: Muckraker movement—meat-packing industry.
Role: As a writer and socialist, Upton Sinclair fought against social injustices in the United States. He was a muckraker, a writer who aimed to expose corrupt and unsanitary conditions in early twentieth-century society. In *The Jungle,* Sinclair brought to the attention of millions of Americans the corrupt, unclean practices of the meat-packing industry.

and scurried into hiding when they saw the light; so they must be mashed quickly. (Sinclair, p. 4)

Sinclair's mother, Priscilla, could not have been more different from her alcoholic husband. Not only did she not touch alcohol, she condemned self-indulgence in any form and even abstained from coffee and tea because they were stimulants. As an adult, Sinclair followed his mother's lead—he never tasted a drop of alcohol during his lifetime. Because Upton, Sr., was away often on sales trips or extended drinking binges, Sinclair and his mother formed a close relationship. She fostered a love for literature in her son, supplying him with books and frequently reading to him. As he grew up, literature occupied an incredible amount of his time—he sometimes read fourteen hours a day. In his *Autobiography,* Sinclair recalled reading all of William Shakespeare's works and John Milton's poetry during a two-week Christmas holiday.

Shaping of a Social Rebel

"[I describe] my psychology as that of a 'poor relation.' It has been my fate from earliest childhood to live in the presence of wealth that belonged to others.... All my life I was faced by the contrast between riches and poverty, and thereby impelled to think and to ask questions. 'Mamma, why are some children poor and others rich? How can that be fair?' I plagued my mother's mind with the problem, and never got any answer. Now I plague the ruling-class apologists of the world with it, and still have no answer." (Sinclair, p. 99)

Priscilla, who came from a wealthy southern family, also ensured that Sinclair's childhood was not spent entirely in miserable poverty. On visits to his mother's relations, Sinclair slept in luxurious beds and ate like a king. Priscilla's father was the secretary-treasurer of the Western Maryland Railroad, and her sister had married a man who would become one of the richest in Baltimore, Maryland. Although these visits were a relief from the squalor of the boardinghouses, Sinclair came to hate the snobbery and greed that he witnessed at his uncle's house. "I do not know why I came to hate it," he later wrote, "but I know that I did hate it from my earliest days. And everything in my later life confirmed my resolve never to 'sell out' to that class" (Sinclair in Harris, p. 9).

Education. By age five, Sinclair had begun finding an escape from his life in books such as *Gulliver's Travels* and the stories of Horatio Alger. He did not begin school, however, until he was nearly eleven years old, after the family had moved to New York City.

Within two years, he had caught up with his classmates, quickly completing eight elementary grades.

In 1892 Upton went on to study at City College of New York, entering into a five-year program that equaled a high-school education and two years of college. At the same time, he showed an enthusiastic and intense interest in religion, studying under the guidance of an Episcopal minister named William Wilmerding Moir. Reverend Moir strongly influenced the young boy with his highly moralistic and puritanical teachings. He believed that if people could successfully stifle their sexual desires, their creativity and spirituality would be that much stronger. Although Sinclair had a crisis of faith before he was twenty and abandoned his religious beliefs, he never forgot Moir's teachings.

Early writings. While still in school, Sinclair began his career as a writer, penning jokes and puzzles that he submitted for pay to children's magazines, newspapers, and other publications. The steady income he received for his efforts enabled him to move into his own apartment. From the age of sixteen, Sinclair was able to support himself—though sometimes barely—exclusively from his earnings as a writer.

By the late 1890s, Sinclair had graduated from the city college and enrolled at Columbia University to study literature and philosophy. While in school, he continued to earn a living at writing, hiring stenographers to take dictation for him. He wrote a popular adventure series—weekly action and adventure stories of a fictional West Point cadet. By the time he was twenty, Sinclair was churning out more than two million words a year, according to one biography.

Although he was making a good living, Sinclair grew bored with this kind of writing. He longed to write of more serious and important subjects. In the spring of 1900, when he was twenty-one, Sinclair abandoned his thriving career and moved to a cabin in the woods of Quebec, Canada, to write "the great American novel."

First marriage. While in Quebec, Sinclair fell in love with Meta Fuller, the daughter of one of his mother's friends. Three years Sinclair's junior, Meta was a beautiful woman who longed to live a creative and intellectual life. She looked to Sinclair as a teacher who could help nourish her intellectual development, and

▲ Meta Fuller Sinclair

he willingly filled the role. They married on October 18, 1900, but from the start, the marriage was an unhappy one.

Influenced in part by Reverend Moir, Sinclair tried to stifle sexual desires for the sake of creative energy. Placing his writing above all else, he generally refused to do anything that would diminish his strength. There were occasional exceptions, however, and Meta became pregnant in the first year of their marriage.

From 1900 to 1905, Sinclair completed several books, including *Springtime and Harvest, Prince Hagen, A Captain of Industry,* and *The Journal of Arthur Stirling.* In spite of his productivity, his ability to support his family was constantly challenged. Meta and their son, David, lived mostly with her parents during these years, and at one low point, Sinclair had to move back in with his own parents. In 1903 he moved with his wife and child to a farm a few miles north of Princeton, New Jersey. Here Meta tried to care for David in a run-down, leaky cabin surrounded by mud while Sinclair wrote in a tent near the house. Overwhelmed and lonely, his wife grew increasingly unhappy. Sinclair was meanwhile mostly blind to her unhappiness, as he spent the majority of his waking hours working at his writing.

Participation: Muckraker Movement

Socialist. When Sinclair was twenty-three, he became devoted to a political philosophy that would shape his life's work. At the offices of one of his publishers, he met Leonard Abbot, a young Englishman who was involved in the socialist movement, which called for workers to own the businesses that produce and distribute the goods in society. Abbot gave Sinclair pamphlets to read and introduced him to prominent socialists such as John Spargo, editor of the socialist journal *The Comrade,* and Gaylord Wilshire, a wealthy publisher who was to become one of Sinclair's closest lifelong friends. After this time, Sinclair became dedicated to the socialist cause. He viewed capitalism, a system of individual ownership, and competition as corrupting American society and took on the task of promoting social welfare and justice.

The Jungle. In 1906 Sinclair wrote his most well-known work, a book about life among Lithuanian immigrants working in the meat-packing plants outside Chicago, Illinois. With this effort, Sinclair became one of the most famous "muckrakers" of his time—a term coined by President Theodore Roosevelt for people who searched out and exposed political or industrial corruption. The author spent seven weeks in the meat-packing towns faithfully researching the story.

In *The Jungle* Sinclair writes of a fictional family of immigrants who come to the United States to pursue the American dream, but their optimistic hopes for success soon turn to bitter tragedy. The story begins on a happy note, at the wedding of Jurgis Rudkis and his bride, Ona. Jurgis has an unshakable faith in his ability to succeed in his new country through honesty and hard work. Circumstances, however, challenge his faith and ultimately destroy it.

The family finds itself in financial straits. They struggle to meet the payments on a house they have purchased but find it increasingly difficult. Some family members lose their jobs, and Ona, after giving birth to a son, goes back to work too early, which causes her to become sick. An ankle sprain forces Jurgis to miss work for two weeks; when he returns to work before the ankle is healed, he cannot fully perform his job and is fired. Meanwhile, Ona's boss forces her into prostitution under the threat of losing her job, and later she dies in childbirth, old and worn-out at age eighteen. Their son, Antanas, drowns in a mud hole in the street. In despair, Jurgis leaves Packingtown, wandering the countryside and becoming a bum. Finally, he attends a socialist meeting, which changes his life for the better.

This tragic story is set against the filthy and inhumane conditions of the Chicago meat-packing plants. In *The Jungle,* Sinclair describes almost unimaginable horrors: diseased cattle processed for human consumption; rotten sausage rejected in Europe and treated with chemicals to be sold in America; rats racing across piles of meat; workers falling unnoticed into cooking vats and becoming an ingredient in lard sold to the public; and workers whose hands had been deformed by acid or knives.

The effect of the book was immediate and widespread. Readers were horrified and demanded reform. Newspapers across the nation filled their front pages with the meat-packing scandal. Even President Roosevelt, who hated muckrakers, was affected by the book. In the end, *The Jungle* had a great deal to do with the passage of the Pure Food and Drug Bill in May 1906. In some ways, Sinclair was surprised at the public's reaction: "I aimed at the public's heart, and by accident I hit it in the stomach" (Sinclair in Bloodworth, p. 58).

Worldwide fame. With the publication of the novel, Sinclair became internationally famous and even more actively involved in social causes. He investigated the working conditions in other industries, such as glass-making and steel, and continued to lobby for meat-packing legislation. He also invested $30,000 of his earnings from the book into a highly publicized experiment in community living called Helicon Hall.

On property in Englewood, New Jersey, the Sinclairs, along with some forty adults and fourteen children, lived cooperatively. The place had once been a boys' school and included a swimming pool, a bowling alley, a theater, and a greenhouse. In the socialist-inspired arrangement, families had their own cottages but shared land and community space, such as a kitchen, living room, and meeting rooms. After four and one-half months, the experiment came to an abrupt end when a fire destroyed the entire community.

From *The Jungle*

There would be meat that had tumbled out on the floor, in the dirt and sawdust, where the workers had tramped and spit uncounted billions of consumption germs. There would be meat stored in great piles in rooms; and the water from leaky roofs would drip over it, and thousands of rats would race about on it. It was too dark in these storage places to see well, but a man could run his hand over these piles of meat and sweep up the dried dung of rats. These rats were nuisances, and the packers would put poisoned bread out for them, they would die, and then rats, bread, and meat would go into the hoppers together. (Sinclair in Yoder, p. 40)

Divorce. Over the years, Sinclair's marriage became increasingly unhappy. He and Meta spent more and more time apart. In the fall of 1908, Sinclair traveled alone to Carmel, California, and fell in love with the West. In Carmel, he played tennis and tried a variety of fad diets. (Sinclair's interest in food and healthy eating was lifelong; he wrote a book called *The Fasting Cure* and a number of magazine articles on the subject of diet.)

While in Carmel, Sinclair also tried his hand, mostly unsuccessfully, at writing plays. In 1910 he wrote *Love's Pilgrimage,* a fictional but almost autobiographical story describing the history and breakup of his marriage. By now both he and Meta realized that their marriage was heading toward divorce. With this awareness and a sense of Meta's deep unhappiness, Upton encouraged his wife to have love affairs. The arrangement worked for a brief while but then strained their relationship. In August 1911, Sinclair filed for divorce. Because of his fame and his unusual approach to marriage,

▲ **Sinclair and his son, David, 1905**

the divorce became an enormous scandal. The press eagerly published stories of the estranged Sinclair couple, turning to *Love's Pilgrimage* for some of their material.

After the divorce, Sinclair traveled in Europe for a while with his son, David. In the spring of 1913, he married Mary Craig Kimbrough, a young southern woman whom he had met years before at J. H. Kellogg's sanitarium, a health retreat in Battle Creek, Michigan.

Other books. During his lifetime, Sinclair published a large body of works. Besides *The Jungle,* some of his better efforts include *King Coal,* published in 1917, about labor problems in the coal mines of Colorado; *Oil!,* published in 1927, a novel based in part on oil scandals during the Warren G. Harding administration; and *Boston,* published in 1928, a novel about the Sacco and Vanzetti trial in that city, in which two men were executed for murders they did not commit (see **Bartolomeo Vanzetti**). During the 1920s, most of his works were nonfiction, dealing with subjects ranging from modern life to education to corruption in the media.

In spite of his great productivity as a writer and his early fame, by the 1920s Sinclair was popular only among socialists. After 1918 he published most of his own books. Today he is not considered one of America's great writers but is remembered mostly for his muckraking efforts.

Aftermath

California. A few years after their marriage, Sinclair and Mary Craig settled in Pasadena, a pleasant community in southern California. He and his second wife enjoyed a happy marriage, untroubled by the melodrama and frustrations of his first marriage. Although Mary suffered from poor health, she was an extremely active woman and was a great help to Sinclair in his work.

After World War I, America's economy boomed and socialism lost its attractiveness and influence as a force in American politics. Sinclair resigned from the Socialist Party but applied for readmission a few years later. Meanwhile, his writing became less radical and he began to turn his attention to such issues as prohibition, the movement to ban the manufacture and sale of alcohol.

Run for governor. In 1933, Sinclair became a registered Democrat so that he could have a chance at being elected governor of California. Although he had run for political office several times before on the Socialist ticket, he devoted himself energetically to winning this campaign. At the core of the campaign was Sinclair's movement to End Poverty in California (EPIC). He published a pamphlet detailing EPIC's twelve principles that sold to hundreds of thousands of people, and he became very popular with California voters. Among other things, he promised to repeal the sales tax and increase income tax for the rich while reducing it for the poor. Sinclair was so popular that he won the primaries, getting more votes than all the other Democratic candidates combined. Among his allies, Sinclair counted actors such as Charlie Chaplin, Jean Harlow, and James Cagney.

Other people in the movie industry, however, pitted themselves against Sinclair. After the primary elections, the opposition, led by rich movie studio heads in southern California who wanted to protect their fortunes, mounted a $10-million campaign against Sinclair. Some threatened to move the industry to Florida if Sinclair were elected. California newspapers also worked to ensure that the famous muckraker would not get elected, labeling him a communist and a dangerous radical. Though Sinclair won a respectable number of votes, in the end he lost the election; he received 879,537 votes to Republican Frank Merriam's 1,138,620.

Final decades. During the last three decades of Sinclair's life, he continued to be busy and productive with his writing. He wrote forty-five books; however, they are considered less powerful than his earlier works. Increasingly, his subjects moved away from the common people and toward the upper classes. Between 1940 and 1953, Sinclair wrote a series of historical novels that traced world history from 1913 to 1946. The lead character in these eleven volumes is Lanny Budd, a wealthy Connecticut man born in 1900; he travels the world and meets famous historical figures. The series proved to be widely popular in America and around the world.

In addition to writing, Sinclair remained politically active well into his old age. He spoke out against McCarthyism in the 1950s, when Senator Joseph McCarthy and other politicians accused many prominent Americans of being communists and working to undermine American government and society. And in 1967, sixty-one years after writing *The Jungle,* Sinclair was invited to witness President Lyndon Johnson's signing of the Meat Inspection Bill.

In 1962, a year after Mary had died following a long illness, Sinclair remarried a third time, to a woman named May Hard. In that same year, he published his autobiography. Sinclair's lifelong interest in diet and nutrition may have served him well, for he outlived his third wife and died peacefully at the age of ninety in a New Jersey nursing home on November 25, 1968.

For More Information

Bloodworth, William A., Jr. *Upton Sinclair.* Boston: Twayne Publishers, 1977.

Harris, Leon. *Upton Sinclair: American Rebel.* New York: Thomas Y. Crowell Co., 1975.

Sinclair, Upton. *Autobiography of Upton Sinclair.* New York: Harcourt, Brace & World, 1962.

Yoder, Jon A. *Upton Sinclair.* New York: Frederick Ungar Publishing Co., 1975.

Ida Tarbell

1857-1944

Personal Background

From Hatch Hollow to Titusville. Franklin Tarbell had planned to move his family from Pennsylvania to Iowa and establish a farm there. He was in Iowa clearing land and working in a sawmill when his wife Esther gave birth to Ida Minerva Tarbell in a Pennsylvania log cabin on Hatch Hollow, the farm of Esther's parents. The first child in the family, Ida was born on November 5, 1857. It was a year of financial panic in America. Large insurance companies collapsed, and the railroads these companies were financing stopped laying down tracks. Franklin was left without a job or enough traveling money to return home. So Franklin, a resourceful man, walked home across Illinois, Indiana, and Ohio, earning a little money as he traveled by taking temporary teaching jobs. Ida was eighteen months old when she first saw her father.

Oil riches. It was a time of depression but also a time of hope. Just forty miles from Hatch Hollow, Edwin Drake had dug a well in hopes of getting more petroleum from land on which pools of oil oozed to the surface. His venture was so successful that a new market arose for the oil that had been used for medicines and lubricants. Now it could be gathered in such quantity that the crude petroleum could be refined to make a cleaner and brighter-burning lamp oil. Franklin saw an opportunity in the new industry. He would

▲ **Ida Tarbell**

Event: Muckraker movement—exposing the trusts and protecting the independent businessman and laborer.

Role: Ida Tarbell, a writer for *McClure's Magazine,* carefully researched practices in the oil industry. A muckraker, or writer who exposed corrupt practices, Tarbell focused on the monopoly of the oil industry that was attempted by John D. Rockefeller. Her writing encouraged resistance to large, monopoly-style trusts and enforcement of antitrust laws.

▲ An oil field

perfect a wooden tank that would hold large amounts of the oil until it could be refined.

Runaway. When Ida was just three years old, Franklin moved his family by wagon over muddy and rocky roads to Cherry Run (Rouseville), Pennsylvania, the middle of oil country. It was a dismal town; the oil prospectors had built it right among the drilling towers and working pumps of the oil fields. On her grandparent's farm, Ida had been used to running freely and playing with the farm animals. Now she hardly dared go outside. Open pits filled with oil were near their home, and an oil- and debris-littered creek passed through the yard. She hated the change so much that, at age three, she ran away from home—with her mother's approval. She got as far as a hill but was too small to climb over the steep embankment.

An early experiment. Still rebellious, and jealous of the attention demanded by her baby brother Will, Ida decided to take him for a walk. There was a footbridge over the creek, and that was where she headed. Once there, she pushed her brother into the creek. Only his billowing skirt and the quick response of a workman to Will's screams saved him from drowning. Many years later, Ida would describe this event as an experiment to see if the boy's dress would keep him afloat.

Pithole and Titusville. For a time, her father's tank business flourished. He moved it to some new fields at Pithole and rode the ten miles to work and home on horseback. By this time, Franklin had built the family a home on a hill away from the grime of the oil fields. When Ida was thirteen, the family moved to a big new house in Titusville.

Ida attended school—somewhat unwillingly at this point, and only when she had to—and church. Her favorite school subjects were geography and science. She would enjoy studying with a microscope nearly all her life.

Ida soon proved to be an independent thinker, good at gathering information and forming it into her own ideas. By the time she was ten or eleven, she had decided for herself that Christianity was her true religion, but her belief in religion would later be shaken by the newly described idea of evolution, the idea that living things change and give rise to other forms over time. Ida was one of the early believers in this new idea about the origins of life.

College. The Standard Oil Company had begun to absorb independent oil companies by the time Ida graduated from high school. Metal tanks encouraged by Standard Oil started to replace the wooden tanks her father's company built. However, the new oil business provided opportunities everywhere. Franklin began to invest in oil property, which yielded large profits to the investors. There was one problem, however: the lone customer for the oil from the fields that Franklin owned was Standard Oil.

When the fields of Pennsylvania produced too much oil, John D. Rockefeller of Standard Oil took advantage of the situation. He stored large amounts of oil and then began to cut the prices he offered field owners for new oil. Franklin's company suffered greatly. Although the suffering was caused, at least in part, by the owners overproducing oil, Rockefeller was blamed. Ida never overcame her conviction that Rockefeller had caused her father's losses.

Still the family scraped together enough money to send the children to college. Ida enrolled in Allegheny College in nearby Meadville. She proved to be a good writer but preferred to spend her time studying life through a microscope. She began to accept the idea of evolution, and to question a religion that taught her that the earth and all living things were created in seven days.

First job. When Tarbell graduated from Allegheny College, she was offered a position there. She refused the job, instead taking a teaching position at Poland Union Seminary in 1881. Her love for the microscope had to be put aside for her new duties, and Tarbell felt trapped by the job. After a year, she resigned.

Editor. The Tarbell family had frequently spent their summers at nearby Lake Chautauqua, New York. In 1883 Tarbell became associate editor of the town magazine, *The Chautauqua Assembly Herald.* A Reverend Flood produced this magazine from his home in Meadville, Pennsylvania. It seemed that Tarbell would be close to home and have time to resume her microscope study and practice investigative journalism.

Reverend Flood, however, had other interests that interfered with the regular publication of the *Herald.* Soon Tarbell found herself writing, editing, laying out pages, and dealing with the printer. Before leaving the *Herald* in 1891, she had learned nearly every phase of magazine publishing. In the end, Reverend Flood decided to leave the magazine and put his inexperienced nineteen-year-old son in charge. Tarbell was unhappy with this change and left the paper. Although she seldom talked about the move, Tarbell's comments in later life suggest that she was fired.

Tarbell meets McClure. Tarbell decided to become a freelance writer, but first she would visit Europe. She sailed for Paris, France, where she lived nearly a pauper's life while studying at the Université de Sorbonne and Collège de Paris. Determined to make her own way, she hired a tutor to improve her French. She would soon make her tutor the hero of a piece of fiction called "France Adorée." Meanwhile, Tarbell found writing assignments for *Harper's Bazaar, Scribner's Magazine,* and a relatively new publication, *McClure's Magazine.* Samuel Sidney McClure, a New York newspaper publisher and owner, had decided that he could compete against the more expensive literary magazines (thirty or thirty-five cents a copy) with a lower-cost magazine to be read by a larger audience who could afford to pay fifteen cents an issue. In 1890 Tarbell met McClure in Europe and agreed to write for his magazine. Her first assignment was to write a biography of Madame Roland, a French author active at the time of the French Revolution. Tarbell followed this with articles about chemist and microbiologist Louis Pasteur and the writer Émile Zola. She also investigated a new method of identifying criminals that later became fingerprinting.

After Tarbell spent three years freelancing, McClure finally persuaded Tarbell to become an editor in a new youth department at *McClure's.* He paid a great salary to win her to the new task: Tarbell's costs for returning to America and a business wardrobe. She would then be paid $2,100 a year. Tarbell began her new work in July 1894.

Life of Napoleon. The famous artist Gardiner Hubbard had prepared some beautiful etchings of the life of French Emperor Napoleon Bonaparte, and McClure had agreed to publish them. Tarbell's first assignment as a *McClure's* editor was to research the life of Napoleon and prepare an article to accompany the etchings. When published, the article and the etchings proved so popular that *McClure's Magazine* sales rose from 24,500 for the previous issue to 65,000. McClure later published *A Short Life of Napoleon Bonaparte* in book form in 1895, and Tarbell followed it up with *A Sketch of the Life of Josephine,* about Napoleon's wife, in 1901.

The year that *A Short Life of Napoleon Bonaparte* was released in book form, Tarbell began a series in *McClure's Magazine* about Abraham Lincoln. This series was even more popular than the story of Napoleon. It too was released in book form by McClure as *The Life of Abraham Lincoln.*

Some of the Books of Ida Tarbell

A Short Life of Napoleon Bonaparte, 1895
The Life of Madame Roland, 1896
The Early Life of Abraham Lincoln, 1896
The Life of Abraham Lincoln, 1900
The History of the Standard Oil Company, 1904
He Knew Lincoln, 1908
Father Abraham, 1909
The Tariff in Our Times, 1911
The Business of Being Woman, 1913
The Ways of Women, 1923
The Life of Elbert H. Cary: The Story of Steel, 1925
A Reporter for Lincoln, 1927
Owen D. Young: A New Type of Industrial Leader, 1932
All in the Day's Work: An Autobiography, 1939

Muckraker. Tarbell was now a well-known and popular author, but she was not satisfied. Early in her writing and editing career, she had persuaded Reverend Flood to include information about social issues in his *Chautauqua Assembly Herald.* She was still interested in exposing problems in society and by 1900 had come to feel that giant trusts, or supercorporations, were beginning to monopolize industries and cause great pain and financial loss to competitors. Richard Armour was building a "beef trust" based in Chicago, Illinois. The giant United States Steel Corporation was ruthlessly trampling its competitors. And, of course, Tarbell had long felt that the practices of Standard Oil should be investigated.

Although he, too, was alarmed by the growing "trusts," President Theodore Roosevelt branded social-action reporters and writers, calling them "muckrakers." The term became a popular name for such activists as Tarbell, and Roosevelt used it over and over again in his speeches. The term did not bother Tarbell.

The frequent absences of McClure from the office, however, did interfere with her work. Tarbell really wanted to investigate Standard Oil, but McClure was never around to approve such a story. Finally, the acting manager of the magazine told Tarbell to prepare an outline of the intended article and take it to McClure, who was vacationing in Europe. She prepared the outline and caught up with McClure overseas. Rewarded for her efforts, Tarbell received approval from McClure for a three-installment article of 25,000 words examining the practices of the Standard Oil Company.

Participation: Exposing the Trusts

Tarbell's plan. Tarbell began to gather information. She had lived in Titusville and had seen the hardship of her father as he struggled to protect his interests against Standard Oil. Titusville, she thought, would be a good place to start her research. Beginning her investigation, she was surprised to learn that few of the old-timers in the town were willing to talk with her about John D. Rockefeller. Also, news articles that might have been useful to her had been destroyed. Tarbell began to feel the power of the gigantic business enterprise.

Other writers had already written smaller and less-well-detailed articles about trusts. Henry Demerest Lloyd had written "Wealth Against Commonwealth," a description of wealth and power that used Standard Oil as the example but without naming it. His article was really a plea for socialism, or worker ownership of the means of producing goods. In early 1901, Ray Stannard Baker wrote about oil practices, but also without naming any names.

Tarbell was determined to strike harder at Rockefeller's empire. She would not only name the company in her reports, she would ask the company to review her writing in hope of gaining additional information.

The investigation. For a start, Tarbell needed to look into an earlier venture of Rockefeller, the South Improvement Company. There had been a review of this company written in 1873, but all copies in Pennsylvania and Ohio had disappeared. Tarbell finally found a copy in a New York library.

About 1870 the state of Pennsylvania had issued a permit to organize the South Improvement Company. The charter gave the company the right to engage in any business of any kind in Pennsylvania except for banking. Rockefeller may have organized the company; certainly, as Tarbell's research proved, he was a member of the board of directors. In 1871 Rockefeller bought control of the South Improvement Company.

With capital of $1,000,000, Rockefeller then began to buy up oil interests in the state and to persuade smaller oil companies to join him. With a greater supply of oil to ship, he was able to negotiate discounts from the railroads and to demand rebates (returns of part of the amount paid) not only on his own shipments of oil but also on those shipped by competitors as well. This action was against a federal law that demanded that all customers of railroads be treated equally.

The local oil men who had not joined Rockefeller soon organized to fight his company and succeeded in destroying it in the courts. By that time, however, Rockefeller had used the South Improvement Company to bring pressure on refiners in Ohio, where he soon controlled two-thirds of the oil business. This was the beginning of Standard Oil Company.

Pressure to back down. As she gathered more information, Tarbell was warned not to continue the project. Some thought Standard Oil people were so ruthless that she might be killed. Others, including Tarbell's father, believed that Standard Oil would use its power with the banks to destroy *McClure's Magazine.*

The original charter for the South Improvement Company to do business in Pennsylvania had not included banking. Rockefeller had overcome this obstacle by buying control of the National City Bank. Through this company, he was able to influence the bankers who helped finance *McClure's Magazine.* The vice president of the bank personally warned Tarbell of Rockefeller's weapon, to which Tarbell responded, "Well, I'm sorry, but of course that makes no difference to me" (Tarbell in Brady, p. 106).

Tarbell had another reason to attack Rockefeller aside from her belief that Standard Oil had ruined her father. As she wrote in her articles, her brother Will was struggling with Standard Oil over rights to sell oil in Europe through his own company, the Pure Oil Company. Her findings were at first reviewed by a Standard Oil executive Henry Rogers. Through him, Tarbell met one of the earliest partners, Henry Flagler. She also received important information about tariff rates that influenced the oil companies from Martin Knapp, chairman of the Interstate Commerce Commission. Tarbell was determined to be as fair as possible in her articles. She hired a lawyer to review all her facts and organized the *McClure's* staff to check and rewrite each article three times before publication. She let her old feelings surface only at the beginning of her writing; she chose to start the series with a story about her own father.

The report and its consequences. By the close of 1902, the article was ready for *McClure's.* The first installment was released in November. The second, titled "A History of Standard Oil Company," reached the market in December. The third, an account of the bitter battle of independent dealers to drive off the South Improvement Company, was published in January 1903. Early word had gotten out about the pieces, however, and other articles exposing United States Steel and Jacob Armour's beef monopoly were also published.

The press had a field day. William Randolph Hearst, publisher of the *Examiner World,* saw the news value of such explosive issues and began inventing trusts for headlines—a coal trust, a book trust, an asphalt trust. (When industrialist J. P. Morgan started International Harvester Company, Hearst even labeled it a trust.) Hearst's rival, Joseph Pulitzer, headlined the *New York World* with such leads as "Billion $ Yankee Trust in Europe," "J. D. Rockefeller's $4,000,000 Check—His Share of Standard Oil Dividends for the Last Quarter of 1902."

On November 11, 1902, just before Tarbell released her first installment, President Theodore Roosevelt promised an alarmed Congress that he would break the trusts. He began with an attack on the "beef trust" that finally resulted in the Food and Drug Administration. Then the railroads came under attack, and they too became the subject of stronger government regulation.

Among the earliest targets of government was Standard Oil. Based in Cleveland, Ohio, and growing at such a rapid rate that many felt it must be operating illegally, Standard Oil had come under government fire as early as 1880. In 1892 government scrutiny of the company in Ohio had grown so strong that Rockefeller moved its headquarters to New Jersey and broke off several parts from it. The company had many enemies. One of them was Frank Rockefeller, John D.'s brother and an original partner in the company. Early in Standard Oil history, brother had quarreled with brother, and Frank had been forced out of the company. He provided much useful information to Tarbell.

From *The History of the Standard Oil Company*

Tarbell wrote that Rockefeller won power by carefully studying everything connected with the oil business and also by plotting with the railroads to crush other oil companies. "For fifteen years he ... worked with the railroads to prevent other people getting oil to manufacture, or if they got it he worked with the railroads to prevent the shipment of the product. If it reached a dealer, he did his utmost to bully or wheedle him to countermand [cancel] his order. If he failed in that, he undersold until the dealer ... was glad enough to buy thereafter of Mr. Rockerfeller." (Tarbell, *History of Standard Oil*, pp. 216–217)

The History of the Standard Oil Company. In 1904 the *McClure's* articles were brought up to date and published in book form as *The History of the Standard Oil Company*—the title of the first article. Tarbell had uncovered evidence that Standard Oil was guilty of industrial espionage. Spying on other oil companies to learn about their plans, Standard would cut its prices at the right times to drive its competitors out of the oil market. Also in 1904, Tarbell published another article for *McClure's* about the spying, "Cutting to Kill." The article stirred the government to action.

The breakup of Standard Oil. Efforts to curb monopolies were not new to the United States government. As early as 1890, Congress had passed an antitrust act. But in 1895, when the courts were asked to apply the Sherman Anti-trust Act to break up a sugar monopoly, the Supreme Court said the act did not apply to manufacturers. Nevertheless, President Roosevelt tested it again against J. P. Morgan's United States Steel Company and won a decision to break up that company. As a result of Tarbell's exposure of Standard Oil, that company too was taken to court under the Sherman Anti-trust Act. It was not until 1911, however, that a Supreme Court decision forced Standard Oil to break up. Parts of Standard Oil of New Jersey became Exxon, Mobil, Chevron, and SOHIO, among other companies. Tarbell had succeeded in breaking up the oil monopoly. She had won the battle, but in the end she lost the cause. World War I soon came, and the oil companies decided, with government approval, to pool their resources, and the parts of the giant company were together again. Besides, even though the original "holding" company was broken up, Rockefeller and his partners still sat in control of the individual companies.

Aftermath

American Magazine. Tarbell continued as editor for *McClure's Magazine* while Samuel McClure explored more publishing projects. He began, among other ventures, a new magazine called *National Geographic.* Eventually, however, he lost interest and sold his publishing companies. Tarbell and some of the rest of *McClure's* staff started a new journal, *American Magazine.* When that was sold to Crowell Publishing Company in 1915, she returned to writing independently.

World War I. In her later years, Tarbell was regarded as one of America's wisest citizens. She was popular as a public speaker and continued to write and publish. A champion of peace, she stayed behind when other peace advocates led by Henry Ford decided to charter a ship and voyage to Europe to settle the war peacefully. Perhaps because of her moderate and thoughtful actions she became an adviser to presidents.

Women's suffrage. On one issue, Tarbell was at odds with other important women activists of her day. She would not join the suffragists, women campaigning for the right to vote. Tarbell saw no value in campaigning for the ballot; women, she thought, were already in control of the country as heads of their own households.

Autobiography. In her autobiography, *All in the Day's Work,* published in 1939, Tarbell remembered a visit to a church attended by Rockefeller:

> My two hours' study of Mr. Rockefeller aroused a feeling I had not expected, which time has intensified. I was sorry for him. I know no companion so terrible as fear. Mr. Rockefeller, for all the conscious power written in his face and voice and figure, was afraid, I told myself, afraid of his own kind. (Tarbell, *All in the Day's Work,* p. 236)

Tarbell died on January 6, 1944, at the age of eighty-six. The muckraker had continued to write, speak, and edit until her last few years.

For More Information

Brady, Kathleen. *Ida Tarbell: Portrait of a Muckraker.* New York: Putnam Publishing Group, 1984.

Tarbell, Ida M. *All in the Day's Work: An Autobiography.* New York: The Macmillan Company, 1939.

Tarbell, Ida M. *The History of the Standard Oil Company.* 1904. Reprint, New York: W. W. Norton, 1966.

Tompkins, Mary E. *Ida M. Tarbell.* New York: Twayne Publishers, 1974.

World War I

1912

Woodrow Wilson is elected president.

1914

World War I breaks out in Europe. Poison gas introduced as a weapon.

1915

German submarine sinks British liner *Lusitania,* killing 1,200, including 120 Americans.

1916

Germany stops unlimited submarine warfare. Wilson is reelected. Tanks introduced in warfare.

1917

Espionage and Sedition Acts limit freedom of speech in the U.S.

1917

German foreign secretary sends telegram to win Mexico as an ally. Germany resumes unlimited submarine warfare.

1917

Russian Revolution results in communist takeover of Russian government.

1917

U.S. declares war on Germany, selects **John J. Pershing** to command American forces. Congress passes selective service act, begins to draft 2.8 million soldiers.

1918

New Russian government officially drops out of the war.

1918

Wilson introduces Fourteen Points. Americans fight at Cantigny, Belleau Wood, and Chateau-Thierry and then in final Allied offensive. Germany sues for peace.

1919

Schenck v. *United States*: Supreme Court Justice **Oliver Wendell Holmes** develops "clear and present danger" doctrine.

1919

Wilson attends Paris Peace Conference, which ends war.

1919-1920

Fear of communism results in "red scare" in the United States; hundreds of Americans are arrested.

WORLD WAR I

World War I broke out in Europe in 1914, but the United States stayed out of the fighting until 1917. Its entrance at this point helped tip the balance. Both sides in the fight were experiencing enormous losses with little gain. The fresh supply of American troops gave the Allies a desperately needed advantage.

The Two Sides—A Partial List

The Allies	The Central Powers
France	Germany
Britain	Austria-Hungary
Russia (until 1917)	Turkey
United States (after 1917)	Bulgaria
plus twenty-four others	

There was great brutality in this first truly modern war. New weapons and fighting tactics brought death tolls never before imagined. Over eight million soldiers would die before the fighting stopped, robbing Europe of a whole generation of young men. With years passing, the trench warfare dragged on and on. Neither side seemed able to win.

At first President **Woodrow Wilson** called for strict neutrality (not taking sides), a stand that was supported by the majority of Americans. Wilson was reelected in 1916 with the slogan "He Kept Us Out of War."

World War I was about the division and redivision of empires in competition with one another and seemed at first not to concern America. As the slaughter continued, however, many Americans began to feel their country should enter the war. The feeling mounted when German submarines sank ships carrying American passengers. The most famous was the British liner *Lusitania,* sunk in May 1915 with the loss of 1,200 lives, including over 100 Americans. Germany protested that the *Lusitania* was also carrying war weapons. But, under pressure from the American public and President Wilson, it agreed to stop sinking passenger ships without warning.

Anti-German feeling resurfaced in 1917. Americans learned of a German offer to return to Mexico the territory of Texas, New Mexico, and Arizona if it would join the Germans in war against the United States should the need arise. Also, Germany again declared unlimited submarine warfare. After German submarines sank several American ships, President Wilson asked Congress to declare war on Germany. Wilson and Secretary of War Newton Baker settled on General **John J. Pershing** to command the American forces that would be sent to Europe to fight on the Allied side.

New Ways of Making War

World War I saw the introduction of more new weapons than any other war in history. Aircraft, submarines, tanks, explosive artillery, poison gas, and new U.S. Browning machine guns—all were used for the first time in combat in World War I. Soldiers would crouch in trenches, deep muddy ditches defended by coils of heavy barbed wire. From the trenches, they could rake their attackers with deadly machine gun fire, losing relatively few soldiers themselves.

Pershing faced an incredible task. The U.S. Army, at about 200,000 men, was in no shape to fight a war in which that number might be killed in just one week's time. Congress passed the Selective Service Act in 1917, outlawing the hiring of substitutes, a practice used during the Civil War. In the end, 75 percent of the U.S. forces, or 2.8 million men, were drafted. Pershing brought these raw American soldiers to Europe. The huge force had to be trained, equipped, transported, fed, and supplied. On top of that, Pershing was determined to resist the Allies' constant demands that he allow them to use the Americans as replacement troops in their own exhausted armies. He insisted instead that the Americans, like the British, French,

▲ **Soldiers wearing masks to protect themselves from poison gas**

and Russian armies, fight as an independent force. With Wilson's and Baker's full support, Pershing held to this policy and led the Americans in victories against the war-hardened Germans. At one point, the general did agree to let four African American regiments fight for the French army. Three of these black regiments won the Croix de Guerre, the highest military honor a French fighting unit could receive.

Assigned a section of the front, Pershing's force helped in the final successful drive against the Germans near the

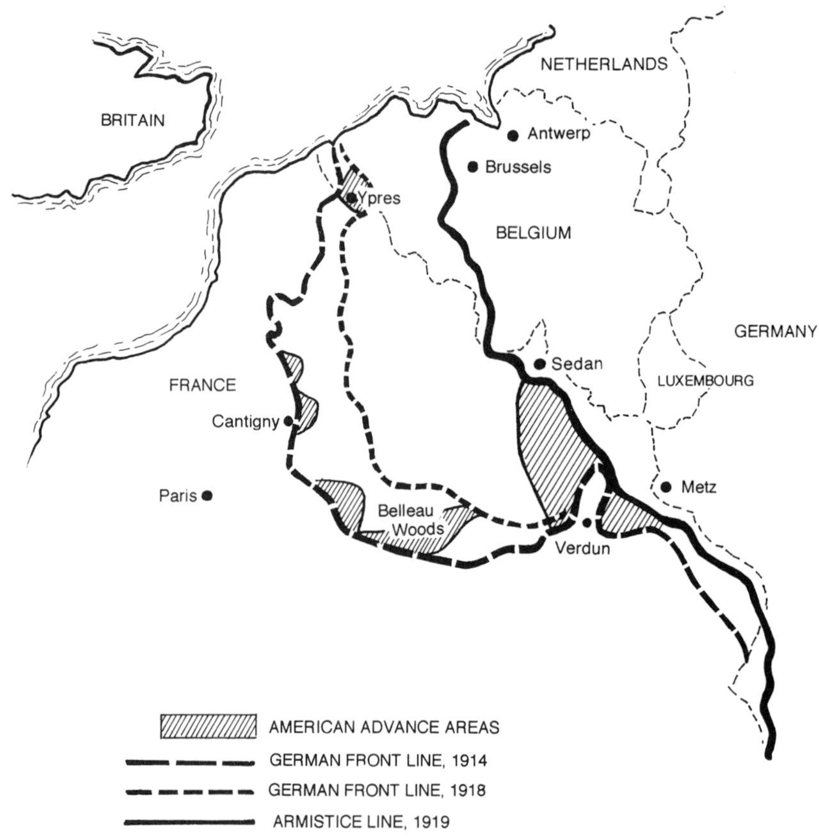

▲ **American advances in World War I**

Meuse River and Argonne forest in September 1918. American military successes proved less important in the defeat of Germany than the seemingly unlimited supply of American manpower. Facing this threat along with battlefield defeats, Germany sued for peace in November 1918.

Throughout the war, President Wilson had struggled to negotiate a peace settlement. In January 1918, in a speech to Congress, he had presented his famous Fourteen Points to promote a fair and lasting peace. Germany requested peace on the terms Wilson laid down in the Fourteen Points, but the actual treaty had to be worked out among the Allies.

Wilson went to Paris to join in these negotiations in early 1919. There, at the Paris Peace Conference, he faced French Prime Minister Georges Clemenceau, who wanted to grind Germany down in defeat so that his country would never again be threatened by its old enemy. Wilson, by contrast, believed that imposing harsh terms on Germany would only bring trouble in the future. He wanted to break out of the old pattern of European warfare, in which defeated countries were forced to accept blame and pay huge amounts of money to the victors.

After almost four months of often stormy negotiations, Wilson and the Allied leaders reached a compromise agreement which included some but not all of the Fourteen Points.

While not as shattering for Americans as for Europeans, the war still had important social consequences for the United States. The need for arms, vehicles, uniforms and other goods spurred the growth of northern industrial cities like New York and Chicago, Illinois. The expansion of industry, in turn, increased tensions between workers and factory owners. Labor leaders, representing the workers, pressed for better wages and working conditions. Many were socialists—that is, they believed that the public should own and control the factories. Though few shared the socialists' views completely, a good number of workers were prepared to offer them a degree of support in order to win a better life. Some labor leaders were prepared to use violence to achieve their goals, as were antilabor businessmen.

Old Ways of Making Peace

After the Franco-Prussian War of 1870–71, the victorious Germans forced France to pay heavy "reparations," or cash payments from the loser that would make up the cost of the war to the victor. Over President Wilson's objections, at World War I's Paris Peace Conference, France, in turn, insisted on payments from Germany. But war had become much costlier. The payments crippled the German economy in the 1920s, opening the way for the rise of the Nazi leader Adolf Hitler. Reparations no longer play a part in most peace treaties.

Meanwhile, a socialist revolution in Russia had succeeded in a takeover of government there. Fears mounted in America. People were afraid of violence in their own backyard and afraid that labor leaders would win control of industry. By 1919 such fears had combined to create a reaction against the socialists. Since red is the international color of socialism, this reaction was called a "red scare." In an atmosphere of near panic, socialist leaders and other reformers were arrested and jailed by the hundreds.

Soon after America's entry into the war, Congress had passed laws against the expression of "disloyal" views. It was under these laws, the Espionage and Sedition Acts, that the arrests were made. Prisoners challenged their arrests in court. Because most had been arrested for expressing their views in speeches or pamphlets, the court cases centered around freedom of speech.

The arrested leaders claimed that the laws violated their rights of free speech, rights guaranteed in the First Amendment to the Constitution. Not until 1919 did such cases come before the Supreme Court, one of whose main members was Justice **Oliver Wendell Holmes.** In his writings for the court about these cases, Holmes laid down ways of thinking about free speech that continue to be used in courts today.

In the first case, *Schenck* v. *United States,* Holmes wrote that freedom of speech is not absolute—it does not exist without any limitations. A man, for example, "falsely shouting fire in a theatre and causing a panic" did not come under free speech protection. If a person's views created "clear and present danger" to society, society had the right to prevent him from expressing those views (Liva Baker, *The Justice from Beacon Hill,* [New York: HarperCollins, 1991], pp. 523-24). Charles T. Schenk had circulated leaflets encouraging Americans to resist the draft, a clear and present danger to a nation at war and a violation of the Espionage Act of 1917, which made it illegal to cause the refusal of military duty.

In *Schenck,* Holmes upheld the government's right to limit free speech. In a later case, *Abrams* v. *United States,* he wrote that this right was in itself limited: the government could only go so far. Only in extreme cases was there "a clear and present danger," and it was important for the government to prove that such a danger existed before arresting someone for expressing his views. Otherwise, society benefited from the free expression of all ideas, whether popular or not.

▲ **Everyone helped with the war effort; here two young women waterproof rockets**

Such concerns had not arisen since the early days of the republic, but they have remained important since Holmes wrote his opinions. Similarly, Woodrow Wilson and John J. Pershing encountered problems that had never before faced American presidents and generals but would continue to come up as America kept its new position of world leadership. In domestic affairs as well as relations abroad, therefore, World War I marks a central turning point in U.S. history.

Woodrow Wilson

1856-1924

Personal Background

Thomas Woodrow Wilson was born in Staunton, Virginia, on December 28, 1856. He grew up in a very religious household, for his father, Joseph Ruggles Wilson, was a minister and his mother, Jessie Woodrow Wilson, a minister's daughter. Married in 1849, the Wilsons had two daughters, Marion and Annie, before the birth of their first son, whom they named after Jessie's brother, Thomas Woodrow. He would be called Tommy until he finished college. When he was two, the family moved to Augusta, Georgia, where Joseph Wilson had been offered a position as minister at the First Presbyterian Church.

"Dream life." Tommy was a shy, quiet boy who passed many of his hours in fantasy worlds created by his imagination. As he later said, "I lived a dream life ... when I was a lad and even now my thought goes back for refreshment to those days when all the world seemed to me a place of heroic adventure" (Heckscher, p. 13). He seemed lazy in school, not learning to read until the age of eleven or twelve, and would be slow in maturing as a young man. The slowness was perhaps encouraged by his mother, who has been described as overprotective of her son, and by two sheltering older sisters, who constantly read him stories, probably making it less important for him to learn to read on his own.

▲ **Woodrow Wilson**

Event: Entry into World War I; Paris Peace Conference.
Role: Elected president in 1912, Wilson brought the United States into World War I in 1917, helping the Allies (France, Britain, and Italy) win the war. For six months in 1919, he pressed Allied leaders in Paris to accept his famous "Fourteen Points," which would establish a fair peace with defeated Germany and create a League of Nations to ensure future peace.

"Tommy Wilson is improving." When Tommy was fourteen, his father won a post as professor at the seminary (a training college for ministers) in Columbia, South Carolina. Uncle James Woodrow, another brother of Jessie's, also taught at the seminary. Tommy continued to do poorly in school, and his father and uncle grew concerned over his lack of progress.

Tommy did learn quickly, however, when he was interested in a subject. At sixteen, he became fascinated with shorthand, a system that uses symbols instead of words to increase the speed of writing things down. He put great effort into mastering shorthand and would continue to use the system in later life. Such accomplishments led Uncle James to write (in a family letter), "Tommy Wilson is improving" (Heckscher, p. 21). Tommy also became fascinated by naval ships. He spent hours at his desk making complicated drawings of various warships and dreaming up sea battles fought and won by Admiral Thomas Wilson. Over the desk hung a picture of British Prime Minister William Gladstone, the daydreaming sixteen-year-old's leading hero. When he grew older, Tommy told a friend, he wanted to be a statesman like Gladstone.

Davidson and Wilmington. In 1873, when he was seventeen, Wilson began his higher education at Davidson College, in North Carolina, where he finally began to do well in classes. He took an interest in debating, beginning to polish the skills that would make him into a superb public speaker. Wilson only spent one year at Davidson. His father had changed jobs again, taking the family to Wilmington, North Carolina, and his parents wanted their son with them.

North to Princeton. In 1875, after a year at home, Wilson went back to school, this time venturing north to the College of New Jersey in Princeton. Renamed Princeton University in 1896, it would play a central role in Wilson's life. He would teach there and then serve as the most effective president in the university's history, using his presidency as a springboard onto the national political scene. All of this lay in the future, however, when the shy eighteen-year-old arrived to begin his four years as a college student.

"Magical years." Wilson loved Princeton. By his second year, he had overcome his childhood shyness. At college, he was elected to student leadership offices and gained wide admiration for his debating and public speaking skills. Wilson developed his own unique style of giving a speech, more conversational and relaxed than the gesture-filled style of the day. Though not a natural athlete, he became involved with football, coaching the team occasionally and helping them achieve an undefeated 1878 season. He also began the serious study of history and political science, thinking and writing about the forces that shape great events and the efforts of statesmen and leaders to control those forces.

By the end of his time at Princeton, Wilson had begun to discover his own intellectual powers and was one of the most respected students on campus. These years of growth and self-discovery would always be, as he later called them, "the magical years" (Heckscher, p. 36).

Lawyer. In 1879, the year he began going by the name Woodrow at his mother's suggestion, Wilson graduated from Princeton. The next year, following the wishes of his father, he began studying law at the University of Virginia Law School. A year and a half of law school was followed by a period of doubt about practicing law. With his father pressing him, Wilson finally moved to Atlanta, Georgia, and set up a law practice there in 1882. However, he was not really happy as a lawyer. Believing himself more suited to being a scholar, he continued reading and writing about history and political science.

Graduate studies and courtship. In 1883 Wilson began graduate studies in political science at the Johns Hopkins University in Baltimore, Maryland. Before leaving Georgia, he had met and fallen in love with a pretty young twenty-three-year-old painter named Ellen Louise Axson. The daughter of a minister (a friend of Wilson's father), she had captured Wilson's heart just as he was deciding to go to Johns Hopkins. In September she agreed to marry him, and the two exchanged letters and visits as Wilson worked at his studies. They were married in June 1885, just as Wilson finished the book *Congressional Government,* which won him his doctoral degree. Published that year, the book received wide praise as an outstanding analysis of Congress's workings. It also won its young author a teaching job at a new women's college called Bryn Mawr, near Philadelphia, Pennsylvania.

Teacher. The Wilsons spent two years at Bryn Mawr, where Wilson continued his progress in the academic world, writing articles and beginning another book. He grew increasingly frustrated with the college's administration, however, and when offered a job at Wesleyan University in Connecticut, he accepted it eagerly.

He taught at Wesleyan until 1890, becoming one of the university's most popular professors. For years afterward, students remembered his enthusiasm and humor in class. "He had a contagious interest—his eyes flashed," one later recalled. "I can see him now, with his hands forward, the tips of his fingers just touching the table, his face earnest and animated" (Heckscher, p. 94–95). Others remembered his jokes or the choice of words he used to describe a subject. In teaching, Wilson truly seemed to have found the calling that was his destiny. Yet below the surface, he felt—as he had since childhood—the stirring of desire for political leadership, for great deeds, for the heroic adventure.

Return to Princeton. Now a slender thirty-four-year-old teacher with a narrow, long-featured face and a quick, lively way of moving, Wilson accepted a job at Princeton, his old college, in 1890. Highly respected for his book and articles as well as for his teaching style, he was something of a star even before he arrived, with 124 out of 238 juniors and seniors signed up for one of his classes in his very first term.

By this time, the Wilsons had three daughters: Margaret, born in 1886; Jessie, born in 1887; and Eleanor, born in 1889. After the move to Princeton, the couple decided not to have any more children. They rented a large house, and Ellen busied herself in the role of mother (having given up painting when they married) while Wilson wrote and taught his classes. He also had great fun with his daughters, playing games and telling favorite stories in which he acted out the parts.

In 1893 Wilson published a second book, *Division and Reunion,* about the Civil War era. Like his earlier work, this one was also widely praised, establishing a reputation for Wilson as a leading historian. Two years later, the Wilsons had a bigger house built for themselves, with a roomy study upstairs. At exactly nine o'clock each night the family would hear a click from the study as Wilson locked his desk, and he would spend the rest of evening with them, talking, playing, or singing songs.

University president. The Princeton board of trustees (the university's governing body) in 1902 unanimously elected Wilson president of the university. Almost immediately he began work on a series of reforms intended to improve the school's performance. He won agreement from trustees and alumni, or former students, in reorganizing the departments, teaching methods, and selecting of classes. Wilson began what became known as the "preceptorial" system there, adding more than forty young teachers (preceptors) to the faculty to act as informal advisors to the undergraduates. Still in place at Princeton, the system is known for its effectiveness.

In other areas Wilson was overruled, however. For several years he struggled to win approval for two plans. One would have linked the graduate and undergraduate schools more closely; the other would have given Princeton a "college" organization similar to the great English universities of Oxford and Cambridge, in which a number of colleges are administered as one university. Though popular with both students and teachers, the plans were bitterly and successfully opposed by wealthy alumni and trustees. In the long struggle, Wilson made powerful enemies and suffered his first taste of defeat. (When the college plan was finally adopted at Princeton in the 1980s, the first college was named for Wilson.)

Governor. His well-publicized battle with the alumni and trustees brought Wilson to national attention. Seen as a "progressive," a champion of the common people who fought against the wealthy and powerful, he gained wide popularity. He was approached by the New Jersey Democratic Party bosses, and with their support won the Democratic Party's nomination for New Jersey governor in 1910. Throwing off the influence of the crooked political bosses, he went on to easy victory in the race and served as governor for two years.

As he did at Princeton, Wilson shook up New Jersey politics with an immediate series of progressive reforms. Showing remarkable leadership, he pushed most of his ideas through the state legislature soon after taking office. The new laws gave voters a stronger voice in electing state officials, regulated public utilities like electricity and gas, reorganized the school system, established workmen's compensation (payment for on-the-job injuries), fought corruption in state politics, and banned industrial monopolies from the state.

To the presidency. Wilson's triumphs as governor won him the Democratic presidential nomination in 1912. He based his campaign on a promise of national reforms similar to those he had passed in New Jersey. Called "The New Freedom," the program helped him win a close and exciting three-way race against President William Howard Taft and former president Theodore Roosevelt. As before, he pushed through the reforms as soon as he took office. Many of them survive in some form today.

Among other laws, The New Freedom limited child labor; set up the first income tax; established the Federal Reserve, the government organization which still regulates banking; offered better working conditions to sailors and railroad workers; and established the Federal Trade Commission to prevent unfair monopolies in business. Yet with all his success at home, President Wilson still faced huge problems in international relations. European countries had meanwhile moved quickly down the road to war with one another.

Participation: Entry into World War I; Paris Peace Conference

Challenges abroad. At age fifty-four, Wilson had switched from an academic career to a political one, and he had risen to the highest office in the land in two short years. As governor and then president, he had won victories that were nothing short of amazing. Great challenges remained, though, especially abroad, where he faced greater difficulties than any president had for decades. The most immediate problem came when revolution broke out in Mexico in February 1913, a month before Wilson's inauguration. Wilson's opposition to the new dictator of Mexico, Victoriano Huerta, led to years of conflict, ending with the invasion by the United States of its southern neighbor under General John J. Pershing (see **John J. Pershing**).

Then, in 1914, after decades of growing tension among the European powers, World War I broke out in Europe. It was a new kind of war. For the first time, technology (such as the recently invented machine gun) allowed both sides to kill huge numbers of the enemy more quickly and in greater numbers than before. By 1915 the Allies and the German enemy had descended into a slow and costly type of trench warfare, with territorial gains of a few yards being paid for by thousands of lives. The war's brutality shocked the world, scarred Europe for generations, and cost eight million dead by its end in 1918.

House on Fire

Wilson suffered from an image as a cold man who lacked a sense of humor. Yet his friends and family knew him as a warm man and a great storyteller with a keen sense of humor. The following incident occurred while the Wilsons were on vacation in Pass Christian, Mississippi, and became part of his legend.

Returning from a golf game one day, Wilson and his Secret Service agents saw that the attic of a house they were passing was on fire. While the agents ran to put out the fire, Wilson went to the entrance, where he found the lady of the house. "Oh, Mr. President," she said, amazed, "it is so good of you to call on me. Won't you please walk into the parlor and sit down?"

"I haven't time to sit down," the President answered dryly. "Your house is on fire."

Rewarded for his service, Wilson was made an honorary fireman by the Pass Christian fire department. (Heckscher, p. 322)

Neutrality. On August 6, 1914, a few days before the war broke out, Ellen Wilson died after several months of illness. "God has stricken me almost beyond what I can bear," Wilson wrote to a friend (Heckscher, p. 334). Facing both personal tragedy and the chaos of war, Wilson behaved with typical courage and restraint. His foremost aim was to keep the United States out of the conflict. The British and the Germans made it difficult to remain neutral, however. The British Navy often illegally took over American ships at sea, and beginning in 1915 the Germans began using submarines to attack Allied merchant and passenger ships. In both cases, American rights and even lives were at risk. In 1915 the Germans torpedoed and sank the British passenger liner the *Lusitania,* killing (among others) more than 100 Americans.

Wilson so firmly demanded that the German submarine attacks stop that his secretary of state, William Jennings Bryan, resigned, fearing Germany would declare war on the United States. Wilson, however, had calculated perfectly. The Germans promised to stop sinking passenger ships.

▲ **"Drifting," a cartoonist's satirical comment on Wilson's neutrality policy in 1915**

Struggle for peace. Wilson worked not only to keep the United States out of the war but also to end it. In 1915 and early 1916, he sent his closest friend and advisor, Colonel Edward House, to Europe to discuss possible peace terms with Allied and German leaders. After being narrowly reelected later that year (with the slogan "He Kept Us Out of War"), he again sent House to Europe. Wilson's hopes of staying out of the war were shattered in early 1917, however, when Germany announced unrestricted submarine warfare against all ships, Allied or neutral. On April 2, after a number of American ships had been sunk, the president went before Congress. Declaring that "the world must be made safe for democracy" (Heckscher, p. 440), he asked for a declaration of war against Germany. Four days later, the United States was at war.

Wilson and the United States at war. U.S. participation actually had little immediate effect. With an army of barely over 200,000, the country was poorly prepared for war. Wilson's leadership carried the day, however. The president set up a variety of war agencies to mobilize U.S. resources, bringing major industries and services under government control. In May 1917, he pushed a selective service bill through Congress, which would lead to nearly three million men being drafted into the army by the end of the war.

As the country mobilized for war, Wilson had to decide what part the United States would play in the Allied effort. He wanted to help win the war, but he also knew that each of the other Allies wanted to come out of it with territorial gains. He was not interested in helping them win more territory—indeed, he viewed such pursuits as part of the problem that had caused the war in the first place. He also faced the question of command. Should the Americans fight on their own, or as part of a team? Wilson agreed to American participation in Allied war planning but was uneasy about putting U.S. troops under foreign command. Instead, he selected General John J. Pershing to command the American soldiers as head of the American Expeditionary Force. Pershing planned to have one million American soldiers in Europe by 1918.

Fourteen Points. Still hoping to make peace even while waging war, in January 1918 Wilson outlined a program of fourteen peace proposals in a speech to Congress. Among other demands, the "Fourteen Points" called for open diplomatic and economic relations (instead of secret treaties and trade barriers), arms reduction, self-government for various peoples, and finally a League of Nations to oversee world affairs. The ideas were not new. Wilson himself had already pressed for a League of Nations, an international body that would have some authority over international relations. In joining these ideas together, however, Wilson presented the world with an organized proposal for handling international relations differently than ever before. The Fourteen Points appealed to common people on both sides, giving the Allies a powerful moral advantage in the war of words that went with the armed struggle.

Later that year, after long and difficult negotiations by Wilson, Germany requested peace under the terms of the Fourteen Points.

Paris Peace Conference. The Armistice (cease-fire) was signed on November 11, 1918. The two sides still had to agree on the terms of the peace, to be ironed out in Paris early the following year. On December 4, Wilson and a large group of advisors sailed for Europe. Wilson himself headed the American delegation to the conference.

In Europe Wilson was greeted as a hero by huge crowds, who lined the streets to catch a glimpse of him. The Allied leaders with whom Wilson met gave him a cooler reception, however. In all, twenty-seven victors were represented at the conference; none of the defeated nations was allowed to take part. Dominating the discussions were the "Big Four": U.S. president Wilson, British prime minister David Lloyd George, French premier Georges Clemenceau, and Italian premier Vittorio Orlando. The three others did not share Wilson's commitment to the Fourteen Points. Clemenceau in particular was eager to take the greatest revenge possible on Germany. During the six months in Paris, Clemenceau and Wilson disagreed strongly, with Lloyd George often taking the middle ground between them.

Leadership for a New Age

Wilson's presidency brought the United States to the position of world leadership, which it occupied for most of the twentieth century. Looking back, his ideas appear well suited to the role. Many of them seemed daringly new in his own day yet are commonly accepted today. No longer are wars ended with the harsh terms, customary up to the twentieth century, that the Allies imposed on defeated Germany.

It took a second world war for the world community to organize the United Nations, directly modeled on Wilson's League of Nations. (U.S. refusal to join had fatally weakened the League.) It is tempting to wonder how the century would have been different if the world had accepted Wilson's ideas a little earlier.

Senate fight. The final version of the treaty went against most (but not all) of the Fourteen Points, as the Allies' desire for revenge overcame Wilson's efforts. Germany was forced to admit guilt for the war, to give up territory, to disarm, and to agree to pay heavy reparations (payments to the victors to help make up the war's costs). Yet Wilson won agreement to his point that called for a world organization, the League of Nations. Also, without his influence Germany would have suffered harsher penalties.

At home, however, even stiffer opposition waited. Wilson's most powerful opponent, Senator Henry Cabot Lodge, led the Republican-dominated Senate, whose approval would be needed in order for the United States to ratify the peace treaty. Lodge, attacking the idea of American participation in the League of Nations, blocked the treaty's passage in the Senate. Rising to the fight, in September 1919 Wilson went on a speaking tour of the West, hoping public support would persuade the Senate to vote for the treaty.

From Wilson's Last Speech as President

(Pueblo, Colorado, September 25, 1919)

"It always seems to make it difficult for me to say anything, my fellow citizens, when I think of my clients in this case. My clients are the children; my clients are the next generation. They do not know what promises and bonds I undertook when I ordered the armies of the United States to the soil of France, but I know. And I intend to redeem my pledges [keep my promises] to the children; they shall not be sent again on a similar errand" (Wilson in Heckscher, p. 608).

Collapse. Wilson had suffered mild health problems in the past, probably including one or more minor strokes. Now, in just over three weeks, he traveled 8,000 miles and delivered forty speeches. During the first part of the trip, his efforts won praise from newspapers and the public. But the rest of his travels progressed less happily. On September 25, 1919, after a long speech in Pueblo, Colorado, Wilson collapsed in his private railroad car. With shades drawn, going slowly to lessen the bumps, the train returned to Washington. There, on October 2, Wilson suffered a massive stroke that paralyzed his left side and left him weak and bedridden.

Aftermath

Slow decline. Wilson would never again be up to the full duties of his office. Instead of resigning, however, as was expected under the circumstances, he stayed in office. Much of the responsibility fell on his advisers—and on his second wife, Edith, whom he had married in 1915. Without him to fight for it, the treaty failed to make it through the Senate. Unable to run for reelection, Wilson demanded that the treaty be the main issue of the 1920 election. The Democratic nominee, James Cox, lost badly to Republican Warren Harding, a well-known treaty opponent. Under Harding, the United States made a separate peace with Germany (outside the plan of the Paris Peace Conference) and never joined the League of Nations.

In 1920 Wilson won the Nobel Peace Prize for his work as president. His health slowly fading, Wilson continued to live in Washington, D.C., cared for by his wife. He died on February 3, 1924.

For More Information

Collins, David R. *Woodrow Wilson: 28th President of the United States.* Ada, Oklahoma: Garrett Educational Corporation, 1989.

Heckscher, August. *Woodrow Wilson.* New York: Charles Scribner's Sons, 1991.

Randolph, Sallie G. *Woodrow Wilson, President.* New York: Walker and Co., 1992.

John J. Pershing

1860-1948

Personal Background

John Joseph Pershing was born on September 13, 1860, in the small town of Laclede, Missouri. The Pershing line had been founded in America by Frederick Pfoershing, who had come to America in 1749 from the French- and German-speaking region of Alsace in Europe. Shortening the family name to Pershing, Frederick had settled as a craftsman in Pennsylvania. His great-grandson, John Frederick Pershing, left Pennsylvania for the West in 1858. During his travels, he met and married a young Tennessee woman named Anne Elizabeth Thompson. The two settled in Missouri, naming their first child John Joseph.

Civil War childhood. The Civil War dominated the boy's early years, lasting until he was five. His father bought a small store during the war, building it up and in time becoming one of the town's leading citizens. The Pershings continued to prosper until John Frederick owned a lumber yard, a new home, and several other real estate properties, including a farm near town. Aside from John Joseph, the family grew to include two younger brothers and several sisters.

Close call. The children played together, the boys often going on nighttime raccoon hunts during the hot summers. John was interested in the family's hunting rifles and took charge of cleaning

▲ **John J. Pershing**

Event: World War I—American soldiers fight in Europe.

Role: After President Woodrow Wilson chose him to command the American Expeditionary Forces (AEF) in World War I, John J. Pershing organized the 2,000,000-man army almost from scratch. Leading the army to victories on the battlefield, he also managed to keep it independent, though French and British leaders wanted the American troops as replacements for their own dead or wounded soldiers.

them. When the boys found a pair of rusty old army pistols, he scraped, oiled, and polished them until they gleamed. Then he loaded one to see if the cartridges fit properly, waved it like a soldier—and *crack,* the hammer slipped and the gun went off. Luckily the only damage was to their mother's favorite mahogany bedstead. The close call made a deep impression on John, and he never again played with a gun.

Hard work and pranks. When John was thirteen, the Pershings' finances suffered badly due to a national depression, the "Panic of 1873." Sadly his parents said that they could no longer afford to send him to college, as they had planned to do in a few years. Instead of college, John would have to work on the family farm and be satisfied with local public schools. For the next four years, he worked hard, doing farm chores early in the morning, going to school during the day, then performing another round of chores in the evening. Life was not all serious, though. John, who was fond of mischief and practical jokes, also became a bit of a prankster. He and his friends crowned their high school careers by locking all the teachers out on the last day of school and conducting classes themselves.

Teacher. Despite the family's best efforts, the Pershings were unable to keep paying the mortgage on their farm. They lost it to the bank, and John was forced to find a job elsewhere. He had performed fairly well in school and had also done a lot of reading outside school. He loved to read, devouring classics like the Shakespeare plays along with biographies of heroes such as Daniel Boone and Davy Crockett. The seventeen-year-old decided to become a teacher, passing the examination for his teacher's certificate in August 1878. He got a job teaching in Laclede's school for blacks.

Discipline. Blacks in town protested against a white teacher, keeping their children away from the school. Then, when the children finally began coming, Pershing faced prejudice from his old high-school friends, who gathered outside the school with shouts of "Nigger! Nigger!" (Vandiver, p. 14). One burst into the classroom, and Pershing calmly told him that President Abraham Lincoln had given rights to blacks and Pershing's job was to see that his students were educated. The intruder left without further trouble. To both rebellious students and hostile neighbors, Pershing showed a tough but patient firmness that prompted troublemakers to obey him.

A few months later, Pershing landed a higher-paying job at a school ten miles outside Laclede. There again he faced discipline problems. Rowdy older students—some older than their new teacher—had scared off the previous teacher. Told by Pershing to stay after school, one older boy deliberately started to leave with the other students at the end of the day. Standing squarely in front of him, Pershing told him "that if he didn't take his seat I would give him a thrashing then and there" (Pershing in Vandiver, p. 15). The boy sat.

"The Normal." While continuing to teach in the summers, Pershing also enrolled the next year in the Missouri State Normal School, known as "the Normal," about sixty miles away. (Normal schools were early two-year colleges for teacher training.) For several years, he divided his time between studying and teaching. The Normal lacked the advantages of a college, however, and Pershing still thought of getting a college education and perhaps even going on to law school. One day he saw in the newspaper an advertisement for an exam to be held nearby for selecting one cadet, or student officer, for the military academy at West Point. Pershing decided to give it a try. He hadn't considered military life, but West Point, where army officers were educated and trained, seemed to offer his best hope for college.

West Point. Pershing won the competition. He spent four years at West Point, gaining almost instant success when he was elected class president halfway through the first year. Though above average academically, his lack of ability in two subjects would also play a part in his future. Try as he might, he never learned to speak French, nor was he ever comfortable addressing an audience. Yet when the "makes" were announced at the end of the year, Pershing was made the class's senior cadet corporal, the highest ranking officer in his class. He kept that position for the rest of his West Point career, graduating in 1886 as senior cadet captain.

Both classmates and teachers saw a mature leader in the lean, blond young man with the square jaw and slightly downturned mouth. It was downturned, that is, until he smiled. Then his whole face lit up. Young women, in addition to his friends and superiors, responded to his charms, and Pershing began to develop a reputation as a ladies' man. He never lacked for female company at the many balls and parties West Point had to offer. By the time he graduated, he was enjoying military life, though he was still not sure he wanted to stay in the army for long.

Cavalry service. Success at West Point allowed Pershing, now a lieutenant in the U.S. Army, to choose his assignment. He asked to be posted to the Sixth Cavalry Regiment, then nearing the end of operations against the Apaches in the Southwest. With the capture of their leaders Geronimo and Mangus, the last bands of independent Apaches were brought to the reservations by late 1886. For the next few years, Pershing trained and performed other jobs with the cavalry. He did well leading his men in war games across the desert. He also scored a notable success by leading an expedition that constructed a "heliograph" over 175 miles of rocky, mountainous terrain. The chain of signaling stations used reflected sunlight to send messages from one fort to another.

In late 1890, Pershing and the Sixth Cavalry were called to the Dakotas to help in operations against the Sioux. Arriving after the massacre of the Sioux at Wounded Knee on December 29, the Sixth remained in the Dakotas until mid-1891.

Instructor. From late 1891 to 1898, Pershing served mostly as a military instructor, first at the University of Nebraska (where he shaped the relaxed cadets into an award-winning outfit) and then at West Point. In 1895 and 1896, however, he took a break from teaching to command a black cavalry unit, the Tenth Regiment, in Montana. Winning a position as instructor at West Point in 1896, he ran into trouble soon after for his tendency to be extremely harsh on his students. He grew highly unpopular among the cadets, who nicknamed him "Black Jack" because of the Montana command. The nickname stuck. Nebraska had taught him the value of tough discipline, but his unhappy time as a West Point instructor showed him that toughness could go too far.

Spanish-American War. In 1898 the United States went to war with Spain over the Caribbean island of Cuba. Unprepared, the army was a mess. Volunteers brought chaos to unready training camps. Pershing, still in command of the Tenth Cavalry Regiment, struggled against a mountain of red tape—army paperwork—to organize his men, their supplies, and their departure. They finally sailed from Florida with the rest of the American expedition in June.

The inexperienced Americans faced heavy opposition from the Spanish in Cuba. The Tenth fought bravely, taking many casualties. Nearly one in five of the American men was killed or wounded, of the officers nearly one in two. Pershing and his men helped Colonel Theodore "Teddy" Roosevelt and the Rough Riders in the famous battle for San Juan Hill. One of Pershing's commanding officers called him "cool as a bowl of cracked ice" in battle (Smythe, p. 2). His courage under fire brought a promotion to major.

Philippines. With promotion came a new assignment, one of three that would take Pershing to the Philippines. These Pacific islands had been part of the Spanish empire and were taken over by the United States after Spain's defeat. Islanders had fought hard against the Spanish and were now unwilling to accept American authority. Pershing's first assignment, in 1899, took him to the southern Philippine island of Mindanao to deal with the warring Moros there. In 1902 he was promoted to captain and given command of Camp Vicars, a small outpost in Moro country. Though Pershing battled the Moros in war, he aided those struck by disease. His fairness led them to vote him honorary *datto,* or chief. He also won wide praise from his superiors, who now regarded him as the leading expert on the Moros.

Marriage. In 1903 Pershing returned to the United States for assignment to Washington, D.C. There the new governor of the Philippines, future president William Howard Taft, asked for his advice on the Moros. Theodore Roosevelt—now U.S. president—also heard of Pershing's success with the Moros, and remembered him from the war in Cuba. Roosevelt wanted to promote Pershing to general, but army traditions dictated that more senior men get promotions first. Meanwhile, at a Washington dinner party one evening, Pershing met a young woman named Frances Warren, the daughter of a powerful senator from Wyoming. Back in his apartment later that night, Pershing shook his roommate awake. "Charlie," he exclaimed, "I've met the girl I'm going to marry" (Pershing in Vandiver, p. 333). He courted Frances for two years. True to his prediction, they married in 1905.

"Jump." The two spent their honeymoon in Tokyo, where Pershing was assigned to the American embassy. For the next two years, he acted as an official observer of Japan's war against Russia, which resulted in Russia's defeat. Then, in 1906, Roosevelt promoted him to general, "jumping" him ahead of more than 900 officers who were in line for promotion ahead of him. Though popular, Pershing briefly caused jealousy due to his spectacular promotion and the special attention from the president.

Philippine command. The new general was given command of Fort William McKinley at the Philippine capital of Manila, then the largest American outpost beyond U.S. borders. He held the command until 1908, when he was appointed military governor of the Moro Province, which included the southern island of Mindanao. Pershing preferred talking to fighting. Yet as governor for the next four years, he fought several tough military campaigns against dissatisfied Moro groups, whose traditional love of independence inspired them to resist American rule. Gradually Pershing won control of the island while managing to avoid heavy bloodshed.

Tragedy in San Francisco. Assigned in 1914 to command the Eighth Brigade, stationed in San Francisco, California, Pershing was soon ordered to take the Eighth to Texas. Civil war had broken out in Mexico, and Pershing and the Eighth stayed for two years in El Paso, Texas, on the Mexican border. Frances remained in San Francisco with their children, three little girls and a boy. On August 27, 1915, Pershing received news that a fire had broken out in the Pershing home there. Frances and the girls were all dead, suffocated by the smoke. Only their son, Warren, survived. Shattered, Pershing took what comfort he could in his son's survival. Promoted again in 1916, to major general, Pershing told a friend, "All the promotion in the world would make no difference now" (Pershing in Smythe, p. 2).

Punitive Expedition. In early March 1916, the Mexican rebel leader Pancho Villa, angered by U.S. support for his enemies, killed eighteen Americans during a raid on Columbus, New Mexico. Immediately President Wilson ordered Pershing to lead the

Punitive Expedition (as punishment) into Mexico. The orders were to capture Villa if possible, and to break up his band of men. For almost a year, still grieving over the loss of wife and daughters, Pershing chased Villa deep into the Mexican desert. Unable to capture the Mexican leader, Pershing did succeed in breaking up his guerrilla army. With Villa no longer a threat to American border towns, the expedition withdrew in February 1917. President Wilson declared himself perfectly satisfied with Pershing's results.

Choosing Men to Serve

Pershing realized the importance of choosing a capable staff in order to manage the huge job that faced him. Some had served with him in the Philippines or Mexico. From the Philippines campaigns, for example, came Major James Harbord, Pershing's friend and chief of staff.

Some young men rose to fame after staff duty with Pershing. George C. Marshall, a brilliant young graduate of the Virginia Military Institute, led American armies as a World War II general before serving as secretary of state after that war. A young lieutenant named George Patton had begged to be Pershing's aid during the Punitive Expedition into Mexico and for a time worked for him in Europe, later becoming a leading general in World War II.

Though many of his staff and often the officers he appointed to command were personal friends, Pershing never hesitated to remove anyone who lacked efficiency. During the Argonne offensive in particular, he removed a number of generals whom he felt were not advancing fast enough.

Participation: American Soldiers Fight in Europe

United States declares war. In response to German submarine attacks, the United States declared war on Germany on April 6, 1917, shortly after Pershing's return from Mexico. Wilson and his able secretary of war, Newton Baker, began the delicate task of finding the right man to command America's armed forces against Germany (see **Woodrow Wilson**). Pershing's commands in Mindanao and Mexico meant that he was now one of the country's most experienced generals. Meanwhile, at fifty-seven, he was young and fit enough to take the stress of such a command and to tackle it with the necessary energy and boldness. Wilson and Baker settled on Pershing, his performance in Mexico still fresh in their minds. With a staff of thirty-one, Pershing sailed for England on May 28th.

"Lafayette, we are here." The small group arrived on June 8th to a heroes' welcome, met British military and political leaders (including King George V), and crossed to France on June 13th. An even more celebratory welcome awaited them there. At

▲ **A captured German fighter plane**

the dock, they were met again by politicians and soldiers, then they boarded a train for Paris, where huge cheering crowds thronged the station to catch a glimpse of the Americans. Covered in thrown flowers, amazed by what looked like thousands of little American flags waving from every possible perch, ears ringing with the "Star-Spangled Banner," the small group slowly made its way from the station through the packed streets. In the next few weeks, a dizzying round of visits followed as the Americans and their stern, dignified general toured various sites, meeting French leaders along the way.

On July 4th, they attended a ceremony at the grave of the Marquis de Lafayette, the French noble who had done so much to help the cause of American independence during the Revolutionary War. Now the Americans felt they might finally repay an old debt. Several speeches were given. "Lafayette," one of Pershing's aides said, ending the last speech, "we are here" (Vandiver, p. 724).

A war of manpower. When the Americans arrived, World War I had already been going on for almost three years. The first German attack in 1914 had been stopped along France's eastern border by the Allies: the French, commanded by General Philippe Pétain, and the British, who had sent an expeditionary force under General Douglas Haig. New technology, such as the machine gun, made it easier to defend than to attack, and defensive trenches, or networks of deep, connected ditches, were dug by both sides along the front. From these heavily fortified positions, defenders could rake attackers with deadly machine-gun fire. It was a new kind of war. Technology for the first time made it possible for hundreds of thousands of men to die in a few days. It seemed to come down to which side would run out of men and supplies first.

German offensive. Germany had also attacked to the east, towards Russia. Russia had resisted, and Germany had thus fought on two fronts. But in 1917, after years of social unrest at home and massive losses in the war, Russia's new communist government sued for peace. Suddenly, with the Russian front gone, Germany had extra manpower to throw against the Allies. It would launch the expected offensive in 1918. The question now was whether the Americans could enter the war soon enough to make up for the extra Germans. Had Pershing arrived too late?

Pressure from the Allies. The excitement of a heroes' welcome soon gave way to grim reality. Three years' slaughter in the trenches had exhausted both sides. Almost as soon as he came, Pershing was asked by Haig, Pétain, and others to put his American soldiers under their command. That was the only way the raw, untrained Americans could be ready in time, Allied leaders argued. Almost until the end of the war, they would keep demanding "amalgamation," or a joining of the Americans with their armies. Up to the end, over and over, Pershing would refuse. When the Allied leaders complained to Washington, Secretary of War Baker defended Pershing's stance. Pershing had been given complete authority to run the American war, and it was his decision alone. The Allies fumed, especially French Prime Minister Georges Clemenceau, whose flashing eyes gave him the nickname Le Tigre (the Tiger). Yet Pershing held firm. Once, his own eyes flashing, he even pounded the table, exclaiming he would not be forced.

Building an army. To justify his flat refusal, Pershing had to make good on his promise that the Americans could quickly pro-

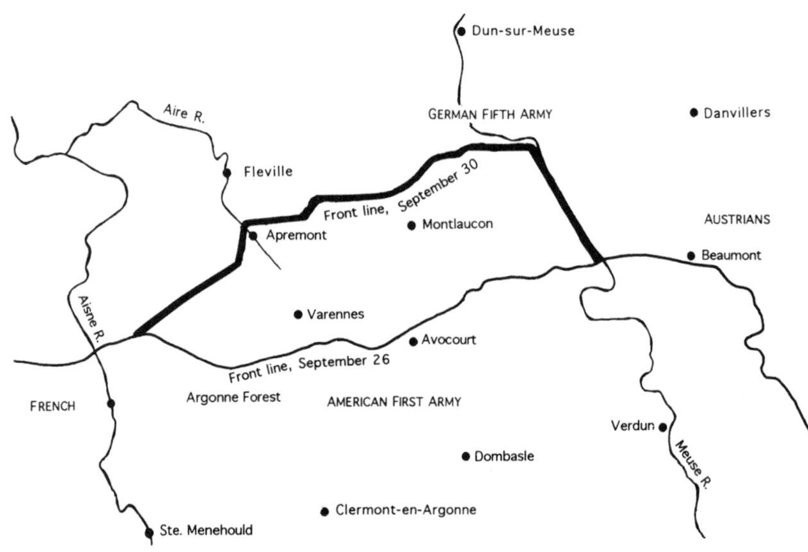

▲ **The Meuse-Argonne Battle, September 26-30, 1918**

vide an effective fighting force on their own. No such force existed when he went to France. The U.S. Army stood at about 200,000 men, insignificant compared to the Allied and German forces. Even these few must be used carefully, for they would be needed to train the soldiers brought in by the newly established draft. As they left for Europe, the Americans had not really understood the size of the clashing armies and the need for men. Pershing, however, soon decided he wanted 1,000,000 men in France by the middle of 1918, with more to follow. Through the summer, fall, and winter of 1917, Pershing and his hard-working staff began the massive job of creating, training, equipping, supplying, and transporting an army.

First tests. The German offensive began in the spring of 1918, with hammer blows against the British lines in the north then against the French lines in the south. The Allies fell back, dazed. The Germans had taken huge bites out of Allied territory and still came on. At their moment of need, Pershing rushed reinforcements to the French and British armies. In fighting at Cantigny, Belleau Wood, and Chateau-Thierry in France, the Americans tested themselves for the first time against the battle-hardened Germans. At

▲ **Troops in a western trench**

Belleau Wood, the U.S. Marines lost over 5,000 men in a few weeks but drove the Germans from defensive positions deep in the woods. At Chateau-Thierry, the U.S. Third Division stopped a German advance across the Marne River, despite heavy casualties and a French retreat on their flank. There the Thirty-eighth Infantry became known as "the Rock of the Marne."

A place in the trenches. By the summer of 1918, Pershing had persuaded the Allies to give the Americans a section of the front. The newly created American First Army held a position at the nose of a German wedge that cut deeply into Allied territory, to Saint-Mihiel on the Meuse River. By late August, Pershing wanted to attack on both sides of the wedge, catching the Germans in middle. Ferdinand Foch, the French general who was Supreme Allied Commander, demanded he call off his attack so that the Americans could take part in a general Allied offensive planned for September. Refusing, Pershing promised that the Americans could crush the Germans and still be ready for the offensive. Foch reluctantly agreed.

Pershing's plan worked. The First Army crushed the German wedge in only two days, taking 16,000 prisoners and almost 500 German artillery guns. Within two weeks, Pershing managed to move 600,000 of his men 60 miles away to their new position at the Argonne Forest for the Allied offensive.

Victory. Foch had assigned the Americans an especially tough area to attack, densely wooded with rugged hills and valleys. In a month and a half of nonstop combat, the Americans withstood everything the Germans could throw against them, drawing valuable German divisions away from the exhausted French and British. With their entire front depending on this central region, the Germans held on grimly. By early November, Pershing's men had advanced as far as Sedan, close to the Belgian border. Elsewhere, the Allies also uprooted the now dispirited German armies. Germany sued for peace, and the Armistice (cease-fire) was signed on November 11, 1918.

Aftermath

General of the Armies. In the celebration that followed German surrender, old rivalries were forgotten. Pershing and the Allied generals praised each other's achievements. Now a teenager, Warren Pershing made a trip to Europe to spend time with his father. Back home in September 1919, Pershing marched at the head of a victory parade down Pennsylvania Avenue. A new rank was created for him: General of the Armies. He served as army chief of staff until 1924, when he reached the official retirement age of sixty-four.

Pershing remained active despite retirement, serving on a special diplomatic mission to South America in 1925 and holding a lifetime appointment as head of the American Battle Monuments Commission. He returned to Europe many times, often taking part in commemorations of the war with men such as Pétain and Foch. His health strong, Pershing survived to see Germany defeated once again in another world war. Pershing died in Washington, D.C., on July 15, 1948. He was buried at Arlington National Cemetery.

For More Information

Smythe, Donald. *Pershing: General of the Armies.* Bloomington: Indiana University Press, 1986.

Vandiver, Frank E. *Black Jack: The Life and Times of John J. Pershing.* 2 vols. College Station: Texas A & M University Press, 1977.

Oliver Wendell Holmes

1841-1935

Personal Background

Oliver Wendell Holmes, Jr. (called Wendell, he dropped the Jr. on his father's death in 1894) was born in Boston, Massachusetts, on March 8, 1841. His father was the famous doctor and writer Oliver Wendell Holmes, a popular author of light poems and the friend of literary figures such as Ralph Waldo Emerson and Nathaniel Hawthorne. Both his father and his mother, Amelia Jackson Holmes, descended from Puritans who came to Massachusetts in the 1600s. They belonged to the small group of upper-class families that had dominated Boston society for generations. Dr. Holmes called this local aristocracy "Brahmins," after the upper level of Hindu society, and the name stuck. Throughout his long life, Wendell would often struggle against the narrow views of the Boston Brahmin world, even as he found comfort in its privileges and traditions.

Skeptics on Beacon Street. The family lived on Beacon Street, where all the best Brahmin families made their homes. By the time Wendell was five, he had a three-year-old younger sister named Amelia and a baby brother, Edward, called Ned. His best friend was a cousin, Johnny Morse, older by a year. The two would grow up together and remain friends all their lives. Morse was a very proper Boston Brahmin. Later in life, he would write conventional biographies of American heroes such as John Adams and Abraham Lincoln. (Morse also wrote a biography of Wendell's father, Dr. Holmes.)

▲ **Oliver Wendell Holmes**

Event: Supreme Court decisions on freedom of speech.

Role: After the Espionage and Sedition Acts of 1917 made it unlawful to criticize the government or to speak out against World War I, several cases challenging the acts came before the Supreme Court. Oliver Wendell Holmes, one of the most influential Supreme Court justices ever, wrote classic opinions in these cases that helped define just how far the government could go in limiting the constitutional right to freedom of speech.

Though friends, the two differed when it came to Wendell's constant need to question everything. Wendell might ask, for example, if it was ever right to tell a lie. "Of course not," Johnny would answer, without any doubt. "Suppose a man came running along here with terror in his eyes and panting for breath and hid in this thicket," Wendell would ask. "Then the pursuers came along and asked us if we had seen him. Which would be better, to give the man away or to tell a lie?" (Baker, p. 50). And Johnny would have to admit that in some cases maybe it was better to lie.

Wendell had perhaps inherited his skeptical mind—or refusal to accept other people's certainties without questioning them—from his father. Dr. Holmes outraged the medical community in the 1840s by suggesting that childbed fever, at that time killing many young mothers after delivery, was spread by the doctors and nurses themselves. Though Dr. Holmes had examined all the evidence very carefully, the experts spoke out angrily against his conclusion. Then, in the 1850s, the microbe (germs) was discovered, and the medical world began realizing the importance of cleanliness. Doctors and nurses began washing their hands routinely, and Dr. Holmes's theory was accepted as correct—as he had always maintained, despite the opposition of others.

Harvard and Darwin. In 1857, at sixteen, Holmes went to the only acceptable college for Boston's Brahmins: Harvard, in nearby Cambridge. At this time, Harvard was still very much bound by old ways of thinking, though that would change soon. Its teachers favored memorization over independent thought in school subjects, and dogma (accepted beliefs) in religious matters. Despite a love for books, Holmes had never been an exceptional student. At Harvard, he became interested in subjects such as art and history, though he usually pursued them on his own rather than through his classes. He also wrote several articles for student publications, complaining of the school's unwillingness to accept new ideas.

The most troublesome new idea was that of an English scientist named Charles Darwin. Darwin's theory of evolution appeared in 1859, with the publication of his revolutionary book *The Origin of Species.* Though not especially interested in science, Holmes was fascinated by the scientific reasoning Darwin had used to arrive at his idea that man and other animals had evolved from earlier forms of life, which most Harvard scientists rejected at first. In the end, Darwin's work changed the entire scientific world. It also changed the way people thought about society and would later influence Holmes's own revolutionary view of the law.

War years. In 1861, just before his Harvard graduation, the Civil War broke out, and Holmes enlisted in the Union Army. Serving for three years, he fought in the great battles of Antietam and Fredericksburg, at both of which he was badly wounded. He was also wounded earlier in his first battle. His three periods of recovery were mixed with periods of waiting and of battle under the harshest conditions. He became used to waking up wet from sleeping on the ground, to eating only salted beef and dried biscuits, and to stepping over the dead bodies of fallen friends and enemies. He would carry the experience of war with him for the rest of his life. Even as an old man, he could remember details of each battle.

Young lawyer. After the war, now a slender and handsome young man in his early twenties, Holmes looked around for a suitable career. He thought about medicine but did not want to choose the same profession as his father. He finally decided on the law and enrolled at Harvard Law School in 1864. He worked hard in law school but made time for a growing circle of friends. They included William James, later to be one of the founders of modern psychology, and James's younger brother Henry, later a famous novelist. He also became friends with Fanny Dixwell, the quietly charming daughter of his favorite childhood schoolmaster.

On finishing his studies, Holmes took the fashionable "Grand Tour" of Europe, especially enjoying a five-week stay in England. There his upper-class Boston connections brought him introductions to many famous people, including Prime Minister William Gladstone. Back in the United States in late 1866, Holmes began his career as a lawyer in the small but high-powered law firm of Chandler, Shattuck & Thayer.

Legal scholar. Almost right away, Holmes began writing and lecturing on the law as well as practicing it in the courtroom. The new president of Harvard, Charles Eliot, was, according to Dr. Holmes, who taught medicine there, turning "the whole University over like a flapjack" (Baker, p. 206). Part of Eliot's program of updating Harvard was to hire the younger Holmes to lecture on law, which he did from 1870 to 1873. During this time, Holmes also worked on a new version of a standard law textbook, James Kent's *Commentaries on American Law.* The book was published in 1873, with Holmes's name as editor. In fact, his contribution came close to rewriting the old book completely. Widely praised, it established his reputation as a leading legal scholar.

Marriage. In June 1872, Holmes married his old friend Fanny Dixwell, herself of the same Brahmin background as he. A shy woman who nevertheless could come out with sharp, witty comments from time to time, Fanny was an accomplished artist. Several years later, she won recognition for a show of her embroideries at the Boston Museum of Fine Arts. One critic described her work as "delicately poetic" (Baker, p. 261). The Holmeses never had any children. Their marriage was a close and loving one, though now and then Fanny had some comments to make about her husband's habitual mild flirting.

Holmes was a great conversationalist and loved to be surrounded by a crowd. His distinguished good looks and sparkling conversation made him in great demand at dinner parties. He also loved to have long conversations with friends such as William James. Holmes and James would stay up late drinking whiskey and "twisting the tail of the Cosmos" (Baker, p. 174), as they described their philosophical talks.

The Common Law. In 1881 Holmes published his major work, *The Common Law,* on which he had spent five years of hard work. In it, he argued that instead of being unchanging rules that were simply passed on from generation to generation (as was believed), laws in fact had changed and developed through the ages. Holmes thus applied Darwin's ideas to the history of law. He backed his conclusions with detailed research, and his book revolutionized the way legal scholars viewed their subject. Its first sentence sums up the book's message: "The life of the law has not been logic: it has been experience" (Holmes in Baker, p. 257). In other words, laws are rooted not in ideas (such as good and bad), but in the actual daily needs of the communities that make them. As those needs change, Holmes showed, so do the laws. This view of law would play a major role in his future work on the Supreme Court.

Massachusetts Supreme Court. As a result of his growing reputation, in 1882 Holmes was named to the Massachusetts Supreme Court, where he served for twenty years. Like the rest of the country in the late 1800s, Massachusetts faced increasing tensions between workers and the companies they worked for. The tensions resulted from growth brought about by the Industrial Revolution, as large corporations with thousands of employees sprang up for the first time. New laws had to be made to deal with this new situation, and old laws had to be interpreted in new ways. The cases coming before him were a perfect illustration of what Holmes had written about in *The Common Law.*

For twenty years, as he slowly developed his ideas, Holmes enjoyed the usual round of dinner parties, visits to Europe, summers in the country, and lectures at various institutions. Meanwhile, he grew older and even more distinguished looking. The long, bushy mustache he had worn as a young man became snowy white.

Participation: Supreme Court Decisions on Freedom of Speech

Joining the court. In 1902 President Theodore Roosevelt chose Holmes for the United States Supreme Court as a replacement for Horace Gray, who had died earlier that year. It was an appointment the ambitious Holmes had dreamed of winning for some time. He had been approached years earlier as a possible candidate for the Senate but refused to consider running. He had no interest in being a senator, he explained to his friends. He wanted to sit on the Supreme Court, and that was that.

Independent voice. As often happens, Roosevelt made his choice because he thought Holmes would support his political goals. In particular, Roosevelt was in the middle of his famous "trust-busting," trying to break up the large corporations that had come to hold monopolies on and thereby control important industries such as railroads, oil, and the like. A major way of breaking up the trusts was for the government to sue the large corporations in court. Holmes had written some opinions for the Massachusetts Supreme Court that seemed sympathetic to Roosevelt's aims. In the first trust-busting case to come before the Supreme Court after his appointment, however, Holmes angered the president by disagreeing with the government. In other cases, he agreed. A complicated and independent man, Holmes insisted on judging each case by his own standards rather than by anyone's political aims.

The Supreme Court

The Supreme Court of the United States is one of the three branches of the federal government, the judicial branch. Its nine judges, called justices, are appointed by the president and serve for life. They include a chief justice who assigns court work to the others and acts as chairman of the group. Each justice has a vote, with the majority deciding. For each case, the chief justice chooses one of the justices in the majority to write out the court's decision on the case. Whether agreeing with the majority or not, other justices may write out their own opinions.

The losing side in a lower court may appeal its case to a higher court, which will either uphold the lower court as right or overturn it as wrong. The losing side in *that* decision may also have the right to appeal to a still higher court. The final step in this process of appeals, the Supreme Court is the highest court in the land and the guardian of the Constitution.

"Great Dissenter." A dissenter is a person who disagrees with a particular position. Holmes's independent views—and the strength and smooth language with which he presented them—led to his being called "the Great Dissenter." In fact, his dissents numbered fewer than 200 out of almost 6,000 cases, or about 3 percent of the total. But his elegant writing style and clear logic made his opinions stand out more than those of other justices.

In *Lochner* v. *New York* (1905), for example, the court declared unconstitutional a New York law establishing a sixty-hour work week for bakers, saying that it limited the economic freedom of the bakery owners. Holmes in dissent defended the state's right to experiment with such legislation, which was thought to be more fair to bakers, though it went against the economic ideas of individual ownership and capitalism. Remaining true to his idea of a living law that changes to follow the needs of society, he wrote that the Constitution "is not intended to embody a particular economic theory" but to defend the rights of people who have widely differing views (Holmes in Baker, p. 419). Those rights included the right of the people of New York to decide what they thought was fair.

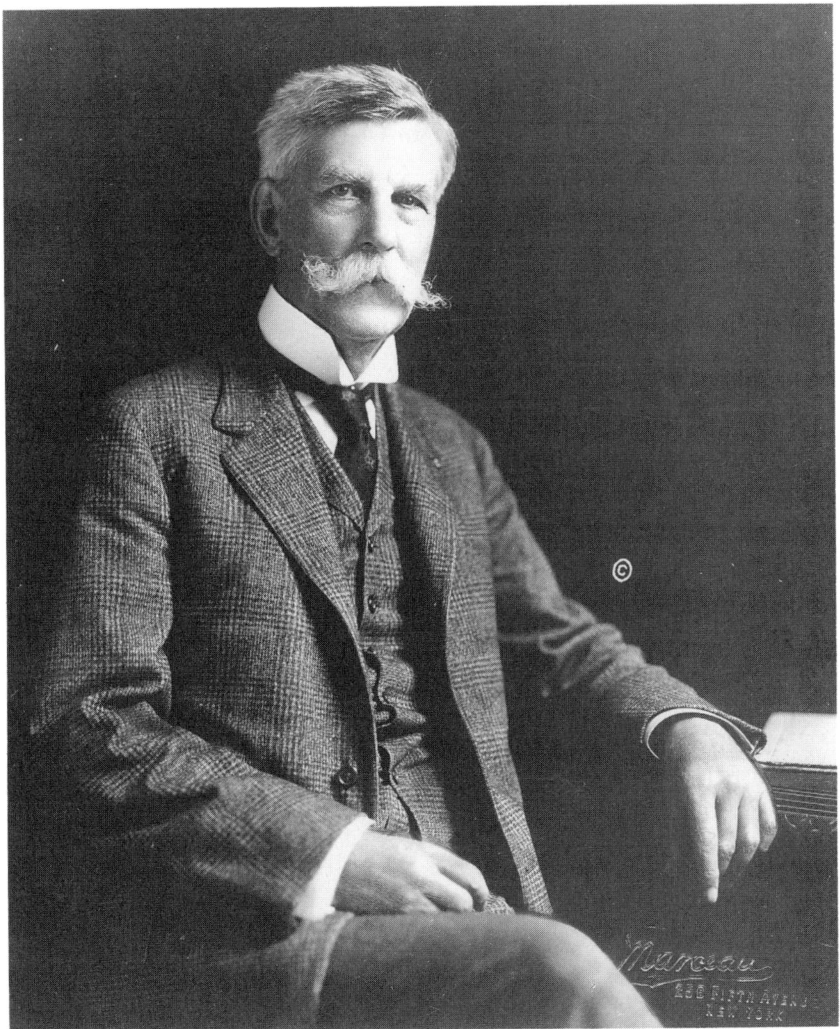

▲ Holmes

Wartime fears. When the United States entered World War I in 1917, wartime enthusiasm led to a "red scare." Fears about socialists, many of whom opposed the war, swept the nation. They were considered a danger to the survival of capitalism and democracy in America. Reflecting the popular mood, Congress passed laws to prevent such antiwar activists from spreading their views, which were also thought to be dangerous to the war effort. They could, it was feared, weaken the fighting spirit of the soldiers. The Federal

Young friends

One way that Holmes seemed to preserve his sense of youthfulness as he aged was through friendships with younger lawyers and intellectuals. These included lawyers Felix Frankfurter and Louis Brandeis, both of whom also ended up on the Supreme Court.

Brandeis, fifteen years younger than Holmes, fought before the Supreme Court for causes such as workers' rights, often taking the cases without pay. Appointed to the Supreme Court by President Wilson in 1916, Brandeis became its most liberal justice at the time. He disagreed with Holmes's "clear and present danger" standard for free speech; Brandeis thought it left the government too much power and might be abused in peacetime. Mostly, though, Brandeis and Holmes voted together, often in dissent from other more conservative justices. Frankfurter, over forty years Holmes's junior, taught law at Harvard and was appointed to the Supreme Court by President Franklin D. Roosevelt in 1939.

Holmes and such young men had long discussions and wrote letters to each other constantly. Holmes himself was never really a liberal. His views were too complex to be labeled so easily. Yet as they rose to fame, friends such as Frankfurter helped create a public image of Holmes as a liberal hero. Though not exactly accurate, that image remains strong today.

Espionage Act of 1917 set stiff penalties for interfering with the recruitment of soldiers. An amendment to the act, known on its own as the Sedition Act, set similar penalties for "disloyal or abusive language" about the government, the war effort, or such national symbols as the flag or the Constitution (Baker, p. 511). Nearly 2,000 people, mostly socialists, were arrested and prosecuted for speeches and writings under these two laws.

Not until 1919, after the war's end, did several of these cases come before the Supreme Court. It was the first time since the days of Thomas Jefferson (though far from the last) that freedom of speech became a major issue in this way. The Court's decisions influenced how the issue would be viewed for the rest of the century, and Holmes's contributions were of crucial importance. Sometimes he wrote the majority opinion, sometimes he dissented. His majority opinions set the standard for future decisions; his dissents, in the end, carried more weight than the decisions they opposed.

Schenck* v. *The United States. During the war, the secretary of the Socialist Party, Charles T. Schenck, had been arrested under the Espionage Act. He was convicted of trying to cause insubordination, or disregard for authority, in the army and for interfering with the draft by sending leaflets to drafted men that urged them to oppose the draft and the war itself. In a unanimous decision, the Supreme Court in 1919 upheld Schenck's conviction. Writing for the majority, Holmes admitted that in ordinary times Schenck's leaflets would be protected under the First Amendment to the Constitution, which guarantees freedom of speech. Yet, as Holmes had written in *The Common Law,* the "character of every act depends upon the circumstances in which it is done" (Holmes in Baker, p. 523). War, Holmes wrote now, changed the circumstances of Schenck's acts, giving the state the right to limit them.

"Clear and present danger." As Holmes put it in his majority opinion:

> The most stringent [strictest] protection of free speech would not protect a man in falsely shouting fire in a theatre and causing a panic.... The question in every case is whether the words used are used in circumstances and are of such a nature as to create a clear and present danger that they will bring about the substantive evils which Congress has the right to prevent. (Holmes in Baker, pp. 523-24)

As always, Holmes's writing style gave his opinion an extra punch. The image of a man falsely shouting fire in a crowded theatre has since become commonplace. And the phrase "clear and present danger," which would help decide similar cases in the future, has become equally wellknown. Like Shakespeare, Holmes had a gift for coining phrases that were so well put they would be adopted by others in conversation.

Abrams* v. *The United States. In two other cases in 1919, Holmes and the Supreme Court handed down similar decisions: *Debs* v. *The United States* and *Frohwerk* v. *The United States.* But Holmes, perhaps under influence of his younger friends, was coming to the end of his willingness to see free speech restricted.

Jacob Abrams, a self-described anarchist and revolutionary, had printed leaflets attacking President Woodrow Wilson, the war, and what he saw as U.S. interference in the Russian Revolution (see **Woodrow Wilson**). He and several others had distributed the leaflets by throwing them out of the window of a weapons factory. Though none of the factory workers took the leaflets seriously, Abrams and the others were convicted under the Espionage Act. Abrams was sentenced to twenty years in prison.

Again the Supreme Court voted to uphold the conviction, but Holmes was not available to write the majority opinion. This time, despite strong objections from other justices, Justice Holmes planned to dissent.

"Free trade in ideas." In *Schenck,* Holmes had focused on circumstances that might give the government a right to limit an individual's freedom of speech. In *Abrams,* on the other hand, he focused on the individual's right to be free from unfair interference. He did not believe that Abrams and his friends—whom he called "poor and puny" (Holmes in Baker, p. 538)—posed any threat to the government. They were not "a clear and present danger." As long as there is no threat, he wrote, American society chooses to allow differing views. The people as a whole believe:

> That the ultimate good desired is better reached by free trade in ideas—and that the best test of truth is the power of the thought to get itself accepted in the competition of the market, and that truth is the only ground upon which their wishes can be safely carried out. That at any rate is the theory of our Constitution. (Holmes in Baker, p. 539)

Holmes thus offered a logical (and Darwin-style) argument in favor of the free expression of thought. If an opinion is valuable, it will survive, went the argument; if it is not, it will die out on its own. There is normally no need for restrictions. Worthless opinions and lies pose little threat since they won't survive anyway. Only in highly unstable circumstances (as in a crowded theatre) does a lie's brief existence threaten society.

Drawing the line. Holmes had drawn attention to the central question in the issue of free speech: where to draw the line between a real threat and a harmless outburst. He had also brought in the idea that circumstances must play a part in drawing that line. Free speech would continue to be a major issue for the Supreme Court, and the line would be redrawn over and over. The problem is an ongoing one in a modern, democratic society. Yet Holmes laid down the basis for approaching it, establishing points that could be used to tackle it in the future.

Aftermath

Dash. In his late seventies at the time of these decisions, Holmes afterward remained on the Supreme Court until the age of ninety-one. He resigned in 1932, after thirty years' service. Holmes never became chief justice. Yet his forceful personality, memorable writings, and easily recognizable appearance gave him a higher profile than other justices. He looked like the public's idea of a judge and lived up to his looks. On his twentieth anniversary on the court, in 1922, his good friend and fellow justice Louis Brandeis wrote: "For O.W.H. Twenty years after—Still the dash of a D'Artagnan" (Baker, p. 565). In other words, the elderly Holmes was still as dashing as the famous musketeer.

Done. Nine years later, in 1931, his ninetieth birthday was marked by a national radio broadcast, in which Holmes spoke live from his study. His beloved Fanny had died two years earlier, and Holmes himself was preparing to retire. It was a time, he said softly into the microphone, "to hear the kind voices of friends and to say to one's self, 'The work is done'" (Holmes in Baker, p. 5). He retired the following year.

Holmes's health remained strong, however, and he continued to have occasional lunches with friends like Brandeis and Frankfurter. In the late winter of 1934, however, he caught a bad cold that turned into pneumonia, weakening him. Holmes died at his Washington, D.C., home on March 5, 1935, just three days short of his ninety-fourth birthday.

For More Information

Baker, Liva. *The Justice from Beacon Hill: The Life and Times of Oliver Wendell Holmes.* New York: Harper Collins, 1991.

Judson, Clara Ingram. *Mr. Justice Holmes.* Chicago and New York: Follet Publishing Co., 1986.

Meyer, Edith Patterson. *That Remarkable Man: Justice Oliver Wendell Holmes.* Boston: Little, Brown & Co., 1967.

Industrial Growth

1882
Thomas Edison opens the first power station in New York to supply businesses and homes with electricity.

1892
Edison General Electric Company merges with Thomson-Houston company to form the General Electric Company.

1893
Charles E. and J. Frank Duryea, brothers, build the first American automobile.

1898
Frederick Taylor sets out new rules for organizing work, called scientific management, to make production efficient.

1903
Henry Ford founds Ford Motor Company.

1908
Ford Motor Company produces the first Model T.

1913
Ford experiments with the moving assembly line, reducing the time to produce a car from 14 to 1.5 hours.

1914
Ford more than doubles a worker's wages to $5 a day.

1915
Businessmen in Toledo, Ohio, experiment with a time-payment plan to sell automobiles.

1919
John L. Lewis becomes president of the United Mine Workers.

1924
Price of Model T drops to $200.

1935
Lewis leads unions out of the American Federation of Labor (AFL), concentrates on organizing unions in industries across the nation.

1936
United Auto Workers stages first sit-down strike against General Motors at Flint, Michigan.

1938
Lewis forms Congress of Industrial Organizations (CIO).

1955
AFL and CIO merge.

INDUSTRIAL GROWTH

Americans, both immigrant and native-born, dreamed of rising from rags to riches in the early twentieth century. And the growth of industry brought real-life success stories that kept such dreams alive. **Henry Ford,** who began as a country boy with little more than raw mechanical genius, amassed a huge fortune. Ford manufactured the nation's first low-cost automobile and in the process perfected the first moving assembly line. Auto parts moved to workers assigned to specific tasks in a car's assembly, reducing the time it took to produce an automobile in 1913 from 14 to 1.5 hours. The quicker process was an example of scientific management, new rules for organizing work introduced by Frederick Taylor, who advised breaking down an operation into its parts, applying careful timing and having the laborer become a step in the operation of the machine. Ford also broke ground by paying a salary of $5 a day, double the amount that other factory owners paid. The raise, he reasoned, would enable the workers to buy his cars and prevent them from quitting.

Ford's methods proved successful—the Model T kept dropping in price from $600 in 1912 to only $200 in 1924. As the cost dropped, cars became available to more Americans, which changed city life. Automobiles allowed families to live miles from work, which contributed to the growth of

▲ **The introduction of electricity into American homes changed society**

suburbs, neighborhoods outside the city. Also, the one-room local schoolhouse declined as buses began transporting students to larger schools. And millions of dollars were spent to build streets and highways, opening up a flurry of new jobs.

Less directly, the automobile affected other industries in America by introducing a new buying procedure. The method, buying a product on time, was first used to sell automobiles in Toledo, Ohio, in 1915. By 1926 three-fourths of all cars were sold on time, buyers taking home the finished car but paying for it over a period of months and years. Soon time- or installment-buying made other items, like refrigerators and sewing machines, affordable to many Americans.

The spread of all these consumer items constituted a second industrial revolution in the United States. At first America manufactured materials, such as cloth, that it sold to other countries, which then produced the finished consumer goods. This changed in the early 1900s, with U.S. businesses going on to produce their own finished goods for consumers.

The power behind this second industrial revolution was electricity, a new source of energy that doubled factory output from 1910 to 1920. Thomas Edison and others invented generators for producing an electric current and ways of using this current to power machinery. Moreover, Edison invented the light bulb, which replaced gas lanterns on city streets and in city homes. Electricity also brought toasters, washing machines, and other appliances into city homes. But Americans in rural areas did not yet have such conveniences, so the gap widened between city life and country life.

Changes in industry, along with entry into World War I, led to population shifts in the nation. America's entry into the war opened jobs to women, blacks, and Mexican immigrants in 1917. Women worked in brickyards, on railroads, and in weapons plants during the war, proving that they could perform jobs once considered fit only for men. It was a temporary victory, however; once the war ended the type of jobs open to women would shrink back to a more limited range. On the other hand, the war had a lasting effect on African Americans. Jobs in industry drew thousands of blacks into a great migration northward. And their departure, in turn, opened up positions on farms and factories to Mexicans who crossed the border for work, especially in the Southwest.

The years 1922 to 1929 were marked by great prosperity in America. A few large firms became dominant in an industry. Ford and General Motors, for example, set the standard in automobile manufacturing, while United States Steel dominated iron and steel making. The Supreme Court approved this trend, ruling in *United States* v. *United States Steel Company* (1920) that a corporation could dominate an industry as long as a few competing companies continued to operate in the industry too. Companies continued to merge, a trend that had already given rise to giants such as General Electric. The modern corporation came into being, dividing a large business into departments run by a management team. Managers began to add vacation time and other benefits to jobs, trying to keep workers happy and uninterested in joining a union.

American Industry and World War I

When America entered the war in 1917, it did not yet have the industry to put out an ensemble of finished products that could fully equip and transport its troops. American soldiers therefore fired French artillery pieces, traveled in British ships, flew French and British planes, and purchased clothing in Europe.

In fact, most wage earners during the 1920s did not belong to a labor union. The American Federation of Labor (AFL), a collection of skilled unions, continued to operate during these years. There was disharmony within the labor movement, though. With the growth of industry, the number of unskilled workers in America had risen by leaps and bounds. Yet the AFL held fast to an early policy—it would not organize unskilled workers or admit unskilled unions into its fold. Another group, the Industrial Workers of the World (IWW), which wanted to seize control of industry altogether, welcomed the unskilled but never grew very large.

More successful was an inside effort to change the policy of the AFL. The United Mine Workers (UMW), one of the largest unions in the AFL, objected to its excluding the unskilled. In protest, UMW president **John L. Lewis** led his own and other like-minded unions out of the AFL. They proceeded to form their own Congress of Industrial Organizations (CIO) despite violent attempts to stop the unskilled from organizing into unions. From shipyards to textile mills, there were instances of employers threatening, beating, even

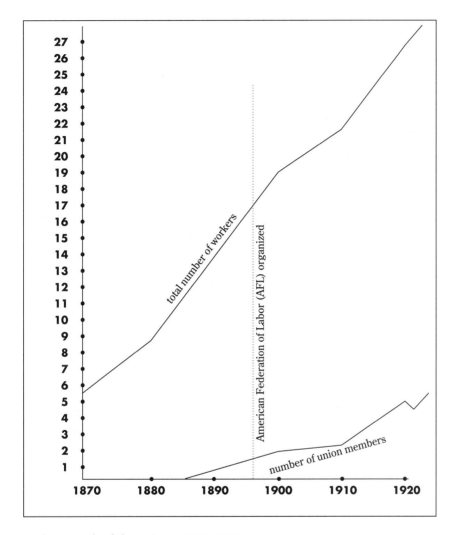

▲ **The growth of the unions, 1870-1920**

killing unskilled workers to prevent them from forming unions. But the workers organized anyway, after which one of their unions, the United Auto Workers (UAW), popularized a new protest technique. UAW members staged a sit-down strike inside General Motors to gain acceptance by management of their union. In response, General Motors signed a pact recognizing the UAW as an official spokesgroup, after which holding a sit-down strike was a tactic used by other companies nationwide.

Henry Ford

1863-1947

Personal Background

The Fords. They came from Cork County, Ireland, escaping from a potato famine there. Sixteen members of the Ford family set sail in 1847, led by William Ford, who would become Henry's father. The party included William, his parents, six brothers and sisters, grandmother, an uncle and aunt, and four cousins. After reaching America, they sailed down the St. Lawrence River to Buffalo, New York, and from there to Detroit, Michigan. The family marched right through the city, going on to the smaller community of Dearborn eight miles away. Three uncles had come to America earlier and described the richness of the soil in Michigan, and the Fords, a family of farmers, were following the paths of these men. William's father bought an eighty-acre farm near Dearborn for $650, and he and the twenty-one-year-old William settled down to work the land.

Eleven years later, William bought half the farmland from his father for $600, married a neighbor girl, Mary Litgot, and added ninety-one acres of her parents farm to his own. It was here that Henry Ford was born on July 30, 1863.

Early life. Life for young Henry was typical of farm boys of his time. He had his share of farm chores to do, along with attending class at the Scotch Settlement School. Many evenings were spent in

▲ Henry Ford

Event: Manufacturing the Tin Lizzie; mass production.

Role: Henry Ford, son of a Michigan farmer, designed and built an automobile that was affordable to the average worker and owned and managed one of the largest automobile manufacturing operations in the world. His treatment of the workers in his factories made him, for a time, one of the most respected men in America.

family card games. As the children grew older, they enjoyed ice skating in winter. They sometimes skated down the Roulo Creek that bordered the farm to the Rouge River, down that river to the Detroit River, and along it to the bustling city of Detroit. There Henry spent many hours watching the workers in Detroit's machine shops.

School and most of the farm work did not appeal to Henry. The one element of farm work that did interest him was maintaining the farm machinery. About the time Henry was born, his father began to buy tools such as the McCormick reaper to improve his farm productivity and take advantage of the increased demand for crops that was created by the Civil War. Early in Henry's life, William Ford began to teach his son to repair these machines.

Neighborhood repairman. By the time Henry was thirteen years old, in 1876, he was lending a hand to neighboring farmers in repairing their machinery. That same year, he was shown a broken watch owned by a friend. Henry had no tools small enough for watch work so he made his own. A nail was hammered into a small screwdriver, and a corset stay was shaped into forceps. With these tools, Henry took the watch apart and made the necessary repairs. From then on, he added watch repair to his help for the neighbors. Ford did not take pay for his work; he was satisfied just to have something mechanical to take apart and put back together.

Henry's mother died before the year was over, and an older cousin came to care for the Ford children. The cousin, Jane Flaherty, was from a family of relatives in Detroit with whom Henry became well acquainted.

Introduction to engines. The year 1876 was marked by still other events that would influence Ford's life. One of the early applications of steam engines was the operation of farm machines. These machines had to be moved wherever needed on the farm. By the 1870s, farmers were beginning to put wheels on their giant steam engines so that they could slowly drive them to the machines they would power. Once in place, wheel gave way to belts to drive the machines. In 1876 Ford saw one of these giant rigs for the first time. Farmers would stand on it, shovel fuel to generate steam, and steer the bulky contraption down the country road. That same year

William Ford attended the Philadelphia Centennial Exposition and returned with stories of the new machines he had seen there. The younger Ford began to think about a powered vehicle to use for transportation.

Detroit. At age sixteen, Ford left the farm for Detroit. There he lived with his Aunt Rebecca and secured a job with the Michigan Car Company making railroad cars. It was his first experience with an assembly line and lasted a week, until young Ford could find work at the Flower and Brothers Machine Shop. He worked at the shop for nearly a year but then returned to the farm to help with the harvest. Farm work still did not interest him, however, and as soon as the harvest was over Ford returned to Detroit, this time to a job with the Detroit Drydock Company. He worked here for two years, during which time he saw an internal combustion engine for the first time.

Late in 1882, Ford left the Drydock Company to join Westinghouse. The move pleased his father because Ford could live on the farm and travel around the area servicing Westinghouse steam engines. The father convinced himself that his son was now interested in farmwork. When the younger Ford became engaged to a neighbor girl, Clara Bryant, in 1886, his father gave the couple a forty-acre farm for an engagement present. His son would later sell this land to advance his continuing interest in machines. Just a year earlier, he had repaired his first Otto internal combustion engine. And a year after his engagement, he built a steam tractor for the farm. Ford and Clara were married in 1888, and the couple moved to Detroit.

Automobiles. Four years later, Ford learned of an automobile built by Charles Duryea. Although this was not the first effort to build an automobile (the first American patents were taken out in 1879), Ford began to think seriously about building automobiles. It would be some time, however, before he could develop his idea. Five years after his marriage, Ford's first child was born. Detroit was in the midst of a serious depression at the time. Twenty-eight thousand workers were unemployed in a city whose population was just over 100,000. Fortunately, Ford had by then established his genius for maintaining machinery and so was steadily employed by the Edison Illuminating Company.

Meanwhile, Ford pursued his interest in engines, building a workshop near his house. By 1896 he had built his first automobile there. It had a two-cylinder internal combustion engine that generated four horsepower. Ford drove it around Detroit for about one thousand miles before he sold it to build other cars.

Race cars. Ford decided to build racing cars and in 1899 constructed three of them. He organized the Detroit Automobile Company to build and sell the cars. They did not create much interest, however, and the company failed within a year. But in 1900, with the help of Barney Oldfield, a bicycle racer who wanted to try auto racing, Ford built another race car named the "999." Oldfield and the 999 made such an impact on racing that Ford became well known. In 1903 he and twelve investors established a company to mass-produce automobiles at a price affordable to workers—the Ford Motor Company. The chief partner in this investment was Alexander Malcolmson. He agreed to put up $3,000 to get the company started. Other investments were pledged totaling $100,000, but only $28,000 was actually invested in the new cars. With this small capital, Ford set out to realize his dream.

The first car turned out by the new company was a chain-driven automobile that sold for $850. In 1903 and 1904, the Ford company turned out 1,708 of these "Fords." Meanwhile, Ford was experimenting with mass production. In the beginning a car was built at one station with workers moving to the station to complete different parts of the building process. Ford felt that workers should remain stationary and that the parts to be assembled and the car-in-progress should instead come to them and be always moving along a line. In 1904 and 1905, his methods resulted in 5,000 new cars. But Ford was still not satisfied. He wanted the company to make a car so low in price that everyone could own one. His was not the first automobile company, but it was the first to put this particular goal into practice. In 1906, perhaps because the initial costs were more than the $3,000 he had promised, or perhaps because he did not approve of the direction the new company was taking, Malcolmson sold his interest for about $185,000. The other partners would remain with the company for several more years. By then, an interest in the company bought for a few hundred dollars brought from $12 million to nearly $40 million as each of the outside investors were bought out by the Ford family. Two of the original investors, the Dodges, would use this money to start a competing automobile company.

Participation: The Tin Lizzie and Mass Production

The Model T. By 1908 Ford Motor Company had developed the car that could eventually be purchased for a very low price—the Model T. The first Model T rolled off the assembly line on October 1 and almost immediately had a great impact on Americans. But there were problems. The car had a crank start, and the fuel to the engine needed to be adjusted by a lever on the steering column. When this was not done correctly, the crank could whip back, and the cranker risked breaking an arm. The Model T also had no shock absorbers, so the ride was rough. It also had some problems going uphill. Fuel did not feed correctly on a slope, so drivers often had to back up hills. Ford joked that this new automobile could be bought by anyone and in any color, provided the car was black. It did, in fact, sell for a lower price than the largest competitor, the Oldsmobile.

Ford's only car. In total control of the company, Ford decided that the company would produce only the Model T. He said:

> I will build a motorcar for the great multitude. The principle is to decide on your design, freeze it, and from then on spend all your time, effort, and money on making machinery to produce it, concentrating so completely on production that, as the volume goes up, it is certain to get cheaper per unit produced. (Ford in Collier and Horowitz, p. 52)

Anticipating a great demand, the Ford company built a large new factory and began to study how to reduce the time required to build the new cars. Using continuously moving assembly lines and breaking the jobs into individual operations, a new Model T could roll off the line every ninety-three minutes. The car was priced so affordably that it became available to many Americans. By the time the Model T was discontinued, the Ford plants could turn out a new car every twenty-four seconds. From its start in 1908 to its end in

▲ **Ford in one of his first automobiles**

1927, the "Tin Lizzie" was changed only reluctantly—except for price. By 1922 the average worker could buy a Ford Model T for less than $500.

Attractiveness of the Model T. There had been other cars before the Model T, but its availability and reliability changed transportation in America and eventually the world. In its lifetime, 15.5 million Model Ts were produced and sold. They were so simple and reliable that about 100,000 of the cars are still being driven today.

Impact on society. The car changed people's lives by making transportation easier. It also changed industry. In the big new plant at Highland Park, Ford and his employees had worked out a method of assembling the parts and then the whole automobile on moving assembly lines. The Model T inspired new mass-production techniques.

The Model T encouraged other changes in the automotive industry too. When the president of Chrysler Motors learned of the dangers of hand cranking, he instructed his engineers to stop everything else and find a better way to start a car. From then on, Chryslers were produced with electric starters. Style became another concern. Car owners began to look at their cars as status symbols, but all Model Ts looked very much alike. Drivers began searching for more style and more options in the car's appearance. This gave Plymouth an opportunity to compete by changing its cars' body style every year.

The Model T had an even greater impact on laborers in America. Workers of the time suffered low pay, long workdays, and dismal conditions. They therefore often felt little loyalty for an employer. As the demand for the Model T grew and the price fell, Ford's company began to suffer because its employees kept quitting. Work on the assembly line was demanding. In 1913 Ford decided to see what could be done to keep the workers on the line. First he asked other automobile builders about their situation and found they were experiencing the same problem. Then Ford began to look at how much job turnover cost him in Model T production. He compared that with the cost of higher salaries. The average worker earned $2.34 a day. What would happen to costs if the salary jumped to $3.00, $3.50, or even $3.75? It was a good time for the Ford Company to ask such questions. That year, the twelve remaining stockholders had earned a total of $12 million in profits.

Some Early American Automobile Companies

Company	Year
Olds Motor Vehicle Company	1897
Buick Manufacturing Company	1902
Cadillac Automobile Company	1902
Oakland Motor Car Company	1907
Chevrolet Motorcar Company	1918
Fisher Body	1919
Pontiac Automobile Company	1926

Ford always acted as the "boss," regardless of vice presidents and shareholders. He imagined himself a sort of grandfather figure to his employees and took a sometimes too active role in their lives.

Now, on January 3, 1914, he called his directors to a meeting to discuss how the employees could better share in the riches of the company. When all agreed with the boss that the Ford workers were not earning a livable wage, Ford began to wonder what would happen if wages were doubled. The meeting adjourned with the directors of the company against the idea. Doubling the wages would bankrupt the business, they said. The boss told them to go home and think about it.

On January 5, the directors agreed with Ford's view. A press conference with three Detroit newspapers was arranged and Ford announced that perhaps for the first time in history, the average worker would be paid $5.00 for a day's work. This salary was affordable to Ford because his assembly line had enabled him to produce cars inexpensively. The Model T had revolutionized industrial economics.

Unable to compete, some of the smaller automobile companies soon closed down and others were absorbed into larger companies. There had been about 175 competitors to Ford in the beginning and the number soon dropped to about 12. The raise in salary paid off as Ford had expected. Workers remained with the company. Having a stable workforce allowed Ford to concentrate on machinery and the assembly line. By 1922 a person could buy a basic Model T for $295. Three years later, a new Model T was rolling off the lines every fifteen seconds. But after 1922, the Model T began to lag in sales.

Death of the Model T. Ford reluctantly made changes in the design of the Model T. For an added price, a buyer could have an electric starter, even though Ford felt that anyone who had trouble with a hand crank did so because it was their own fault. By 1925 Model T options also included a horn, flower vases, and even a foot-fed gas pedal to replace the steering column choke lever. It was, however, too late. Chevrolet and Plymouth were rapidly gaining on the sales of the Model T. In 1927 Ford shut down the plants to retool for a new model. He had held off so long that remodeling stopped production for eight months and cost Ford, who by this time had bought out all his partners, one fifth of the value of the company. The results were the loss of first place in auto sales to Chevrolet and later to Plymouth and the development of a completely new Ford, the Model A. Meanwhile, son Edsel had come into the business and decided to design an automobile as stylish and beautiful as the Model T had been practical. Edsel started a new division of Ford to make Lincolns. At first the Lincoln lost money for Ford and encouraged even more competition.

Aftermath

Ford's image. As the Model T gained popularity, Ford gained respect from his fellow Americans. He also developed a high opinion of himself. This development caused him to attempt some seemingly impossible tasks and to take some very questionable positions.

The peace ship. In 1914 Ford was strongly opposed to the war developing in Europe. He felt that he could personally settle the issues before the Americans got involved. Ford chartered a ship, the *Oscar II,* and set sail for Europe with some peace advocates. Once there, Ford found that the German government did not want to talk with his peace group and that other European leaders questioned his mission. After two weeks, the ship returned home.

Though Ford strongly opposed America's entry into World War I, when the United States did become involved, he turned the Ford Company into a supplier of aircraft. One of his most popular wartime airplanes was the *Ford Trimotor,* used for transporting troops and supplies.

The "international Jewish conspiracy." After the war, in 1919, Ford decided to take up a crusade against what he imagined was an international conspiracy of Jews to upset society. (Throughout history Jews have been made the scapegoats for many of society's ills by those who disagreed with their religious beliefs and differed from them in other ways.) Ford bought a newspaper, the *Detroit Independent,* and used it to publish bitter anti-Semitic accusations based on the idea that Jews were in a giant conspiracy to gain control of world economies. He published pamphlets describing what he thought was the uncommon influence of Jews in America, then he turned his wrath on Aaron Shapiro, a Jew who had attempted to help farmers by organizing farm cooperatives. Shapiro sued Ford. Ford consequently claimed innocence on the grounds that his writings had not hurt anyone.

When challenged to document his idea of a conspiracy, Ford pointed to an editor of the *Jewish Tribune,* Herman Bernstein, whom Ford said had first told him about the Jewish conspiracy. Bernstein denied the charge and, in turn, accused Ford of inciting pogroms (massacres) against Jews in Europe. Ford offered to apologize if Bernstein found any evidence in Europe that Jews had been hurt because of his accusations. Bernstein personally traveled to Europe and did indeed uncover a great deal of such evidence. Ford apologized and went out of the newspaper business, but much damage had been done.

Public benefactor and political leader. At the same time, Ford attempted to help the country beyond his company's activities. When, after the war, there was a great demand for farm tools, he started to manufacture Ford tractors in his factories. He sponsored and paid for experiments with soybeans, feeling that this product had so many uses that it would make farmers financially independent. Upon the death of President Warren G. Harding, Ford was considered for president, but he himself supported Calvin Coolidge. President Coolidge was succeeded by Hoover, whom Ford also supported.

Ford had little use for Franklin Delano Roosevelt. He favored Herbert Hoover and campaigned for his election for a second term. However, by that time Ford—through questionable political activities as well as his anti-Jewish actions—had turned from a national hero into a national villain. His support of Hoover may have led to Roosevelt's victory in the presidential election.

The Great Depression. President Roosevelt struggled to lift America out of a Great Depression in the early 1930s. Part of his effort, the National Labor Relations Act was passed to benefit the working person. Ford strongly opposed this act and refused to join other car makers in adopting its proposals. In his disagreement, Ford fought hard to keep the United Auto Worker's (UAW) union from gaining a foothold in Ford plants. In 1941 Ford received a court order to allow his employees to enroll in the UAW and to rehire twenty-two union organizers whom he had fired for their actions. Forced to allow a union vote, Ford found that his popularity with his employees had dwindled. More than 70 percent of the Ford workers voted to join the UAW. Only 3 percent voted to continue to have no union. The remainder had other ideas for organization.

Withdrawal from the Ford Company. By 1945 Ford had become frail. His son Edsel had died earlier. His grandson, Henry Ford II, was the only one left to take over the company. Ford felt that his grandson had done nothing to contribute to the company's growth. Henry II felt that he had not been given the opportunity. Unhappy when he resigned as president of the Ford Motor Company on September 21, Ford growled at his grandson, "Congratulations. You're taking over a billion-dollar organization that you haven't contributed a thing to" (Ford in Collier and Horowitz, p. 208). Henry II was elected president and immediately dismissed his grandfather's most trusted aides.

Ford died in Detroit on April 7, 1947, about eighteen months after resigning as head of his revolutionary motor company.

For More Information

Collier, Peter, and David Horowitz. *The Fords: An American Epic.* New York: Simon and Schuster, 1987.

Dahlinger, John Coté, and Frances Spatz Leighton. *The Secret Life of Henry Ford.* New York: Bobbs-Merrill Company, 1978.

Gelderman, Carol. *Henry Ford, the Wayward Capitalist.* New York: The Dial Press, 1981.

John L. Lewis

1880-1969

Personal Background

Heritage. John Watkins, a coal miner from Wales, immigrated with his family to America and by 1878 had found work in the coal mines of Iowa. About the same time, Thomas Lewis also came to America from Wales and found work in the mines. In 1878 Thomas married John's daughter, Ann Louisa Watkins. The young couple settled in Lucas, Iowa. So many of the town residents were miners that its chief attractions were a branch of the Knights of Labor, which was a national labor union, and a large miner's hall that served as a school and recreation area. John L. Lewis, the first son of Thomas and Ann, was born in Lucas on February 12, 1880.

Thomas Lewis. Life was hard for the Iowa coal miners in the 1880s. They worked long hours for low pay for nine months of the year and then were unemployed for three months. Often the families found themselves moving from town to town as coal mines closed, opened, or suffered temporary shut downs. For the Lewis family, moving became necessary for another reason as well.

Thomas resisted the poor treatment of miners. John was just two years old when his father led a miners' strike against the coal company in Lucas, White Breast Fuel Company. The strikers fought hard for their demands, but when it appeared the company would win, most of them returned to their jobs. Not only did Thomas

▲ **John L. Lewis**

Event: Organizing industrial workers.
Role: John L. Lewis, president of the United Mine Workers (UMW), saw and acted upon a need to represent the body of American workers created by new mass production techniques. He organized the Committee for Industrial Organization (CIO) and became the labor leader for masses of factory workers in America.

Lewis lose his job at the company, but he was probably also "blacklisted," put on a list that circulated among mine owners to warn them of troublemakers. For several years, Thomas failed to find work in mines anywhere. The family moved around Iowa, to Cleveland, Mahasaka, Cedar, Cedar Mines, Oswalt, Oskaloosa, Colfax, and then to Des Moines. There the family grew to include six sons, two daughters, and an adopted son. Eventually the sons would become miners and help greatly in their older brother's efforts to organize an effective coal miner's union.

Early life. Life for John was not unlike that for any son of poor parents with large families. He attended schools in Des Moines—Grant Park Elementary, Lincoln, and Washington. For a short time, he went to junior high but then dropped out. Stories vary about the extent of his high school education. According to his own story, he had none: "I never went to high school. I got along all right in school, but I was just more interested in outside things than I was in classroom work" (Lewis in Alinsky, p. 16). Those "outside things" included selling newspapers, playing baseball, listening to the tales of the miners, and fighting. John gained an early reputation for testing the fighting strength of bigger boys and for his strength as a public speaker. Most nights were spent listening to his father talk about mine problems and the value of unions.

John's mother, a member of the Reorganized Church of Latter Day Saints, may have been his main link with religion. The Latter Day Saints were very much opposed to drinking alcohol and to sex before marriage. John appreciated his mother's dedication to her church and its rules, although he himself did not become a member.

Coal miner. In 1897 John's father was no longer blacklisted, so the family could return to Lucas and mine. Both Thomas and John went to work for the Big Hill Coal and Mining Company. John, aged seventeen, drove mules and pulled coal for the older miners, earning a reputation as a good and dependable worker.

Myrta Bell. Lewis had grown to be a husky and handsome young man with an abundance of dark, wavy hair and heavy eyebrows. His size and appearance made him a standout at the local parties. At one of these he met Myrta Edith Bell, daughter of a local doctor. Myrta had graduated from high school and taken courses at

Wayne University to become a teacher. Her quiet ways prompted Lewis to gain more knowledge and improve his speech. With Myrta's encouragement, he spent more time reading. Lewis was particularly interested in military history, western adventure, and mystery stories.

At this point, Lewis had no firm idea of what he wanted to do in his life. He seemed disinclined to stay in the mines. Lewis tried practicing carpentry, running a mill, and managing the local opera house. He even served for a time as justice of the peace.

Western travel. In 1901 Lewis left Lucas, the mine, and his family and headed west. For five years, he roamed the West by stagecoach, rail, or foot, taking whatever jobs he could get to support himself. It is likely that he tried other forms of mining in the copper, silver, and gold mines that stretched from Montana to Utah to Arizona. Whatever he did, acquaintances began to create stories about his strength. One story tells how he was trapped in a mine by a mule. He is said to have freed himself by pounding the mule on the head, then killing it with a blow from a piece of heavy mining timber. Wherever he traveled he watched, listened, and took careful note of events. Lewis was in the West, perhaps in Hanna, Wyoming, when a 1905 mine disaster cost the lives of 236 workers. Later he would call his five years in the West his period of formal education.

The United Mine Workers. In 1906 Lewis returned home to Lucas to work in the mines. Much of his life, he had heard about Samuel Gompers, the founder of the American Federation of Labor (AFL). One of the unions under the AFL was the United Mine Workers (UMW). Although the UMW had not been greatly successful against the mine owners, it had grown to nearly two million members. Lewis had not spent many years in the mines, but he understood miners' problems and could explain them well to other people. The miners respected him and soon voted to send him as the Lucas delegate to the 1907 national convention of the United Mine Workers. Attending this meeting gave Lewis a direction for his life; he would devote himself to union organization.

Another decision that year gave him added cause to settle down. He married Myrta Bell, whom he would depend on for advice and support until her death. The couple had three children—John

Jr., Kathryn, and Margaret. Margaret would die at the age of eleven, but John and Kathryn, along with Lewis's father and brothers, were to become strong supporters in his attempts to build strong unions.

Now Lewis had a family to support. He tried a number of other occupations, even running for mayor of Lucas, but none were successful. After a year in Lucas, Lewis and his wife packed their bags and set off for Panama, Illinois. Lewis had decided that to organize a strong union of miners he had to be where there was more mining activity. Illinois mining was booming.

Within a year, Thomas Lewis and the rest of the family had moved to Panama. The Lewises all joined Local 1475 of the United Mine Workers. They gained influence in the local, and John was soon elected its president. In another year, he had become legislative agent for District 12 of the UMW. His first action was to campaign for laws calling for better working conditions in the mines. Mining had always been a dangerous occupation. Lewis had long been aware of this fact, but after an explosion at Cherry, Illinois, killed 160 miners, Lewis felt driven to take action.

Lewis and Samuel Gompers. The American Federation of Labor brought together under one organization many different unions. One of the largest unions in the AFL was the UMW. In 1911 Lewis became an Illinois delegate to the annual conference of the American Federation of Labor, founded by Samuel Gompers. Gompers was a good organizer but had not proven to be a strong champion of some of the union members. By 1911 he was being attacked by various unions in the AFL, particularly because of his indecisiveness about black workers. Lewis considered Gompers to be a groundbreaking labor boss and stoutly supported him at the conference. The two became fast friends, and Lewis emerged from the conference with an appointment as an AFL representative.

Lewis proved to be an excellent agent for the AFL, presiding over strikes and recruiting new union members. In fact, his rise in both the UMW and the AFL was rapid, thanks in part to his family and his own flair for public speaking and theatrics. After holding a number of important positions, Lewis was elected president of the UMW in 1918. He inherited a union in which each local demanded freedom to do their own bargaining. Lewis knew that broken into such small factions, the UMW would be ineffective. He decided that all miners must be organized and that he must resort to any tactic to get them to band together, even hiring armed thugs if necessary to enforce Union rules.

In 1919 Lewis added to his reputation by taking the coal miners into a strike. They had cooperated with the United States government during World War I, signing an agreement not to ask for higher pay or fewer work hours, but now the miners wanted to make up for lost time. They demanded a 60-percent increase in pay, a six-hour day, and a five-day work week. The government wanted to delay the decision, claiming that the war was not yet officially over. In the end, Lewis settled for a 14-percent increase in wages.

Defeat in West Virginia. At nearly the same time, Lewis ordered that the coal miners of West Virginia be organized. That part of the country had been nonunion and therefore was producing coal for sale at a lower price. Union fields in other states were suffering since their higher priced coal had to compete. Finally West Virginia's miners organized and struck. The mine owners fought back, firing union members and throwing them out of their houses. The owners hired gunmen to force the workers to give up the union. At Bluefield, West Virginia, the sheriff and his men fought a battle with the mine owners' gunmen. In Madison, West Virginia, 2,000 well-armed company enforcers fought a war with 6,000 miners. Finally, the United States Army stopped the battles.

Fifty thousand miners had joined the UMW and for their actions had been thrown out of jobs and homes. As a result, West Virginia remained nonunion for the next thirteen years. Lewis had lost his first major battle for the UMW.

President of the UMW. Lewis was tough, eager for a fight, and ruthless both in battling the mine owners and in keeping his own union members in line. He refused to accept defeat. Lewis attempted to reshape the UMW, helping to get its president John White appointed to the wartime Federal Fuel Board. Supported by Lewis, Frank Hayes then stepped into office as union president. Hayes made Lewis a vice president. Some stories claim that Lewis at this point encouraged Hayes to drink more than he should have—and he became ineffective as the union president. Lewis then became acting president while Hayes went to Europe. In any event, Lewis became president of the UMW in 1920. He would remain its president for forty years.

Lewis saw a new opportunity for labor unions. Gompers had formed the AFL from a number of crafts unions. But World War I had turned America into an industrial giant, and men like Henry Ford had designed huge factories where products could be assembled on moving lines by relatively unskilled workers (see **Henry Ford**). The large number of unskilled workers, Lewis thought, could help with struggles between labor and management *if* they were organized. He began to press Gompers to include the industrial workers in his union plans. But unions like the Cigarmakers, the Machinists, and the Carpenters wanted to preserve their own status as skilled workers. Although he still considered Gompers to be a union organizing genius, Lewis began to break with his old friend about organizing industrial workers.

Participation: Founding the Congress of Industrial Organizations

Lewis versus the AFL. For years, the powerful leaders of the crafts unions resisted admitting the unskilled assembly workers into the AFL. They claimed that it would lead to dual union memberships. A machinist or carpenter, for example, would have membership in the craft union and in the union of the workers in the industry for which they worked. Some machinists might, for instance, find themselves in a union of automobile workers. There could be mixed or conflicting goals and the union effort would suffer.

Lewis had for a long time pleaded for the crafts unions to help the industrial workers organize. At the AFL convention of 1935, as leader of the most powerful union in the AFL, he tried again to promote organizing the steel industry:

> Our people are suffering and they are suffering ... for the fact that the American Federation of Labor has failed ... to organize the iron and steel workers.... How long does any one think the United Mine Workers of America will be satisfied with that policy? (Lewis in Zieger, *John L. Lewis,* p. 82)

▲ **Factory and mine owners often built shacks, such as these in "Pottersville," within their compounds to protect and house strikebreakers**

His proposal to unionize the steel industry was voted down 18,000 to 10,000. Again Lewis refused defeat.

Fight with Hutcheson. During the AFL convention three days later, Lewis had an opportunity to dramatize his demand. The rubber workers from Ohio wanted to speak in favor of industrial unions. They were blocked from doing so by the giant president of the Carpenters' Union, William Hutcheson—known as "Big Bill." Big Bill kept the rubber workers at bay by challenging them on one point of order, then another, and still another. Lewis pretended irritation and described Hutcheson's challenges as rather small potatoes. Though they had been friends, the two big labor leaders started to insult each other. Hutcheson began to call Lewis names. That gave Lewis his opportunity. He jumped over a row of chairs and slugged Hutcheson, who was then helped from the conference while Lewis strolled to the stage as if nothing had happened. Lewis had made the point that he intended to fight for industrial unions.

Organizing the CIO. The next day, October 20, 1935, Lewis called a few friends to a meeting at the hotel. Invited were members of the AFL: Phil Murray (of the UMW), Tom Kennedy (UMW), John Brophy (UMW), Sidney Hillman (Men's Clothing Workers), and David Dubinsky (Women's Garment Workers). Non-AFL members present were Charles Howard (representing printers), Thomas McMahon (textile workers), Max Zaritsky (cap makers), Thomas Brown (mine, mill, and smelter workers), and Harvey Fremming (oil workers). These men all agreed to join forces to force the AFL to organize industrial workers. They formed a Committee for Industrial Organization (CIO) to work within the AFL to organize the large industries such as steel, automobiles, and rubber. John Brophy was selected as president of the committee.

Backed by the large treasury of the UMW, the committee began its work. Soon groups of unskilled workers in some large industries were ready to petition the AFL for membership. Meanwhile, president William Green of the AFL wrote to Lewis warning him of the dangers of his actions. Lewis responded by resigning his position as vice president of the AFL. He would continue to direct the movement for industrial unions from his position as president of the UMW. Again the proposal was raised at the AFL conference, this time specifically to admit the auto workers, aluminum workers, rubber workers, and radio workers as industrial unions. On June 4, 1936, the Committee for Industrial Organization organized the Steel Workers' Organizing Committee (SWOC). William Green and the AFL responded by suspending the CIO from the AFL. Lewis continued to support organizing the steel workers with UMW money.

Now Lewis introduced a new technique for forcing company owners to bargain with the unions. Instead of just walking out on strike and picketing the company entrances, union members now began to "sit down" at their work stations. Not only did this stop work, it prevented the company from replacing workers and resuming work. It was tried first against General Motors at its Flint, Michigan, plants and resulted in union and management discussions there. From September 1936 to May 1937, as many as 500,000 workers were engaged in sit-down strikes. Threatened with this action, the United States Steel Company, the largest of the steel factories, agreed to let the SWOC organize the workers.

Other steel companies refused to follow the U.S. Steel example, and union members struck violently. The company managements enlisted armed guards and the local police, and battles were fought viciously. Striking workers beat their replacements and the company managers. Union-hired toughs helped the workers. In one struggle, Republic Steel Company bought better weapons for the Chicago police to use in breaking the strike, and eleven workers were killed. President Franklin D. Roosevelt, who had enlisted Lewis's advice in seeking ways to recover from the Great Depression, refused to help settle matters. Lewis, in response, turned against Roosevelt and opposed some of the president's strongest moves to enlist labor in the country's recovery from depression.

AFL-CIO. The turmoil resulting from the organization of the CIO stirred labor everywhere. AFL membership increased by three million in 1937. Almost one-fourth of all workers outside of agriculture were union members. Still the CIO and AFL were at odds, and the crafts unions were reluctant to support the industrial workers. On November 15, 1938, Lewis took UMW out of the AFL and formed an organization that would actively pursue the interests of industrial unions, the Congress of Industrial Organizations.

In the 1940 presidential elections, Lewis showed his irritation with Roosevelt by supporting Wendell Wilkie. Perhaps partly because of Roosevelt's reelection and partly because he was aging (Lewis was now sixty), he resigned as president of the CIO in late November 1940. He was replaced by his longtime aide, Philip Murray.

World War II was beginning, and Lewis pledged his UMW workers to a no-strike agreement for the rest of the war. He now had time to consider his actions and their effects on unions. In 1942 he proposed to reunite the AFL and CIO.

In the next few years, Lewis held a stormy relationship with both George Meany, president of the AFL, and Philip Murray of the CIO, removing the UMW from the CIO and rejoining the AFL in 1946, then breaking with the AFL again in 1947.

Relationships were also stormy with the government. The UMW had agreed not to strike during World War II, but wartime prices had not been held in check and the country was suffering from inflation. Mine workers with their prewar salaries were suffering. In 1943, groups of mine workers began to strike for better

▲ **Lewis, center, with supporters**

wages. Lewis supported these actions, raising fears in the government that his leadership would spread the strikes to other industries. Lewis fought frequently with the National War Labor Relations Board, the government agency assigned to regulate labor. Still the unions grew, both the AFL and CIO, until by war's end there were more than eighteen million union members. By 1947 big labor had grown so threatening to the government that a law (Taft-Hartley) took away some of the strike weapons used by the unions. Also by then, a new fear had arisen, communism, and the Taft-Hartley Act refused government recognition to any union official who could not prove he or she was not a communist.

In 1955 Lewis's proposal finally resulted in reuniting the AFL and CIO. Lewis continued as UMW president and one of the most powerful labor leaders. His union took over banks to support the mine workers, built hospitals in mine areas, and established retirement and welfare funds for the union members. Lewis retired as UMW president in 1960 at the age of eighty.

Aftermath

Personal fortune. Lewis had been good for American laborers, and his union had been good to him. When the average laborer was earning $1,200 a year, Lewis's salary as UMW president was $12,500. In addition, the union provided a nearly unlimited expense account. Lewis was able to live in luxury that provided three house servants and allowed Myrta to indulge in her favorite hobby, collecting expensive antiques and works of art. The union also provided good jobs for other family members. Lewis's brother George was an executive in the Illinois mining district; his brother Dennis was in charge of hiring "enforcers" for the union; his brother-in-law Bill was treasurer of the CIO; and his daughter Kathryn was her father's private secretary. At the same time, when he left the presidency, the UMW treasury had grown to $110 million.

Final days. Although Lewis continued to be a director of the UMW retirement and welfare fund, his last years were spent in almost total isolation. He even refused to participate with Columbia University in recording the history of the labor movement.

When he died on June 11, 1969, Lewis had been isolated for so long that some former associates reacted as if they thought he had died long ago. In fact, the Lewis image had long since died, and important members of the family were gone. His wife Myrta had died in 1942, his mother in 1950, and his daughter Kathryn and brother Dennie had died within three weeks of one another in 1962.

For More Information

Alinsky, Saul. *John L. Lewis: An Unauthorized Biography.* New York: G. P. Putnam's Sons, 1949.

Lichtenstein, Nelson. *Labor's War at Home: The CIO in World War II.* Cambridge, U.K.: Cambridge University Press, 1982.

Zieger, Robert H. *John L. Lewis: Labor Leader.* Boston, Massachusetts: Twayne Publishers, 1988.

The Scopes Trial

1859

Charles Darwin publishes *The Origin of Species,* presenting his theory of evolution.

1896

William Jennings Bryan loses the election for U.S. president to William McKinley.

1900

Bryan loses presidency to Theodore Roosevelt.

1908

New York City has 400 movie houses, which run silent half-hour films. Bryan loses presidency to William Taft.

1910

Readership of several low-cost magazines rises to more than 500,000.

1910–1915

Religious leaders publish *The Fundamentals,* twelve volumes of essays against the theory of evolution.

1919

World's Christian Fundamentals Association is founded.

1920

Bryan and others call themselves "fundamentalists." Public radio broadcasts begin.

1924

Clarence Darrow wins fame as a defense lawyer in Chicago murder trial.

1925

Tennessee enacts law to forbid the teaching of evolution; John T. Scopes challenges the law.

1925

Darrow and Bryan oppose each other in the Scopes Trial.

1968

U.S. Supreme Court declares antievolution law unconstitutional.

THE SCOPES TRIAL

American values and beliefs were changing in the 1920s. With the introduction by industry of consumer items and of benefits such as paid vacations, pleasure became a priority. The spread of entertainment media—movies, low-cost magazines, and radio—in the early 1900s strengthened this trend.

Among the ideas being adopted in cities and towns at the time was the theory of evolution, which held that humans and apes had descended from common ancestors. Already accepted by scientists, the theory was deeply upsetting to some others, who feared that new notions and values would displace old commitments to hard work, family, and the Bible. Clashes surfaced in society between champions of the new and of the old. One such clash was the trial of John Thomas Scopes.

In 1925 the Tennessee legislature passed a law forbidding the teaching of Charles Darwin's theory of evolution in the state's public schools. On the publication of Darwin's *Origin of Species* in 1859, certain religious leaders had reacted angrily to the theory's seeming contradiction to the Bible. Years passed, and still some religious leaders refused to accept the theory. In 1920 these leaders began calling themselves "fundamentalists"—they were committed to preserving the "fundamentals," or basics, of their beliefs. Fundamentalists believe that every statement in the Bible is literal truth. So they rejected Darwin's theory that people and apes evolved from common ancestors over millions of years; they held instead to the biblical statement that God created man and the animals separately. The Tennessee legislature, mostly fundamentalists, worried that children who were taught a scientific theory of creation would stop believing in the Bible. To prevent this, they passed an antievolution law.

Antievolution Law

"Be it enacted—that it shall be unlawful for any teacher in any of the universities, normals, and all other public schools of the state ... to teach any theory that denies the story of the Divine Creation of man as taught in the Bible, and to teach instead that man has descended from a lower order of animals." (Weinberg and Weinberg, pp. 317-18)

A prominent leader of the fundamentalist movement was **William Jennings Bryan,** a popular speaker and three-time candidate for president. Bryan's political support had always come from rural areas, the farms and small towns where people shared his deep religious views. In cities, where new ideas more easily took hold, some of the religious leaders began to view the Bible as more of a guide than an exact blueprint. Stories like that of Adam and Eve, they argued, could be seen as symbolic. That is, Adam and Eve's creation might represent the creation of humans as a race, and the six days of God's work might stand for a much longer time. God might even have chosen to do his work *through* evolution, some suggested.

Growing rapidly, the cities were emerging as the new leaders in American culture and politics. The countryside, which became associated with fundamentalists, meanwhile was losing its influence on American life. Still, both sides made up strong forces in the early twentieth century. After Tennessee banned the teaching of evolution in its schools, Bryan predicted that other rural states would soon do the same. The American Civil Liberties Union (ACLU), an organization devoted to protecting free speech and other constitutional rights, offered to support anyone who challenged the law in court.

▶ **The press had a field day with the Scopes Trial**

Orator, Statesman and Student of Bible

Here is Mr. Bryan, wearing the sheepskin apron of the Master Mason. The picture was taken after he led the prayer at the laying of the cornerstone for $300,000 Scottish Rite Cathedral at Miami.—International Newsreel photo.

At left above Mr. Bryan is shown making a speech at the pinnacle of his career as an orator, when his silvery voice charmed thousands. At right, the Commoner is reading the Bible in the yard of the home of Richard Rogers at Dayton, where he passed away. Last photo by International News Service.

Mr. Bryan on the day he arrived in Dayton to appear as the champion of the fundamentalists at the Scopes evolution trial. —Photo by International Newsreel.

HEAT AT TRIAL TEST TO BRYAN

DAYTON, Tenn., July 26.—(By the Associated Press.)—Shortly before William Jennings Bryan died today he remarked he had never felt better in his life and was ready to go before the country to wage his battle against modernism.

The great Commoner had returned to Dayton this morning after completing arrangements for the publication of the address he had prepared to deliver in closing the trial of John T. Scopes, who was recently convicted of violation of Tennessee's anti-evolution law.

Publication of this speech at an early date was to mark the opening of the crusade in behalf of fundamentalism Mr. Bryan planned to carry before the entire country.

Despite the fact that Mr. Bryan had spoken yesterday at Jasper and Winchester, Tenn., and had traveled over 200 miles, he appeared in the best of health and unfatigued. He attended services at the Southern Episcopal Church and led the congregation in a prayer which citizens of Dayton tonight described as one of the most beautiful ever delivered in the church.

During the days of the Scopes trial the heat in Dayton was most oppressive and the courtroom crowded to the doors. Mr. Bryan was of necessity seated inside the rail at the counsel table, where there was very little air. While he carried a palm leaf fan, there was little circulation of breeze through the room and he seemed to feel the heat exceedingly. However, as far as known, he made no complaints, and there was nothing to indicate

'BIBLE ENOUGH,' HE DECLARED

NEW YORK, July 26.—(By Universal Service.)—"The Bible is good enough for me," was William Jennings Bryan's final national message as revealed in the current Colliers' Weekly, in which he replied to an earlier article on evolution by the son of Charles Darwin.

"Darwinism enthrones selfishness" Bryan says in the article.

"The Bible crowns love, the greatest force in the world.

"Christianity places before man infinite possibilities and invokes him to improve them to the uttermost.

"Jesus brought into the world the gospel of hope and taught that one could be born again, reborn in an instant.

"There is a spiritual gravitation that can draw all souls toward heaven; a law the existence of which can be demonstrated as clearly by its results as the law of gravitation in the physical world can be demonstrated by its effect on matter.

"I would propose the Bible as a substitute for a more materialistic doctrine because the Bible is not only the foundation of our present standard of morals, but also gives us our only conception of God, and tells us of Jesus, the Christ."

Coal Miner, Crazed, Kills Family, Then Self

PITTSBURGH, July 26.—Crazed by his inability to find work, Levi Sterner, a coal miner, killed his wife and his 11-month-old daughter a d then shot himself to death

Schoolboys Enlisted to Oust Groundhogs

Soon after, a group of friends who were against the Antievolution Law met at Robinson's Drug Store in the small Tennessee town of Dayton. Testing the law, they agreed, would also be a good way of bringing national attention—and business—to Dayton. They were joined by biology teacher John T. Scopes. Scopes, twenty-four years old and unmarried, seemed a fine choice for the role of defendant. He intentionally told his class about evolution, then informed Dayton authorities that he had done so. It was the drugstore owner, also the chairman of the school board, who notified the press of Scopes's arrest for teaching evolution.

Right away, the ACLU promised money and publicity for Scopes's defense in the coming trial. Bryan volunteered to act as lawyer for the state, while the famous defense attorney **Clarence Darrow** and Dudley Field Malone offered their services free to the ACLU on Scopes's behalf.

Billed as the "Great Monkey Trial" (a reference to Darwin's theory), the legal contest brought swarms of reporters, businessmen, and outright hustlers to the small town. The trial, with all its fanfare, would make the case into a contest between rural and city life. In a way that was unfair, for many in the city as well as in the country still held to the old beliefs, rural life would be turned into a symbol of backwardness, or opposition to science.

The reaction of outsiders far exceeded the expectations of Scopes and his friends, who were pushed into the background by the famous participants. National attention remained riveted on Dayton throughout the trial, which lasted from July 10 to July 21, 1925. Most of the reporters openly favored the defense, portraying the fundamentalist townspeople as superstitious country bumpkins. A carnival atmosphere prevailed, with the audience (often nearly 1,000 people) laughing or applauding despite the judge's warnings.

The highlight came when Darrow, in a surprise move, called to the witness stand none other than Bryan himself, as an expert on the Bible. Darrow's long and grueling cross-examination of Bryan exposed gaps in Bryan's knowledge of

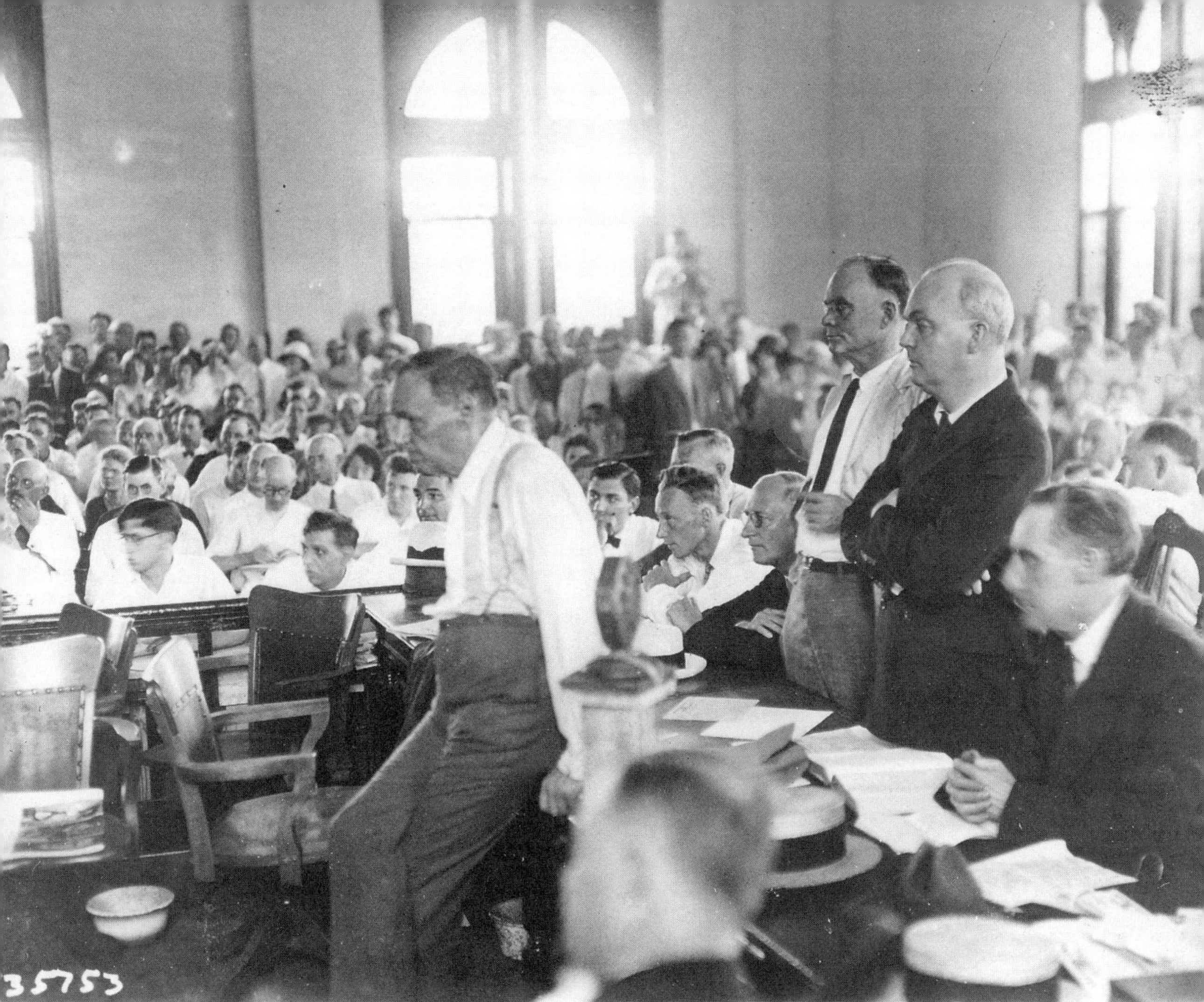

▲ **Darrow, center front, in court**

the Bible and of biology. Bryan looked increasingly ridiculous, and the reporters exaggerated his discomfort in their stories. The trial closed the next day. While the fundamentalists won, much of the nation now saw them as old-fashioned and foolish.

Other states did, as Bryan had predicted, pass similar laws, but no attempt was made to enforce them. Such laws have repeatedly been declared unconstitutional beginning in 1968, despite continued efforts by fundamentalists. Scopes, around whom this controversy raged, soon after gave up teaching.

Clarence Darrow

1857-1938

Personal Background

Family life. Clarence Seward Darrow was born in the small Ohio town of Kinsman on April 18, 1857. His parents' ancestors came from England, settling in New England in the 1600s; both his grandfathers moved west to the Ohio frontier in the early 1800s. His parents, Amirus Darrow and Emily Eddy, met in school, fell in love, and married in 1845. At first Amirus became a preacher, but then he began to lose his religious faith and quit. He became a furniture maker and carpenter instead.

A bit of a dreamer, Amirus preferred to escape into a good book rather than spend long hours at the workbench. The Darrows, consequently, barely scraped together a living. Emily, both a housewife and a women's rights advocate, shared her husband's love of books and his searching attitude to life. Both were quick to ask questions, to reject authority, and to side with the underdog. They passed on these qualities to their offspring—especially to Clarence, the fifth of seven children.

Baseball and coffins. Growing up in the small village, Clarence played a lot with his brothers and sisters. They fished in summer, sledded in winter, and in general spent most of their time outdoors. Clarence's greatest love was baseball. The sport would claim his affection into adulthood, though later it would have to compete with poker as his favorite pastime.

▲ Clarence Darrow

Event: The Scopes Trial (Tennessee Evolution Trial)—defense of John T. Scopes.
Role: A famous defense lawyer, Clarence Darrow volunteered for that position in the Scopes Trial. He saw a chance to support Darwin's theory of evolution, which Scopes was accused of teaching. In the national publicity surrounding the trial, Darrow also saw an opportunity to attack Christian fundamentalism and its hero William Jennings Bryan, a prosecuting attorney.

Clarence's bright, sunlit outdoor world was balanced by a darker one indoors when Amirus, not making enough money as a carpenter, turned to a new profession. He became the village undertaker, using his carpentry skills to make wooden coffins. Clarence found the coffins scary. Death seemed beyond his understanding. Later it often lurked in the background of his thoughts:

> I remember the coffins piled in one corner of the shop, and I always stayed as far away from them as possible, which I have done ever since. Neither did I ever want to visit the little shop after dark. (Darrow in Tierney, p. 9)

As a lawyer for people facing the death penalty, he would spend much of his life struggling to keep others as far away as possible from coffins, too.

Mother's death. When Clarence was fourteen, his mother's death added to this sense of mystery and fear. Emily's passing left a hole that her husband and children would feel for the rest of their lives. Her fourteen-year-old son would always "remember the blank despair that settled over the home when we realized that her tireless energy and devoted love were lost forever" (Darrow in Tierney, p. 16).

"Showy profession." School was a hateful burden to Clarence, whose dislike of it was the major way in which he revolted against his parents. His father kept trying to make him study Greek and Latin, but Clarence saw no reason to learn a language that no one had spoken for almost 2,000 years. Never gaining much formal education, Clarence learned instead on his own. He would come to love books, but by choosing and reading them himself.

A national depression, the Panic of 1873, made Clarence quit school at sixteen. He found a job teaching, which pleased him much more than being taught. He loved to get up in front of a class and explain ideas to them. Clarence also began to study law, spending a year at the University of Michigan Law School. He didn't do very well in his classes. Once again, Clarence thought he could learn better out of school and therefore left to work for a law office, studying law on his own in his spare time. He didn't love the law or even take it very seriously. But he did love to speak in front of an audience and had become a popular speaker in local Saturday night debates. It was this side of the legal profession that attracted him: "A showy profession," he called it, "one that lets a man enjoy the limelight" (Darrow in Tierney, p. 25).

Country practice. When Darrow was twenty-one, he passed the bar examination for would-be lawyers. "The committee did not seem to take it very seriously," he remembered wryly. "I was not made to feel that the safety of the government or the destiny of the universe was hanging on their verdict" (Darrow in Tierney, p. 23). For the next decade, he practiced law in the smalltown courtrooms of Ohio, living first in Andover and then in Ashtabula. Much like the young Abraham Lincoln, he sharpened his speaking and arguing skills before tough country judges, at the same time involving himself in local politics. In 1880 he married Jessie Ohl, the daughter of neighbors from Kinsman.

Chicago. In 1887 the Darrows moved to Chicago, Illinois. Chicago toward the end of the century was a booming, lively city, a dusty, bustling, growing place. Its citizens saw it as America's great city of the future. Darrow would live there for the rest of his life, and the city would always be linked to his name. He took to life in Chicago enthusiastically. Becoming a close ally to the reformer and millionaire John Peter Atgeld, Darrow dove right into big city politics. When Atgeld was elected governor of Illinois in 1892, Darrow became one of the city's most powerful men.

Against capital punishment. Darrow's alliance with Atgeld brought in legal business, and his practice thrived. Most of the cases were ordinary, but a few made headlines. Sometimes unable to say "no" even to a murderer who couldn't pay him a dime, Darrow would come to specialize in lost causes, often fighting to prevent the executions of convicted criminals. In one such case, Darrow unsuccessfully defended Robert Prendergast, convicted in 1894 for the murder of Chicago's mayor Carter Harrison. Darrow hated the death penalty, believing it a savage form of punishment.

Defending labor. Politically as reform-minded as Atgeld, by the mid-1890s Darrow began to make a name for himself by defending labor leaders and other advocates of change. When Socialist Party leader Eugene V. Debs was arrested over his role in a railroad strike, Darrow and the other defense lawyers took the case all the way to the Supreme Court. (They lost.) Darrow also dabbled in politics, in 1896 losing a narrow election to Congress.

Divorce, remarriage. Jessie, a quiet and reserved woman, did not care for her husband's often stormy and controversial public life, for the constant stream of visitors through the house, or for the long hours, days, or sometimes weeks he spent away from home. The two had grown apart by the late 1890s, and they divorced in 1897. Their son Paul, who would be Darrow's only child, was fourteen. Darrow showered his love on the boy, though as his son grew older it became clear that he took after his mother in personality. He, too, disliked the constant controversy of his father's life and shunned publicity as an adult.

Darrow married again in 1903. His second wife, Ruby Hamerstrom, shared Jessie's quiet ways but not her dislike of Darrow's fast-paced life. They remained happily married for thirty-five years.

The Haywood Trial. In 1906 Darrow was hired to defend "Big Bill" Haywood, a miner and labor-union leader charged with killing former Idaho governor Frank Steunenberg. Steunenberg had angered the unions by sending in federal troops to stop disorder during an 1899 miners' strike, a move that led to defeat for the strikers. Five years later, he was killed by a dynamite charge placed outside his house. The leaders of the miners' union were suspected of seeking revenge.

History has left the image of Darrow as a master defense lawyer, unable to make a false step in proving his clients' innocence. In the Haywood case, however, Darrow's performance was less than perfect. His usually clever arguments seemed desperate and clumsy. The prosecution had an ideal witness who swore that Haywood had hired him to kill Steunenberg. Everyone believed the killer, who claimed to have reformed his ways after becoming a devout Christian. Furthermore, Haywood had a violent past and had often called for violence in the cause of the unions.

No one ever knew for sure why, but the jury found him "not guilty."

The McNamara Case. In 1911 two California union men, John and James McNamara, were charged with the disastrous

▲ **Darrow at work**

bombing of the antiunion *Los Angeles Times,* in which almost fifty newspaper workers were killed or injured. The McNamaras, protesting their innocence, were arrested soon after. Union officials cried out that the McNamaras had been framed and hired Darrow to defend them. But Darrow soon found out that the brothers were indeed guilty, and that the evidence against them was ironclad. After persuading them to plead guilty, a move that shocked union leaders, he focused his efforts on keeping the McNamaras from being executed. In a remarkable performance, he succeeded. Yet the guilty plea angered the union leaders, who had expected Darrow to perform miracles. He never again worked for the unions.

Accused. Out of the McNamara case came the most bitter time of Darrow's life: his own arrest and trial in Los Angeles, California, for trying to bribe a member of the McNamaras' jury. In the end he was found not guilty, but then he was tried again for trying to bribe a second juror. The jury in the second trial was divided, and the charges were dropped. By the time the Darrows finally went back to Chicago from Los Angeles a year and a half later, Clarence's reputation had suffered badly, even though he had not been convicted of any crime. His friends avoided him, and he found it hard to get new clients. By now in his fifties, he began to think he was ruined.

Comeback. Darrow, however, made an astonishing comeback over the next decade. Much of his regained popularity came during and after World War I. From the beginning of the war in 1914, he called for America to participate on the side of the Allies. When public opinion, at first against joining the war, finally shifted to agree with him, he was seen as a patriot who had been right all along. Presidents Woodrow Wilson and Warren G. Harding asked his advice, and young lawyers began to look up to him as a hero. His law practice started booming again in the prosperous twenties, and in 1924 he took a case that made his name a household word across America.

Leopold and Loeb. It was called "the crime of the century": two young men from wealthy Chicago families, Richard Loeb and Nathan Leopold, Jr., had been charged with the kidnapping and murder of a boy named Bobby Franks. The Loebs hired Darrow to defend their son. Darrow had read about the case and had assumed the boys were innocent. In fact, they confessed soon after being arrested, telling a grim story of how they had tried to commit the "perfect crime." The murder had been no more than a cold-blooded game to them.

Public outrage exploded against the boys, who were seen as trying to buy freedom with their families' wealth. Darrow had them plead guilty. In a brilliant twist, he argued that their money actually hurt them, by arousing public anger. If they were sentenced to death, he claimed, it would be merely because they were rich, not because of their crime, which he admitted was horrible. In perhaps his most brilliant victory ever, Darrow avoided the death penalty for the two boys, winning sentences of life in prison instead.

Participation: The Scopes Trial

Test case. Soon after "the crime of the century," Darrow took part in a case described as the trial of the century. A public-school teacher named John T. Scopes had been arrested in Dayton, Tennessee, in 1925. He was charged with teaching Darwin's theory of evolution by natural selection, in violation of a state law passed earlier that year. (He had used a textbook approved by the state.) The arrest was no unlucky accident. Scopes and some friends had deliberately brought it about. It would give them a chance to challenge a law they thought was wrong, and it would also bring fame and business to the sleepy Tennessee town. They expected that the issue involved—scientific reasoning versus religious faith in the origin of life forms—would capture public attention. But Scopes and his friends got more than they bargained for.

Monkey Trial. The trial, set for July 1925, became the focus of a clash between two strong groups: Christian fundamentalists, who believe that every word in the Bible is literally true, and those who accept the scientific theory of evolution. It was billed as "The Great Monkey Trial" because the theory of evolution holds that men and apes descended from common ancestors. Fundamentalists, by contrast, believe the Bible's statement that God created humans and other life forms separately.

Academic freedom. William Jennings Bryan volunteered to prosecute Scopes (see **William Jennings Bryan**). A three-time presidential candidate and America's leading public speaker, Bryan stood for the old-fashioned values of the fundamentalist countryside. On the other side, the American Civil Liberties Union (ACLU) had promised to defend anyone charged with breaking the law. The ACLU wished to guard academic freedom, a teacher's right to teach what he believed was true. When he read of Bryan's participation, Darrow volunteered his services for the defense.

Media circus. Such big names brought an immediate flood of media attention to Dayton. Reporters, gawkers, con men, traveling preachers, and small-time salesmen flocked to the tiny town, selling monkey dolls, pins and other souvenirs. Some pins bore the words "Your Old Man's A Monkey" (Weinberg and Weinberg, p. 320). Trainers brought chimpanzees on chains. So many reporters came that dozens of special telegraph lines had to be put up, so the story could be wired out to the newspapers.

Darrow's Popular Image

The importance of the Scopes Trial in American history resulted in large part from newspaper reports that were heavily slanted in favor of Darrow and the defense. Like other reporters, H. L. Mencken of the Baltimore *Sun* constantly made fun of the fundamentalists, painting a picture of Darrow as the defender of reason against the forces of ignorance. Mencken said the citizens of Dayton were yokels, and he scoffed at their old-fashioned beliefs. His report of Bryan's cross-examination was one-sided, making Bryan look more helpless than he actually was. Mencken and Darrow would be close friends for the rest of their lives.

Duel. Bryan and his wife arrived in town before Darrow, and Bryan gave a speech his first night. "The contest between evolution and Christianity is a duel to the death," he stated. "If evolution wins in Dayton, Christianity goes—not suddenly, of course, but gradually—for the two cannot stand together" (Weinberg and Weinberg, p. 320). Darrow and his wife arrived two days later, and Darrow spoke at a similar dinner. He recalled his own small-town roots, but it was clear that the townspeople were on Bryan's side. Scopes and his friends by now had faded into the background, where they would remain.

Opening arguments. The trial began on Friday, July 10, 1925, but opening arguments did not start until the following Monday. Over 900 people jammed the courtroom. A heat wave frayed tempers and soaked shirts. Hardly anyone wore a jacket. Darrow began by attacking the antievolution law itself, calling it a throwback to the sixteenth century, and claiming it was unconstitutional under the First and Fourteenth Amendments. He went on to predict the banning of books and newspapers if the law were allowed to stand. Baltimore reporter H. L. Mencken said the speech "rose like the wind and ended like a flourish of bugles," yet it had no more effect on the religious audience than if Darrow had "bawled it up to a rain spout in the interior of Afghanistan" (Weinberg and Weinberg, p. 322). The next day, the prosecution opened its case, with

Tennessee attorney general A. T. Stewart's speech claiming that Scopes had, in fact, violated the 1925 law.

Contempt. Over the next several days, both sides brought in witnesses to strengthen their cases. The prosecution called students from Scopes's class. The defense tried to bring in scientists and religious scholars to testify that many interpretations of the Bible were possible. Darrow wanted to show that the Bible did not have to be taken literally, and that there need not be a conflict between the two accounts of creation. The judge, John T. Raulston, decided not to allow these witnesses. Darrow complained. He said he did not understand why "every suggestion of the prosecution should meet with an endless waste of time, and a bare suggestion of anything that is perfectly competent on our part should be immediately over-ruled" (Darrow in Weinberg and Weinberg, p. 323). Soon after, the court adjourned for the weekend. On Monday, Judge Raulston cited Darrow for contempt (disrespect) of court. His bond was set at $5,000. Darrow apologized, though in his apology he seemed to mock the judge.

Darrow's Courtroom Style

Though Darrow tried other big cases, his reputation rested not so much on his knowledge of the law, which was rather weak, but on his ability to create doubt and move an audience. Short on patience when it came to research, he was brilliant at giving the impression that horrible consequences would result if the jury should convict his client. His technique was to tie a particular case to general ideas of right and wrong: for example, his claim that the antievolution law would lead to book banning and censorship. Because he was so skillful in arguing about generalities, he was usually able to pass quickly over the details of a particular case.

Cross-examination. The climax of the trial came when the defense stunned the courtroom by calling to the witness stand none other than Bryan himself, as an expert on the Bible. Darrow was famous for his ruthless cross-examinations, in which he did his best to trap the witness into contradicting himself. Calling Bryan as a witness amounted to a dare, which Bryan accepted, stepping up to the witness box confidently. By this time, the trial had moved outside to escape the heat.

As Darrow questioned him, Bryan at first held his own. His responses were sharp and often witty. He defended his beliefs, maintaining that every word in the Bible was literally true. This left the way open for Darrow to point out contradictions within the Bible, which Bryan could not explain. If the first woman, Eve, was literally made out of the rib of the first man, Adam, then where did their son Cain's wife come from? If the serpent was made to crawl on its belly for tempting Eve, how had it moved around before that—by walking on its tail? Did a whale really swallow the prophet Jonah and spit him out whole after three days? How long exactly had it been since the Creation? How long had the Creation itself taken God?—exactly six days, as the Bible says?

Inherit the Wind

The Scopes Trial was the subject of a 1955 play called *Inherit the Wind* by Jerome Lawrence and Robert Lee. The play was later made into a popular movie in which actor Spencer Tracy portrayed Darrow. Both the play and movie helped cement Darrow's image in American popular culture.

"Fool ideas." Bryan began to look more and more foolish. Finally, sweaty and trembling, he accused Darrow of insulting the Bible. Darrow objected, saying "I am examining you on your fool ideas that no intelligent Christian on earth believes" (Darrow in Weinberg and Weinberg, p. 326). Finally Judge Raulston adjourned the court in an open attempt to save Bryan from further embarrassment. The next morning, he ordered that Bryan's testimony be taken out of the record. The defense immediately rested its case, ending the trial and denying Bryan a chance to speak and recover his dignity. Darrow surprised everyone by asking the jury to find Scopes guilty so that they could appeal the case to a higher court. It took the jury only nine minutes to do so. Judge Raulston sentenced Scopes to a fine of $100, which was paid by Mencken's Baltimore *Sun*. Scopes left teaching soon after.

Aftermath

Unconstitutional. Though the fundamentalists had won the case in court, they had lost it everywhere else, as much of the nation ridiculed their ideas. The tragedy of Bryan's humiliation was capped by his death only five days later. He died in his sleep—of a weak heart, many said, caused by his ordeal in the witness box. Scopes's conviction was overturned on appeal, and never again was an attempt made to enforce the antievolution law. Though similar laws were passed in some other states, attempts to enforce them soon stopped as well. In 1968 the Supreme Court ruled such laws unconstitutional under the First Amendment.

Other cases, lectures. Sixty-seven years old at the time of the Scopes Trial, Darrow went on to try only a few more big cases. A lifelong supporter of equal rights for blacks, he took several cases for the National Association for the Advancement of Colored People (NAACP). He also kept up a heavy schedule of lectures and public debates, capitalizing on his popularity after the Scopes Trial.

By the 1930s, when Darrow was in his seventies, his health began to fail and he was forced to give up his heavy schedule. After a long illness, Darrow died in Chicago on March 13, 1938.

For More Information

Tierney, Kevin. *Darrow: A Biography.* New York: Thomas Y. Crowell, 1979.

Weinberg, Arthur, and Lila Weinberg. *Clarence Darrow: A Sentimental Rebel.* New York: Putnam, 1980.

William Jennings Bryan

1860-1925

Personal Background

Father. Silas Bryan worked his way through college as a farmhand and woodchopper. He graduated from McKendree College (a Methodist college in Lebanon, Illinois) in 1949 at the age of twenty-two and went on to earn a master's degree. A year later he married a former student, Mariah Elizabeth Jennings. For several years, he taught and acted as superintendent of schools while studying for the law. At age twenty-nine, Silas began to practice law, which led to eight years in the Illinois state senate and to a final post as circuit judge.

Adding the earnings of his private law practice to his salary as judge (Silas continued to be both a practicing attorney and a judge), he was able to buy a 500-acre farm near Salem, Illinois. He built a mansion on the farm for his family, and Mariah had their fourth child, William Jennings Bryan, there on March 19, 1860. Two more sons and two more daughters would join the Bryan family and live on the farm in Marion County.

Early life. Silas and Mariah had firm designs for their children. Mariah, who did not much believe in public education, taught the children at home until they were ten years old. Her home schooling must have been strict, for when he did enroll in the public school, William was a model student in his behavior and study

▲ **William Jennings Bryan**

Event: The Scopes Trial (Tennessee Evolution Trial)—prosecution of John T. Scopes.

Role: William Jennings Bryan, a lawyer and three times an unsuccessful candidate for United States president, was a dedicated fundamentalist who volunteered to participate in the trial of a teacher, John T. Scopes. Scopes was accused of breaking Tennessee law by teaching about evolution, a scientific explanation of the origin of life forms. Bryan sided with the state.

habits, even though he confessed that he was not much interested in learning.

Silas farmed 250 acres, raising corn, wheat, vegetables, cattle, and poultry. The children were required to help around the farm. William, the oldest son, took on some major farm responsibilities. By the time he was fourteen, he was as capable on the job as most of the adult farmhands. It was William who built and fed the fires in the home, milked the cows, and tended the livestock.

If the judge were strict about farm chores, he was even stricter about religion. He himself prayed with the family or privately at least three times a day and expected the same devotion from his children. He also studied the Bible diligently and spoke about it often. Both parents were religious, and there was no lack of religious education for the children. With his father a stern Baptist and his mother an equally devout Methodist, William attended two Sunday schools each week, one at each church, until he was twelve. Then his mother joined the Baptists, and the family began to attend church together.

William so adored his father that the boy grew up believing the judge's teachings without question. Judge Bryan had said that the individuals who could do most good for mankind were statesmen and ministers, so William decided early to follow a career in politics or religion. In 1872 his father retired as judge and ran for a seat in the United States Congress. Already becoming known for his gift of speech, William campaigned for his father, who nevertheless lost the election. It was the judge's last attempt to gain a political post.

Education. In 1873, when Bryan was a freshman in high school, the nation suffered a severe economic panic and depression. This sapped the Bryan finances so that after graduation from high school, Bryan was sent to Whipple Academy to prepare for Illinois College rather than enrolling in a more renowned eastern college. At Illinois College, Bryan majored in classics studies, and mathematics was his favorite subject. He learned in studying U.S. history that democracy was the best of all possible governments, and he came to believe that as a government by the people, democracy was Christianity in action. Bryan later campaigned for political office under the slogan "Equal rights for all, special privileges for none" (Coletta, p. 11).

Bryan earned good grades and was particularly active as a debater. His powerful voice and well-researched speeches made him class orator and vice president of the junior class. Even in college, Bryan took positions that he would fight for throughout his life, speaking out for the anti-alcohol laws of prohibition, for women's suffrage, and for the elimination of most protective tariffs. (Tariffs are fees placed on imports to protect local industry from low-cost competition. Bryan felt they did not encourage good local business practices.) Still he took time, to his parents' dismay, to "run with the girls." He graduated in 1881, a handsome, powerfully built young man with a reputation for great intelligence.

Beginning to speak. A year earlier, Bryan had met and become engaged to a student from nearby Jacksonville Female Academy, Mary Baird. In that same year, his father had died of a stroke, leaving the family finances in disarray. Nevertheless, it was a family decision that Bryan would attend Chicago's Union College of Law. Bryan began that year to speak seriously on behalf of various political candidates. Full of youthful zeal, his first political speech attempted to cover every subject. It began "If ye have tears, prepare to shed them now," and, after some time, ended, "as for me, give me liberty or give me death" (Bryan in Coletta, p. 16). When asked how he had performed, Bryan's always honest mother responded, "Well there were a few good places in it—where you might have stopped" (Coletta, p. 16).

The Bryan family. By 1883 Bryan was ready to practice law and hoped to earn enough to get married. Fresh out of law school, he joined the firm of Kirby, Brown & Russell in Jacksonville, Illinois. Twenty-three-year-old Bryan was a big man with a full beard that disguised his young age and he positioned himself just inside the firm's door, but he still made very little impression on the people who came into the office. The first month he earned $9.60, mostly by collecting debts. A year later, however, the third partner, Russell, left the firm and Bryan began to work for some of the company's older clients. His fortunes improved and he was able to marry his fiancée, Mary, after a four-year engagement. The inscription on the wedding ring told of his impatience and commitment—"Won 1880—One 1884." Mary and Bryan would have two children, Ruth (1885) and William, Jr. (1889). While raising these children and managing the home, Mary would continue her education and become a practicing lawyer on her own. Bryan became so involved in politics in later years that little was ever recorded about the family's life. We know, however, that he and Mary supported each other at every step. Bryan, for example, sent for Mary to come to Florida to help decide what to do with the regiment he had just led in the Spanish-American War.

Personal habits. As a young lawyer in Jacksonville, Bryan was active in community affairs, playing on a softball team representing the County Bar Association, attending philosophy and temperance meetings, taking active roles in church, watching polls in elections, and serving as president of the Young Men's Christian Association (YMCA).

Bryan's eating habits were particularly bad. He might start a day with a breakfast of fried pig's feet and follow that with more meat, veal, or corned beef at lunch. A pastry carried him through the afternoon, along with radishes. Bryan would eat bunches of radishes at any time as long as they were smeared with butter. And he ate great quantities. It was not uncommon for him to ask a dinner companion if he or she intended to finish the plate, and then eat what that person had left, also finishing his own meal. Sometime in his adult life, Bryan was diagnosed as diabetic and placed on a strict diet—a diet to which he paid nearly no attention.

Move to Lincoln. In 1887 the Bryans took a step that would lead to a life of politics. Jacksonville was old and stable with little opportunity while Lincoln, Nebraska, was young, growing, and as open as the frontier land on which it stood. Bryan proposed to move to Lincoln and join an old friend, Adolphus Talbot, in a new law firm there. Mary agreed, so the family relocated. It was a fortunate move. Not only did the law firm prosper, but even better, Bryan found political opportunity there.

Politics. The Republican Party held control of Nebraska, such tight control that few Democrats wanted to challenge it. Bryan thought Democrats would have a chance in districts that included large cities such as Lincoln. His theory proved accurate when in 1890 he was elected to the United States Congress. No other Democrats had thought it possible to win.

By 1890 Bryan had gained a reputation as an outstanding trial lawyer. He had lost only one case in three years in his practice in Lincoln, and he took time to speak frequently against the tariff, which protected business and permitted high prices. Bryan had favored a change in the income tax to make it a percentage of earnings tax, and he had begun to speak out against the gold mine owners who held that gold should be the standard for the country's money—all positions that he could now press for in Congress. He declared that he would support anything that would promote free citizens, just laws, and an economical government.

Leader of the party. In 1892 the Bryans moved to Washington, D.C. When a depression began in 1893, Bryan proposed to help the economy by taking U.S. currency off the gold standard. Many countries of the world guaranteed the value of their money by keeping reserves of gold. Others kept reserves of both gold and silver to guarantee their paper money. With two different standards, some countries had a difficult time trading with one another. Bryan argued that there was not enough gold in the world to support all the money of the world and that the United States should accept both gold and silver as guarantees. He was certain trade would improve and prosperity return. The question then arose as to what proportion of silver to gold was proper. Bryan proposed a sixteen-to-one ratio, speaking so eloquently that he became the recognized leader of the Democratic Party.

Strangely, his leadership of the party did not bring personal victories. He was defeated for a third term in Congress and was then nominated for president of the United States. Three times, in 1896, 1900, and 1908, he was the Democratic nominee, and three times he was defeated. Although he continued to speak out for any proposal that would help the common person, Bryan never held elected office again. Still, he was recognized as the Democratic Party leader.

The Commoner. Bryan continued to campaign for any legislation that would eliminate special favors for one person over another or one government over another. He had served as a colonel during the Spanish-American War but had spoken out against America's building an empire by keeping the Philippines permanently. He continued to write and lecture, publishing a weekly newspaper, *The Commoner,* that he had started in 1900. His continued pleas for the average person and battles against trusts and tariffs earned him the nickname the "Great Commoner."

Secretary of State. Bryan would once more hold public office, but not an elective one. Just as World War I threatened to break out, Woodrow Wilson was elected president. President Wilson hoped to keep America out of the war and to establish peace through conversations among governments. He felt that Bryan had the same goals and asked him to become secretary of state. Bryan accepted, but then a German shell hit and sank the *Lusitania,* a British merchant ship traveling from New York to Europe with 1,154 passengers, 188 of them Americans. Many in the United States were outraged by this treatment of innocent civilians, and President Wilson was compelled to send a letter of protest to Germany. Pressure grew and, when the president was compelled to send another letter of protest, Bryan felt it would bring the country into the war. He resigned his post as secretary of state amid accusations of cowardice by some and applause by others. Rural Americans mostly supported Bryan for holding to his beliefs.

Bryan's Positions as a Statesman

In Congress and throughout his political career Bryan acted to benefit the commoner.

Bryan spoke out for:

- Child labor laws
- Canceling war debts because they burdened the common person with taxes
- Peace
- Universal disarmament
- Breaking the monopoly of gold as a money standard
- Government ownership of private monopolies
- A tax scaled to income
- Anything to benefit the urban factory worker

Bryan spoke out against:

- Peace agreements that punished the loser
- Expansion of the United States into an empire
- Standard Oil Company and all other trusts

In 1920 Bryan, now out of politics but still a powerful speaker, moved to Florida. In 1924 he was a delegate from that state to the National Democratic Convention. But it was 1925 before Bryan would again make the headlines.

Participation: The Scopes Trial

John T. Scopes. Ever since Charles Darwin released in 1859 his *Origin of the Species by Means of Natural Selection,* a book of science suggesting how living things might have developed, people had been speaking out both in favor and against this theory of evolution. As a lifelong fundamentalist who believed the Bible to be completely accurate, Bryan had been one to speak out against evolution (which suggested that present forms of living things, including humans, had arisen over time from other life forms). He even proposed an amendment to the Constitution making antievolution a national principle. As early as 1922, Bryan had given speeches about what he believed to be the menace of Darwinism. It was better to "trust in the Rock of Ages than to learn the ages of rocks" (Bryan in de Camp, p. 44).

In 1925 the state of Tennessee arrested John Thomas Scopes, a high school teacher in Dayton, Tennessee. Scopes was accused of using a new textbook that described Darwin's ideas—of teaching the theory of evolution in violation of the state law. Trial was set for July 10.

The prosecution's case would be argued for the state by its attorney general, A.T. Stewart; Wallace Haggard, the son of Dayton's mayor; and the law firm of Herbert Hayes. The well-known trial lawyer, Clarence Darrow, would direct the defense (see **Clarence Darrow**). He was to be aided by Arthur G. Hayes and Dudley Field Malone.

Duel to the death. Bryan, now sixty-five years old, decided to help Haggard and Hayes in what he felt was a duel to the death between evolution and Christianity. A famous lawyer, he would help balance the sides, whether the others liked it or not. Haggard was not at all sure he wanted to share the limelight, and his fears may have been justified.

Grand entrance. Bryan arrived in Dayton on July 7 and immediately began to create publicity. A grand parade brought him into town from the train station. He was soon making his first speech for the media. Why wait for the trial, he thought, when he could take his case to the people through the newspapers? During the next three days, Bryan spoke everywhere he could find an audience. His schedule was nearly as hectic as when he first ran for president of the United States.

Bryan in charge. The state attorneys were not convinced that they needed Bryan's help. After all, what Scopes had done

▲ **Bryan meets the press**

using that new textbook was clearly against Tennessee law, and they had a copy of the text for evidence. Bryan tried to appease Haggard at their first meeting:

> Now boy, I want you to feel free to tell me anything you think about this. You disagree with me if I say something wrong. I didn't come down here to tell you boys how to run this case. I have come to win the case and not to take command of it. (Bryan in de Camp, p. 127)

But Bryan did take charge, or at least played a dominant role in the trial. He made the opening presentation for the prosecution. It was clear that he was on a crusade for fundamentalist Christianity.

(Bryan, as a fundamentalist, believed the Bible not only to be totally accurate but also to contain all that a person needed to know about the subjects it addressed.) Darrow, on the other hand, was prepared to fight for freedom of speech and thought in the schools.

Trial by the news. Throughout the trial, Bryan tried it in the news as well as in the courts. He used every opportunity to make the headlines. At one time, he boldly offered $100 to any scientist who would admit to have descended from apes. As soon as the offer reached the newspapers, Dr. R. C. Spangler, a scientist at West Virginia University, made the admission and Bryan dutifully paid the $100, using the event, of course, to ridicule Dr. Spangler and the theory of evolution.

In defense of Christianity. Urged on by the famous Christian crusaders Billy Sunday and Aimée Semple McPherson, Bryan ended the first week of the trial with a spellbinding seventy-minute speech during which, as was his habit, he used every persuasion but reason to convince his listeners of his position. Over the years, he had become so dynamic in his presentation and so apparently organized in his arguments that his audiences paid rapt attention—and later wondered exactly what he had said.

A number of witnesses were summoned. Scientists were called on to explain their theory of evolution. Ministers were called on to defend the religious positions. A member of the school board testified to having seen the textbook and spoken with Scopes about evolution. It turned out that the school board member was also a textbook salesman and had given the book to Scopes, but in the clearly antievolution atmosphere of the court, that act did not discredit, or damage, his testimony.

Bryan the witness. The trial was in its ninth day when Darrow called Bryan to the witness stand. With carefully planned questions, he led the old Bible student to admit that some stories in the Bible are illustrations rather than fact. Darrow asked questions about Jonah and the whale. Did Bryan really believe that a man could be swallowed by a big fish and live inside for three days? He asked about the flood. Could it be that there were fewer types of animals in Noah's day, that two of each could fit on a large boat? Then when he asked about the story of the creation—that God created the world in six days—he succeeded in getting Bryan to admit that even he believed that the Bible was not telling about twenty-four hour days as we have today. Bryan lost ground by this questioning, but his time to shine lay ahead. On the eleventh day of the trial, he would make the closing arguments for the prosecution.

Bryan prepared carefully for what some have estimated would have been a six-hour speech. This would be his finest day. He would play on the emotions of the court, not on its sense of reason. He was capable of preaching and using wit, sarcasm, and false reasoning to persuade any audience, which is what he intended to do. Unfortunately for Bryan, that is what Darrow expected.

Darrow's victory. Darrow had already won his point on the right of teachers to present new and challenging ideas. To him, whether Scopes was or was not guilty was secondary. Having won the day before, he was not about to let the smooth-talking Bryan destroy his victory. On the eleventh day, Darrow rose to tell the court that his client was, in fact, guilty as charged and asked that the case be closed. He would then appeal the case on new grounds before a new court. The judge agreed. Scopes was found guilty of violating Tennessee's antievolution law and fined $100 (soon after he would quit teaching). Bryan lost the opportunity to give his great speech.

Aftermath

Bryan's reaction. Nearly all his life Bryan had crusaded for the rights of the average man. He believed that the greatest possible government was one directed by the people themselves, and that people were inherently good and capable of self-rule. This faith in the common person did not waver even when they refused to elect him president three times. His only reaction was that the people had decided and he would abide by their just will.

Final days. After the Scopes Trial, Bryan was weary and beaten but not ready to surrender. He spent the next two days dictating to his secretary the speech he had not made; two days later he proofread the copy of his undelivered speech.

Five days after the trial, on the evening of July 25, 1925, the Great Commoner arranged a vacation for himself and his wife and made some business telephone calls. He afterward laid down for a nap and died in his sleep.

For More Information

Coletta, Paolo E. *William Jennings Bryan—Political Evangelist, 1860-1908.* Lincoln: University of Nebraska Press, 1964.

de Camp, L. Sprague. *The Great Monkey Case.* Garden City, New York: Doubleday, 1968.

Levine, Lawrence W. *Defender of the Faith.* New York: Oxford University Press, 1965.

Harlem Renaissance

1900-1910

Suburb of Harlem grows in New York City. By decade's end, it is populated largely by African Americans.

1909-1910

National Association for the Advancement of Colored People (NAACP) is founded to promote equality for African Americans.

1912

James Weldon Johnson's *The Autobiography of an Ex-Coloured Man* is published.

1915

William J. Simmons revives the Ku Klux Klan at Stone Mountain, Georgia.

1916

Marcus Garvey establishes Harlem headquarters for his United Negro Improvement Association (UNIA).

1916-1918

Black population in northern cities increases by up to 120 percent.

1917

Race riots break out in Philadelphia and Chester, Pennsylvania, and in St. Louis, Illinois.

1919

Over twenty race riots erupt in U.S. cities as soldiers return from war and job competition escalates.

1920

Garvey holds First International Convention of the Negro Peoples of the World in Madison Square Garden.

1924

Membership of Ku Klux Klan approaches four million.

1926

Zora Neale Hurston and others publish the magazine *Fire!!*

1927

Hurston becomes first black student at Barnard College. Johnson's *God's Trombones* is published.

1929-1930

Great Depression ends financial support from whites for Harlem Renaissance artists.

HARLEM RENAISSANCE

Close to one million African Americans left the South from 1910 to 1930. They streamed north in search of jobs, many of them flocking to the area of Harlem in New York City.

Outside Harlem, there was growing anti-black sentiment in the country. Lynchings of blacks continued in the South, and the Ku Klux Klan was reborn, this time targeting Jews and Catholics as well as blacks. In the North, white workers gave the black newcomers a hostile welcome, with race riots breaking out in Pennsylvania and Missouri in 1917. As the war ended and white soldiers returned to find blacks competing for their jobs, tensions worsened. Twenty race riots broke out in one postwar season, called the Red Summer of 1919.

Meanwhile, more than 100,000 African Americans settled in Harlem from 1916 to 1918, shaping the area into a distinct city within a city. Harlem became a hotbed of political and social activity in the 1920s. Parties, night clubs, musicals, demonstrations, and rallies attracted blacks and whites alike. White New Yorkers attended uptown clubs to hear jazz musicians such as Louis Armstrong, Fletcher Henderson, and Duke Ellington. Also known as the Jazz Age, the 1920s broke ground as talented blacks began moving into the mainstream of American art. At the same time, the National Association for the Advancement of Colored People

(NAACP) took case after case to court to win political rights and fought segregation in government lunchrooms. But in contrast to advances in art, social and political gains for blacks would lag behind.

A term used in Harlem at the time was the "New Negro," meaning black business and professional people of the ghetto who had both racial pride and a fighting spirit. Harlem's artists and **Marcus Garvey** helped develop this New Negro.

Two movements within Harlem spread racial pride and a sense of history among black Americans. One of the movements, built by Garvey, inspired black nationalism—patriotic feelings for the African American community and for Africa. Garvey called on African Americans to support black-owned businesses. He further urged that blacks return to Africa to establish a country and government that was totally their own. Publishing the *Negro World* newspaper and organizing the First International Convention of Negro Peoples of the World, Garvey himself took steps to build solidarity among blacks. He also formed a military-style Universal African Legion whose members paraded in blue and red uniforms, filling black onlookers with pride. Though his back-to-Africa approach was criticized by other black leaders, Garvey won more than 500,000 supporters, followers who took to heart his messages about supporting black businesses and feeling proud of their own heritage.

The second movement, centered in Harlem as well, was a great creative outpouring by black artists, thinkers, and musicians. Called the Harlem Renaissance, it included blacks who took pride in their African roots and their folk tradition in America. But they did not share Garvey's desire to return to Africa. They, by contrast, felt that America was their home and wanted their fair share of American rights.

Harlem became the magnet for artists of every variety in the 1920s. The explosion of artistic talent saw more African American writers being published than ever before in history. A poet and novelist, **James Weldon Johnson** also wrote songs for shows on Broadway that helped open mainstream theater to black artists and served as a lawyer for the NAACP. Though involved in politics through the NAACP, he believed more strongly in the power of art to effect social change. Sharing this conviction, **Zora Neale Hurston** wrote short stories, essays, musical plays, and stage revivals. Much of her writing was based on her own firsthand research in the South, where Hurston collected information on African American folk practices and tales. Who supported her? Harlem was quite the style in the 1920s, attracting whites with jazz music and other novelties. White investors, called patrons, supported black artists while they created songs, stories and paintings, paying grants, scholarships, and prize money to the artists. Unlike Garvey's independent, black-owned businesses, then, Harlem artists operated on funds supplied by whites.

Notable Writers of the Harlem Renaissance—A Sampling

Sterling Brown	"Memphis Blues"
Countee Cullen	"Yet Do I Marvel"
Langston Hughes	*Weary Blues*
Zora Neale Hurston	*Mules and Men*
James Weldon Johnson	*The Autobiography of an Ex-Coloured Man*
Claude McKay	"If We Must Die"
Jean Toomer	*Cane*

Black writers in Johnson's time faced a creative obstacle because they were supported by white patrons. There was conflict in black society over subjects such as someone who was light-skinned passing for white. But the patrons, on whose money the artists depended, had certain ideas of their own. They assumed, for example, that all black people wanted to be white and expected the writers they paid to create such characters. So Harlem artists of the time struggled to be true to their subjects and yet stay in the business of creating art. In 1929 a great depression would befall America, drying up funds for the Harlem artists. Before then, a surprising number managed to capture the African American experience in the rural South and the urban ghetto through notable writings. Johnson's *The Autobiography of an Ex-Coloured Man,* for example, was the first novel to deal with the dilemma, or difficult situation, faced by blacks who could pass for white and to celebrate ragtime music, a form of black folk music until then considered unrespectable.

Marcus Garvey

1887-1940

Family Background

Marcus Mosiah Garvey was born in St. Ann's Bay, Jamaica, on August 17, 1887, to Marcus and Sarah Garvey. The youngest of eleven children, Marcus was only one of two who survived past childhood. Together with his sister Indiana, Marcus grew up amid sugar plantations in the rural, tropical setting of the small port town in the British West Indies.

Maroon blood. Marcus was instilled with great pride in this heritage from the time he was a young boy. He was descended from the legendary Maroons, or "wild ones," Africans brought as slaves to Jamaica who successfully escaped from slavery and won independence from British colonizers in 1739. His father taught him how the Maroons took to the hills to avoid foreign domination and were among the only Africans of the West Indies whose bloodline remained pure, unmixed with the blood of whites.

Marcus, Sr., also exposed his son to great literature and taught him much about world history. A well-read and respected man, Marcus, Sr., kept the largest private library in St. Ann's Bay and, though he was a solitary and largely unaffectionate man, provided his son with a solid education and strong sense of pride in himself and his ancestry.

▲ **Marcus Garvey**

Event: Black nationalism movement.
Role: As a newspaper publisher, leader of the Universal Negro Improvement Association, and founder of the Black Star Line shipping company, Marcus Garvey promoted the concept of black pride in an atmosphere of racial prejudice in America after World War I. Garvey urged his followers to create their own economic power base that was separate from white society, and he sought an independent homeland for African Americans in Africa.

Pride. Unlike black Americans of the nineteenth century who were generally taught little of their African lineage, denied education, and subjected to slavery, Marcus grew up with a positive sense of black history and with great ambition. Sarah, who gave Marcus the middle name "Mosiah" after the biblical figure Moses, encouraged her son to be a leader and had dreams of sending him to a good British university.

Dreams dashed. By the time Marcus reached fourteen, however, both his college ambitions and his inexperience with racism came to an abrupt end. First, a white girl who had been one of his best friends was sent abroad to school. Upon saying goodbye to Marcus, she informed him that she could no longer communicate with him because the outside world did not approve of white girls associating with black boys. Marcus was shocked to learn that the dark skin of which he was so proud was, for many, a reason to discriminate against him. The incident had a major effect on Garvey. "It was then that I found for the first time that there was some difference in humanity, and that there were different races, each having its own separate and distinct social life," he wrote (Cronon, p. 8). Garvey never thought of playing with white girls after that and began to realize the huge problems that racism caused for most dark-skinned peoples of the world.

In that same year, 1901, all hope of sending Marcus to college or even continuing his public education was dashed when his father lost all of the family property except for the house. In order to help support the family, Marcus was pulled from school and apprenticed to his godfather to learn the printing trade.

Relocation. After two years as an apprentice, a hurricane destroyed much in St. Ann's Bay and forced Marcus to move with his mother to the capital city of Kingston. There he landed a higher-paying printing job and supported himself and his mother. Sarah, however, thoroughly disliked city life and was severely weakened by the move. She soon died, leaving Marcus independent at sixteen.

Participation: Black Nationlism Movement

Retraining. On his own and living in a populous city for the first time, Marcus Garvey matured rapidly. Because the Kingston locals made fun of his small-town banter, Garvey determined to learn to speak effectively and began to educate himself in the art of persuasion. To that end, he attended church services throughout Kingston, listening to a variety of preachers, and began to model his own speaking style after those he heard preach. Soon he became a forceful enough orator to be elected president of his printer's union. But success was short-lived when the union folded after a strike in 1907. Garvey was forced to take a government printing job that paid poorly.

Poverty and the birth of a movement. A member of the inner-city poor working class, Garvey for the first time in his life began to realize the many problems that faced urban minorities in addition to racism. He had to deal with low wages, lack of opportunity, and job discrimination because of his dark skin and, what was worse, he knew blacks throughout the British and Spanish colonies of South and Central America were being treated in a similar fashion. Improving conditions for poor working people became a goal of his, and with that in mind, Garvey founded Jamaica's first political association, the National Club, and along with it started publishing *Our Own,* a separatist black newspaper.

By 1910, at age twenty-three, Garvey was publishing two more reform newspapers, *The Advocate* and *The Watchman,* and had begun to travel throughout the colonies to survey the living conditions of his countrymen. He financed his travels by working as a banana picker in Costa Rica, where he was shocked by the living and working conditions of the black workers. They lived in squalor, were paid next to nothing for intense, backbreaking labor, and had virtually no legal or government representation. He traveled to Cuba, Panama, Nicaragua, Honduras, Colombia, and Venezuela and found conditions there equally dismal. Garvey's "brain was afire" (Cronon, p. 16). The more discrimination he saw, the more he began to realize the desperate need for leadership in the black community to remedy the situation.

World education. After beginning two reform newspapers in South America, Garvey traveled to London, England, to better educate himself in order to help the masses back home. He went to work with Duse Mohammed Ali, who ran the *Africa Times and Ori-*

ent Review, and added to his knowledge of African and world history. He became extremely well versed in history and politics and after reading Booker T. Washington's *Up from Slavery,* Garvey decided it was his destiny to become a leader:

> Where is the black man's government? Where is his king and his kingdom? Where is his President, his country, and his ambassador, his army, his navy, his men of big affairs? I will help to make them. (Garvey in Cronon, p. 16)

Garvey was outraged to learn that workers in Africa and the continent's natural resources were being used, just as they were in European colonies elsewhere, to benefit a small minority of wealthy whites. He was further shocked to learn that dark-skinned peoples made up 75 percent of the world population, while the lighter-skinned, 25 percent minority controlled the majority, along with most of the wealth. But Garvey was more than outraged by these statistics; he was inspired. He wrote in the *Asian Times and Orient Review* in October 1913:

> There will soon be a turning point in the history of the West Indies ... the people who inhabit that portion of the Western Hemisphere will be the instruments of uniting a scattering race [and they] ... will found an Empire.
>
> This may be regarded as a dream, but I would point my critical friends to history and its lessons. Would Caesar have believed that the country he was invading in 55 B.C. would be the seat of the greatest empire in the world? (Garvey, *Garvey and Garveyism,* p. 10)

Garvey returned to Jamaica in the summer of 1914 with the dream of "uniting all the Negro peoples of the world into one great body to establish a country and Government absolutely their own" (Cronon, p. 16). With that goal in mind, on August 14, he founded the Universal Negro Improvement Association (UNIA) and the African Communities League.

UNIA. Garvey's UNIA was revolutionary not only because it advocated a return to Africa but because it urged the black community to create and support its own economic base. It sought to teach black history to and instill race pride in Africans throughout the world. Garvey, a stocky man with gleaming ebony eyes, envisioned accomplishing these aims by starting an industrial educational center in Kingston, much like Booker T. Washington's Tuskegee Institute, and by creating a shipping company owned and operated by Africans. In Garvey's mind, the Black Star Line, as it would be called, would unite blacks throughout the world in commerce, taking trade goods and passengers between the West Indies, the United States, and Africa. Garvey had the charisma, or special charm, of a great leader. But his dreams would require a good deal of money to realize, which was why Garvey traveled to the United States in 1916.

Garvey's Flag

Among Garvey's many accomplishments was his creation of the African flag—the red, green, and black striped banner. The black stood for the Africans' skin, the green for their hopes, and the red for their blood. Garvey also established an African government-in-exile, pronouncing himself its president.

Harlem. Garvey's arrival in Harlem, New York, coincided with the greatest migration of blacks from the South to the North in U.S. history. From 1916 to 1918, black populations in northern cities such as Chicago, Illinois, and New York, increased by as much as 120 percent. The mass migration was caused both by job availability in the North due the absence of white males, who were off fighting in World War I, and by the boll weevil, which destroyed cotton crops and farm jobs throughout the South. At first African Americans found a better standard of living in the North and not the outright prejudice they experienced in the South. But soon conditions changed. With the end of World War I and the return of soldiers from overseas, job competition became fierce in the cities and racial tensions rose. Widespread race riots broke out in cities across the country in 1919. Garvey, already strongly instilled with race pride, was uniquely positioned to lead a spiritual revolution in the black community, to address African Americans' frustrations, and to promote black pride in the United States.

Garvey, who had traveled throughout the United States after his March 1916 arrival, set up a New York division of the UNIA in Harlem, in time attracting up to 2,000 U.S. members. In addition to the UNIA, Garvey founded the *Negro World* weekly newspaper, which served to carry his message throughout the globe.

Experiencing racial tensions across the United States and especially in New York, Garvey felt that prejudice would always

▲ **Garvey in uniform as the self-proclaimed president of the Republic of Africa**

exist in the United States as long as the races competed for resources. Further, he felt that as long as prejudice existed, there would be "no hope of social equality" or "progress of the Negro in America" (Garvey, *Garvey and Garveyism,* p. 18). In direct opposition to other African American leaders who were urging desegregation and the mixing of African Americans into mainstream American society, Garvey called for separation:

> There is but one solution, and that is to provide an outlet for Negro energy, ambition and passion, away from the attractiveness of white opportunity, and surround the race with opportunities of its own. (Garvey, *Garvey and Garveyism,* p. 20)

Advocating that Africans of all secondary nationalities move back to Africa, he entered into discussions with the president of Liberia to acquire land there for his vision of a new African "Empire."

Black backlash. Garvey received strong opposition from the National Association for the Advancement of Colored People (NAACP) because of his call for segregation. Likening him to the Ku Klux Klan, a group of white supremacists who terrorize blacks, the NAACP succeeded in temporarily breaking up Garvey's organization and thwarting his land deal with Liberia. But Garvey pressed on, restructuring the UNIA and building up an even greater following. He started meeting with more African leaders to get land and raised money for the Black Star Line. At the same time, he organized the first International Convention of the Negro Peoples of the World, held in New York's Madison Square Garden in 1920.

UNIA conventions. The convention marked a major turning point in U.S. history. For the first time in a massive public gathering, Africans in America boldly asserted themselves as an independent group by creating a Declaration of Rights of the Negro Peoples of the World, in which they listed twelve complaints and made fifty-four demands for fair treatment in the future. Garvey's speech to the crowd further let the world know the UNIA and the "New Negro" were forces to be reckoned with:

> The Negro is not contemplating the initiating of fighting, but we must protect our interests. We are going in for mass organization. In the past we have worked separately and individually, now we are going to organize. (Garvey, *Garvey and Garveyism,* p. 50)

Garvey's speech summed up the attitude of the so-called New Negro. Influencing a whole new generation of African American leaders such as Malcolm X, Garvey was the first to advocate black power and social change by any means necessary. In the Declaration of Rights, Garvey stated:

> We believe in the supreme authority of our race in all things racial; that all things are given to man as a common possession; that there should be an equitable distribution and apportionment of all such things, and in consideration of the fact that as a race we are now deprived of those things that are normally and legally ours, we believe it right that all such things should be acquired and held by whatsoever means possible. (Garvey in Nembhard, p. 34)

Black Worldwide Business

The Black Star Line was not only the first black-owned and black-operated shipping line in the world, it was the first company to offer stock only to blacks. In calling for stockholders, Garvey advertised: "Now is the time for the Negro to invest in the Black Star Line so that in the near future he may exert the same influence upon the world as the white man does today." (Garvey in Cronon, p. 51)

Following the convention, UNIA membership swelled to four million worldwide, and Garvey was the subject of heated debate. Many hailed Garvey as the most remarkable man of the time while others, such as the NAACP's W. E. B. Du Bois, who had a long-running feud with Garvey, denounced him and his message. Du Bois called Garvey the "black peril" and launched a "Garvey must go" campaign (Garvey, *Garvey and Garveyism,* pp. 52, 76). While his supporters saw him as a visionary—the Black Moses—Garvey's critics called him an anarchist, someone who was not in favor of any set form of government, and a man who set back the cause of integration. Speaking of whites, Garvey offended many with his views: "I regard the Klan, the Anglo-Saxon Clubs and White American Societies as better friends of the race than all other groups of hypocritical whites put together" (Garvey in Cronon, p. 126). Garvey made an abundance of enemies with such statements, and their forces eventually took their toll.

Aftermath

Prison. After Garvey founded the Black Star Line in 1919, the company began to suffer great economic setbacks. Though it was a landmark accomplishment—the first black-owned, black-operated shipping line in the world—both a hostile business environment and lack of business leadership on Garvey's part soon plunged the company into near bankruptcy. Moreover, Garvey was convicted of fraud for the overcharging of company stock and sentenced to five years in prison. President Calvin Coolidge reduced Garvey's sentence to two years and nine months, which he served in an Atlanta, Georgia, prison, but Garvey was afterward deported and sent back to Jamaica.

Banishment. Garvey continued to run the UNIA for the next decade, first out of Kingston and then out of London. He lived with his second wife, Amy Jacques Garvey, and had two sons. (He had married his first wife, Amy Ashwood, in 1919. They divorced in 1922. He married his second wife later that year.) In January 1940, he suffered a brain hemorrhage that left him partially paralyzed, and on June 10, 1940, he died.

Like other revolutionary leaders, Garvey was often misunderstood and generated more than his share of controversy. That his effect was powerful is undeniable, though. He certainly contributed, through his *Negro World* newspaper and other activities, to the birth of the black cultural movement in America known as the Harlem Renaissance. Criticized by other black leaders, he nevertheless reached many in the larger African American community. His wife shared her opinion of his impact:

> Marcus Garvey demonstrated to the whole world that the colored people of America and the black people of the world can organize. Under the mighty banner of the red and green and black, almost three million people joined his ranks, captured by a program that appealed both to their heads and their hearts. This vast army with one aim and one idea proved to the Nordic people that the colored people were not to be forever split up and incapable of following one leadership. (Garvey, *Philosophy and Opinions,* p. 189)

For More Information

Cronan, E. David. *Black Moses.* Madison: University of Wisconsin Press, 1969.

Garvey, Amy Jacques. *Garvey and Garveyism.* Kingston, Jamaica: United Printers Ltd., 1963.

Garvey, Amy Jacques. *Philosophy and Opinions.* New York: Antheneum, 1973.

Nembhard, Len S. *Trials and Triumphs of Marcus Garvey.* Kingston, Jamaica: The Gleaner Co. Ltd., 1940.

Stein, Judith. *The World of Marcus Garvey.* Baton Rouge: Louisiana State University Press, 1986.

James Weldon Johnson

1871-1938

Personal Background

James Weldon Johnson was born into a middle class family in Jacksonville, Florida, on June 17, 1871. His father, James, worked as a head waiter and his mother, Helen, as a schoolteacher during the post–Civil War economic boom in Jacksonville. Together they raised two sons, James and his younger brother, John Rosamond (called Rosamond), in a comfortable, loving home.

No slavery. As a boy, James's situation was somewhat unique in that he was raised in the South by African American parents who had never been slaves. Helen, who hailed from Nassau in the Bahamas, had no history of slavery in her family, and James, Sr., who came from New York, had always been a free man. Hence the Johnsons raised their children without fear of being denied opportunities because they were black. They encouraged James and Rosamond in their studies and held high hopes for their futures. There was no doubt that the boys would go to a black college when they finished their primary education—the only question for the boys was which profession to pursue.

For James, that choice was not easy. He dreamed of becoming a lawyer, a doctor, a teacher, a preacher, a musician, and a writer, and amazingly enough, he accomplished most of these goals during his lifetime. But before he chose his path, he had encouragement from a variety of sources.

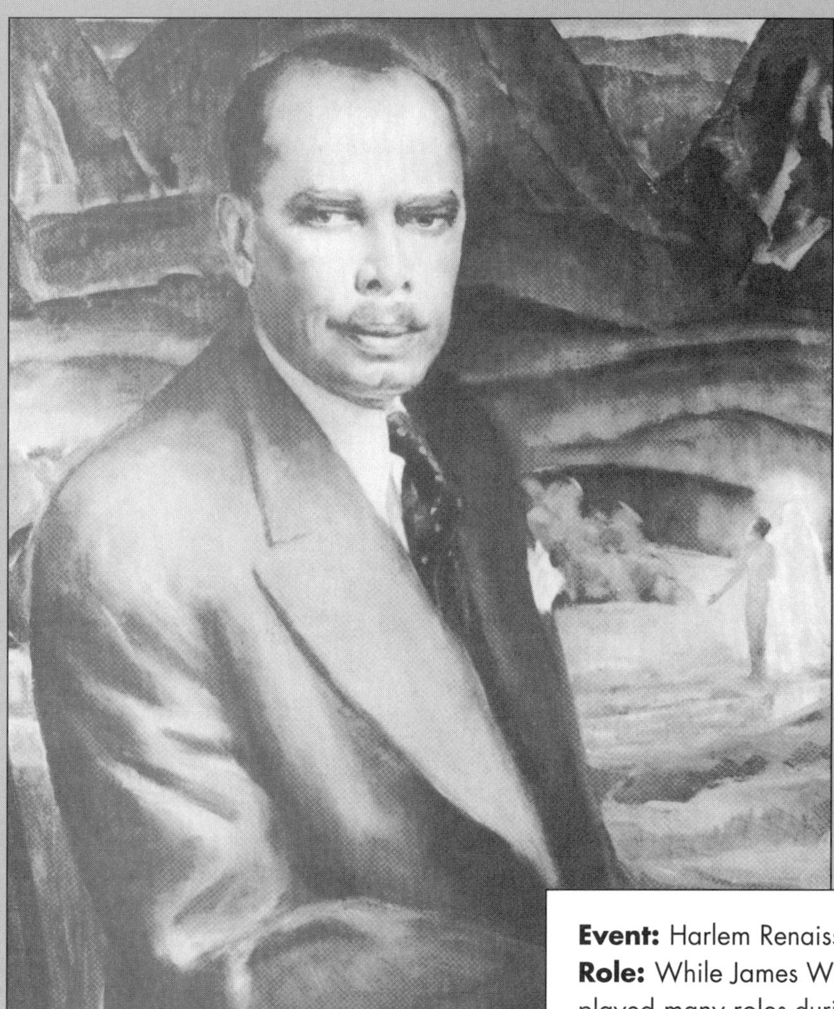

▲ James Weldon Johnson

Event: Harlem Renaissance.
Role: While James Weldon Johnson played many roles during his lifetime, it was his work as a writer and poet that helped usher in what came to be known as the Harlem Renaissance in New York City during the 1920s. Johnson's works reveal the cultural richness of the black American community as well as its struggle during the nineteenth and twentieth centuries.

Grandma Barton. James's maternal grandmother, Grandma Barton, played a key role in his development. Living just down the street from James, she ran a bake shop where he worked while attending elementary school. A very religious woman, Grandma Barton took James to church as often as possible and encouraged him to become a minister. James was inspired by the spirituals sung by the Methodist congregation, and at age ten, he officially joined the church, though his father thought he was too young to make such a decision. But while the church experience made James for the first time in his young life think seriously about religion as well as about music, it also began to wear on him. Grandma Barton's zeal to have her favorite grandchild become a preacher became excessive and at age fourteen James grew exhausted from attending church services three to four days a week. Though he continued to sing in the choir, he stopped attending regularly and became an agnostic like his father, believing in God but not necessarily the church.

Mom and Dad. James's parents taught him to strive for excellence in everything he did. His mother read to her sons from Charles Dickens and other great writers of the day from the time they were small boys, and his father bought James his first collection of books. The boys were taught Spanish by their parents, and their mother, a gifted vocalist herself, also taught her sons to sing and play the piano and guitar. As a result, James and Rosamond both became avid readers, writers, and musicians.

Education. When James graduated from Stanton elementary school at the end of eighth grade, he was sent to Atlanta University because there were no public secondary schools open to black children in Florida. For the next eight years, through preparatory school and four years of college, James was transformed from a boy into a man.

Away from his parents and on his own for the first time in his life, James began developing his talents as a writer and pursuing his interest in public speaking. He read more Dickens, George Eliot, and virtually all of the great Victorian novels and poetry. Inspired by what he read, he tried his hand at writing and found that he possessed talent. He wrote short stories and poetry that met with approval from teachers and other students. James was amazed at the response he received, noting that "the potency possessed by a few, fairly well-written lines of passionate poetry is truly astounding" (Johnson, *Along This Way,* p. 79). He resolved to continue his literary efforts and began to realize the political and social impact writing could have.

Though a good writer, James was not a great speaker. He was still rather shy and was astonished when boys his age would "rise without fear or hesitation [and] discourse upon weighty subjects" (Johnson, *Along This Way,* p. 79). So he determined to make as fine a speaker out of himself as possible and joined a university debate team. By the end of his sophomore year, Johnson had won first prize in an oratory contest and had learned the secret to good oration: rhythm, which came naturally to the musically inclined Johnson. His speaking skills would prove handy in his chosen profession. James was preparing to become an educator.

Prejudice—Jim Crow laws. While school was a very positive experience, the trips home during the summer provided more somber lessons. Johnson had been sheltered from prejudice both at school and while growing up in a black neighborhood of Jacksonville, which itself was known as "the most liberal town in the South" (Levy, p. 8). On the train, however, Johnson had his first of many experiences with the recently enacted Jim Crow laws. These laws, which were enforced in most Southern states, forbade any racial mixing in public places and restricted black train passengers of all classes to a single car, which was usually dirty and half-filled with cargo.

On a trip home one summer, Johnson was traveling first class. When the conductor came to take Johnson's ticket, he suggested that the passenger and his friends move to the "colored car." Johnson, having paid for a first-class ticket, naturally refused. Upon his refusal, a "murmur started in the car and soon became a hubbub" (Johnson, *Along This Way,* p. 85). Threats were made, with some of the passengers promising to lynch Johnson and his friends if they did not move. Recalling from newspaper accounts that just a week earlier a group of black ministers were attacked by a mob in this same part of the country over the same issue, Johnson gave up his seat, gathered his belongings, and moved to the colored car. Instead of making Johnson feel inferior, the experience only insulted his pride. He knew that he was equal to any man on the train, and for the first time in his life he began to realize the tremendous prejudice that existed in America and to regret living in the South.

Participation: Harlem Renaissance

Stanton expands. When Johnson graduated from Atlanta University in 1894, he was offered both a scholarship to study medicine at Harvard College and the principalship of Stanton school, where he had studied as a boy and his mother had taught. Torn between two excellent options, James at age twenty-three decided to return to his home and accept the position at Stanton.

Though young and inexperienced, Johnson quickly rose to the challenge put before him. He not only efficiently administered the school but vastly improved it. Within his first year at Stanton, Johnson expanded the school to include grades nine and ten, making it the first public secondary school open to blacks in Florida. While this alone was a noteworthy accomplishment, it was just the first in a long series of goals Johnson managed to achieve during his adult life.

Newspaper publisher and lawyer. One great advantage of being a school administrator was that classes met for only eight months of the year. That left four months open, and Johnson used the time to further his aims. In 1895 he founded the first black daily newspaper in Florida, *The Daily American.* While he wrote articles and edited the paper by day, Johnson studied law by night and passed the bar in 1896, becoming one of just a handful of black lawyers in the state. As the school year resumed, the newspaper suffered and was closed eight months after it began. But Johnson didn't give up his publishing goals—they would simply be postponed and fulfilled a few years later in a different form.

New York. While Johnson was busy in Jacksonville, his brother Rosamond was hard at work in New York City establishing himself as a singer-songwriter. With Rosamond's encouragement, Johnson traveled to New York on his next summer vacation in 1897,

▲ **Bob Cole, Johnson, and Rosamond Johnson**

joining Rosamond and his partner, Bob Cole. The trio began writing songs together and over the next seven years broke ground for black artists, which laid the foundation for the Harlem Renaissance in the 1920s.

Johnson had been writing poetry since his college days and with his brother's help put these words to music. One of his early efforts was an homage to President Abraham Lincoln—the first to be written from a black man's perspective—and soon came to be known as the "Negro National Anthem." It opens with the lines:

> Sing a song full of the faith that the dark past has taught us;
>
> Sing a song full of the hope that the present has brought us. (Johnson, *Along This Way,* p. 154)

Johnson established the tone that most of his future works would contain. While acknowledging the "dark past" of African Americans, Johnson chose not to dwell on the negative but rather look to the "hope that the present has brought us." He maintained that rather than making African Americans weak or inferior, adversity had made the community strong. Overcoming such hardships was something to feel proud, not ashamed, of.

Marshall Hotel. With works such as the "Negro National Anthem," the trio enjoyed great success. By 1903 Johnson resigned his position at Stanton and moved to New York City permanently. The Marshall Hotel, where the three lived, became a mecca for black artists and drew such individuals as the actors Bert Williams and George Walker and the poet Paul Laurence Dunbar into the city. Before Harlem, the Marshall became a central destination for black artists, and "its importance as the radiant point of the forces that cleared the way for the Negro on the New York stage cannot be overestimated" (Johnson, *Along This Way,* p. 177).

Art Attack

Johnson believed that through art African Americans could "more effectively reach a prejudiced person than [through] any polemical [argumentative] essay" (Levy, p. 301). Hence Johnson sought to and did produce some of the greatest American writing to come out of any era and helped establish Harlem and the black community as a fertile womb.

By 1905 the Johnson-Cole trio had signed a music publishing contract for $10,000 and was writing material for Florenz Ziegfield, producer of the famous Ziegfield Follies on Broadway. With this contract, not only had the trio made it to Broadway, but they had opened the door for other black artists. White actors in black face were now replaced with black actors, and musical plays such as *Blackbirds, Porgy,* and *The Green Pastures*—all based on the black experience—were being produced regularly. In fact, they were becoming the biggest hits on Broadway.

Novel and travel. When the trio dissolved in late 1905, Johnson entered into a new phase of his life. He met and married Grace Nail and was convinced by a friend to go into the government's consular service. Because of his fluency in Spanish, Johnson was appointed by President Theodore Roosevelt to posts in Venezuela and Nicaragua, where he served as the U.S. Consul until 1914.

During his time out of the States, Johnson continued to write and work on an idea for a novel he'd had that would tell of his experience as a successful black man in America. Titled *The Autobiography of an Ex-Coloured Man,* Johnson's book was published in 1912 and made a huge impression on both black and white communities in America. In it, he became the first to openly praise black art forms, such as ragtime music and Negro spirituals, and to show the many positive contributions African Americans made to U.S. culture. He also was the first to illustrate the psychology of the black man and show how the race question kept both black and white Americans from accomplishing goals in other areas, such as politics, the arts, and science.

Johnson's Strategy against Prejudice

As a member of the NAACP, James argued for social equality. He did not, however, favor special treatment or handouts for blacks but rather wanted a level playing field on which they could compete fairly and fend for themselves. He, in fact, argued that "regardless of what might be done for black America, the ultimate and vital part of the work [will] have to be done by black America itself." (Johnson, *Along This Way,* p. 315)

A changed America. Upon his return to New York City, Johnson began writing editorials for the *New York Age* newspaper, the oldest black daily in New York. In addition, he began to get more involved in black politics. Johnson became secretary of the National Association for the Advancement of Colored People (NAACP) in 1916, then worked aggressively for civil rights and the establishment of antilynching laws.

In 1918 black Americans grew seriously disappointed if not outraged by their ill-treatment after serving their country overseas in World War I. Many had assumed they would be treated as equals upon their return from service, but instead most found prejudice to be as common as before and in some areas even heightened by a very active Ku Klux Klan, a group of white supremacists who terrorized blacks. Up to 1,000 lynchings per year were occurring—especially in the South—and few arrests were ever made of the lynchers. As a result, race riots erupted across the nation. It was to this hostile climate that Johnson returned and sought to effect change.

Harlem. Johnson and his wife moved to Harlem, which had recently been established and was fast becoming, as the Marshall

Hotel had been, a mecca for African American artists. The Johnson home itself became a stopping ground for many writers, actors, and musicians. Meanwhile, Johnson, in addition to many other tasks, began to produce more poetry. He also put together anthologies of other black writers' works. According to Johnson:

> This was an era in which was achieved the Harlem of story and song; the era in which Harlem's fame for exotic flavor and colorful sensuousness was spread to all parts of the world; when Harlem was made known as the scene of laughter, singing, dancing, and primitive passions, and as the center of the new Negro literature and art. (Johnson, *Along This Way,* p. 380)

The Color of America's Skin

Johnson hoped that African Americans could preserve their culture and, in turn, influence the American culture as a whole. But he saw that some blending, in all likelihood, would take place: "It seems probable that ... the Negro will fuse his qualities with those of the other groups in the making of the ultimate American people; and that he will add a tint to America's complexion and put a perceptible permanent wave in America's hair.... My hope is that in the process the Negro will be not merely sucked up, but through his own advancement and development, will go in on a basis of equal partnership." (Johnson, *Along This Way,* p. 412)

Aftermath

Final years. Throughout the 1920s and 1930s, Johnson kept up his literary efforts as well as his work with the NAACP. He produced a book of "Negro spiritual sermons" titled *God's Trombones* in 1927; it was a great departure from the dialect poetry usually associated with black sermons. Of the sermons, "The Creation" became the most famous and showed spirituals to be high art and a distinct form in literature. This sermon describes the creation of man, picturing God kneeling in the dust to shape a lump of clay "like a mammy bending over her baby" (Johnson, *God's Trombones,* p. 20).

On June 29, 1938, Johnson died in a car crash at age sixty-seven, leaving behind a grieving widow as well as a grief-stricken world community. More than 2,000 mourners marched through the streets of Harlem in Johnson's funeral procession; both black and white Americans turned out to praise his life's work. New York City mayor Fiorello La Guardia summed up a popular opinion of Johnson, saying:

> His many-faceted genius produced a wide variety of fine things. One of these is a long-remembered song. James Weldon Johnson

wrote "Under the Bamboo Tree" but he didn't lie lazily under it. He went out and worked and fought. He won respect and admiration in every field of endeavor in which he engaged. (Levy, p. 347)

For More Information

Johnson, James Weldon. *Along This Way.* New York: Viking Press, 1933.

Johnson, James Weldon. *God's Trombones.* New York: Viking Press, 1927.

Johnson, James Weldon. *The Autobiography of an Ex-Coloured Man.* Boston: Sherman, French & Company, 1912.

Levy, Eugene. *James Weldon Johnson: Black Leader, Black Voice.* Chicago: University of Chicago Press, 1973.

Zora Neale Hurston

c. 1901-1960

Personal Background

Origin. Zora Neale Hurston was born a strong, outgoing child on January 7, probably in 1901. Because she liked her privacy—even when it came to giving out factual details—no accurate record of her birth was kept. The dates offered by her and her biographers range from 1891 to 1903, with 1901 being the most commonly cited and the one that is engraved on her headstone. In any case, Zora developed into a highly creative child, full of energy and curiosity. Always out-of-doors, she was a tomboy who preferred climbing the chinaberry or citrus trees in her sprawling backyard to playing with the rag dolls she received for Christmas.

Eatonville. Zora grew up in the sunny, all-black town of Eatonville, Florida, where she lived with her parents, Lucy and John, and her five brothers and two sisters. Unique because it was solely governed and inhabited by African Americans, Eatonville provided a secure environment—sheltered from racial prejudice—that aided in Zora's development into a self-confident young woman.

In addition to its supportive environment, Eatonville planted the seeds of Zora's lifelong fascination with African American folklore. She grew up listening to the "lying sessions" in front of her local drugstore, "where people sat around on boxes, benches, and nail kegs, and 'passed this world and the next one through their

▲ **Zora Neale Hurston**

Event: Harlem Renaissance.
Role: Zora Neale Hurston, a black fiction writer, folklore collector, and cultural anthropologist, led the literary movement of the 1920s known as the Harlem Renaissance. Writing plays, novels, short stories, and even an opera, Hurston preserved and made widely known African American folklore and challenged stereotypes, or popular images, of blacks.

mouths'" (Hurston in Hemenway, p. 12). The drugstore was the heart and soul of Zora's community, and the stories told there were part of an oral tradition that dated back to slavery. The folktales Zora heard throughout her childhood served not only to instill in her a strong sense of pride in her heritage, but they also sparked her active imagination. Woven into her childhood experiences, the folklore of the South eventually became the subject matter of and inspiration for the literature Zora produced.

Mrs. Lucy Hurston. Zora was also deeply influenced by her mother, who encouraged her daughter to "'jump at de sun'" because "we might not land on the sun, but at least we [will] get off the ground" (Hemenway, p. 14). A former schoolteacher, Lucy Hurston was a tough, intelligent woman who tried to foster the same qualities in her daughter. She not only encouraged Zora to reach for the sun but also made her feel special, as if the sun and moon illuminated her every footstep. She taught Zora to read before the child entered elementary school, and though her husband was known to have an eye for the ladies, she kept her family together until her death. Unfortunately, however, that day came early in Zora's life. Her mother died when Zora was just nine, and the family fell apart almost immediately after.

For the nine-year-old Zora, the death of her mother was the end of a phase in her life: "That hour began my wanderings. Not so much in geography but in time. Then not so much in time as in spirit" (Hurston in Hemenway, p. 17). Zora had always been a bright young woman and an eager reader. Written or recited, stories created a new world for her, a "hemisphere of the imagination" to which she could safely and happily retreat (Hemenway, p. 16). After her mother's death, this hemisphere became even more appealing.

Zora's father remarried right away and, because Zora strongly disliked her stepmother, she was sent away to boarding school in Jacksonville. Relations with her father grew worse, and by about age thirteen, Zora cut off most ties to her family and began working as a maid around Jacksonville to support herself. In 1915 she joined a touring Gilbert and Sullivan theater company as a wardrobe girl, which lasted eighteen months and provided her with her first real glimpse of the world outside Florida. Zora eventually settled in Baltimore, Maryland, in 1917, where she obtained another domestic service job and enrolled in Morgan State University to get her high school diploma. She graduated in 1918 and entered Howard University the following year.

Writing begins. Hurston began to fully explore her talents as a writer when she became a Howard University student in 1919. Realizing her love of language and creative arts, Hurston became an English major and was accepted as a member of an exclusive campus literary club, the Stylus. It was with this group that she published her first short story, "John Redding Goes to Sea," in May 1921. Though a decent first effort, the tale was overshadowed by Zora's next short stories, "Drenched in Light" and "Spunk," which attracted attention from literary circles in New York. Based on her own Eatonville childhood and the rich folklore she knew so well, the stories were published in National Association for the Advancement of Colored People's *Opportunity,* the NAACP magazine. The stories so impressed editor Charles Johnson that he became one of her most enthusiastic supporters and helped convince her to move to New York City in 1925 to be part of a burgeoning literary movement then called the "Negro Renaissance."

Johnson, as well as many of Hurston's college professors, recognized immediately the importance of Hurston's work. Her folktales and stories of black life in the rural South were not only beautifully written, they offered a glimpse of parts of African American culture that had, up to this point, been largely ignored by the general public—including African Americans. Hurston's work was serving to give the folklore of her ancestors an official place in American literature. Moreover, she was preserving this folklore for generations to come, while at the same time illustrating the proud heritage of the black race.

Participation: Harlem Renaissance

Reputation. Even before her arrival in New York City in 1925, Hurston was becoming well known for both her writing and her high-spirited personality. Firmly at home as the center of attention, Hurston took command of a room when she entered it. She was a master storyteller—having learned the skill during her childhood—and could reproduce dialects, or different ways of speaking, like a professional actor. She captivated crowds at parties with her folktales and stories of life back in Eatonville, and it soon became apparent that she would greatly affect the New York writing scene. Langston Hughes, another up-and-coming writer, described Hurston as "the most amusing" of all the authors in Harlem during the 1920s and considered her an accomplished entertainer, both in person and on the written page (Hughes, p. 235).

> **Their Eyes Were Watching God**
>
> Like many of her characters, Hurston expected events to turn out happily and was a dreamer. *Their Eyes Were Watching God* is a love story by Hurston based partly on her second marriage. In describing the heroine Janie, Hurston states perfectly her own enthusiasm for life: "She pulled in her horizon like a great fish-net. Pulled it from around the waist of the world and draped it over her shoulder. So much of life in its meshes! She called in her soul to come and see!" (Hurston in Hemenway, p. 236)

Renaissance era. By the time Hurston arrived in New York City, Harlem had become the hotbed of literary activity, and black artists were being "discovered" by the entire nation. Harlem, which was built between 1900 and 1910, had a housing surplus due to World War I, so the area was desegregated. From 1916 to 1918, Harlem's African American community swelled to 100,000 due to the "Great Migration," the mass movement of African Americans from the South who came North in search of jobs in industry and a more liberal environment. By 1920 Harlem's population had topped 200,000 as the town became, in effect, a city within a city and was considered the "Negro capital of the world" (Hemenway, p. 30).

Known for its writers and entertainers, its night life and rich cultural mix, Harlem attracted people of all races during the 1920s. More black writers were published than ever before in U.S. history, and Harlem became the destination for hopeful black artists, who arrived in droves, dreaming of becoming part of the Negro Renaissance movement.

As one of these hopeful artists, Hurston moved to Harlem and, for the first time since her mother's death, felt a sense of belonging. Like Eatonville, the black-dominated and creative environment of Harlem immediately appealed to her and became a warm, nonthreatening home where she could grow as an artist. In fact, Harlem welcomed Hurston with open arms. Not only were her stories in all the "correct" publications—including the NAACP's *Opportunity* magazine and the anthology of the movement, *The New Negro*—but her work was highly original and celebrated black Southern culture, a subject few had, up to this point, written about so well.

Hurston's work ranged from short stories and essays to musical plays and stage revivals. She believed that Negro material was eminently suited to drama and music. The world and America in particular, Hurston felt, needed what this folk material held. Hurston, like James Weldon Johnson, believed that art could fight racism and produce positive social change more effectively than reason or heated debates (see **James Weldon Johnson**). Art's advantage was that it humanized events and drew emotional responses from people. For example, in her early work "Drenched in Light," which tells of a young girl growing up in an Eatonville-like town, her heroine asserts:

> I am not tragically colored. There is no great sorrow damned up in my soul, nor lurking behind my eyes.... I do not belong to the sobbing school of Negrohood who hold that nature somehow has given them a lowdown dirty deal. (Hurston in Hemenway, p. 11)

Hurston believed, like her heroine, that being black was something to be proud of, and she wanted to show the world, and particularly white Americans, that there were black Americans who grew up "drenched in light," utterly happy being themselves and not envious of any white person's lot. In fact, the white elderly woman in this story begs to keep the heroine, Isie, around in order that her "light" may rub off on the old woman. Like "Drenched," most of Hurston's work is in part autobiographical and challenges the notion that African Americans are or feel inferior to Anglo Americans. Meanwhile, the work illustrates a rich cultural heritage.

Though her writing had political impact, Hurston did not wholly support any of the political movements of the era. She was opposed to Marcus Garvey's separatist philosophy (see **Marcus Garvey**). At the same time, she had reservations about the NAACP goals of desegregation and full integration. She felt that "negroness" was being rubbed off by close contact with white culture, and she thought that segregated towns like Eatonville, where she had grown up, helped preserve black cultural identity. Because of these views, Hurston sought more and more to get away from politics and concentrate on her art.

Fire!! Hurston thought of herself as an artist first and foremost, as did Langston Hughes, Gwendolyn Bennett, Aaron Douglas, Wallace Thurman, and Bruce Nugent. This group of writers decided to produce their own magazine that would be a "non commercial product interested only in the arts"—an "outlet for Negro fire"—which they appropriately called *Fire!!* (Hemenway, pp. 44–45). Unfortunately, the writers' school activities and finances limited *Fire!!* to just the one issue, in late 1926, but it was a literary success. Hurston contributed the short story "Sweat," which portrayed the struggles of a poor working couple in the South. Widely praised, it illustrated how Hurston's small-town tales could reveal larger truths about life in general.

Where Hurston Found the Money to Write

Black writers were well received but not necessarily well paid in the 1920s. Hurston, like other writers of the time, was forced to rely on outsiders for a steady income. She had two backers, Fanny Hurst and Charlotte Osgood Mason, both wealthy white women. They provided a valuable service to Hurston but by no means made her wealthy, and each earned a sizable return on their investments. In fact, for only $200 a month Mason owned the rights to the folklore recorded by Hurston, whose loss of control later led to her financial ruin. The writer did not have the rights to republish these stories when she fell on hard times.

Anthropology and art. During her first year in New York, Hurston was accepted to Barnard College as its first African American student and the following year, in 1927, secured patronage, or financial support, for her work from Charlotte Osgood Mason, a wealthy white woman who backed many Harlem artists. Known as "Godmother," Mason bought a car for Hurston and funded a folklore-collecting trip to the South. Besides gathering anthropological information for Barnard College and Columbia University, Hurston found the trip to be a rich resource for her own creative work. It became one of many trips south, which would yield four novels, two books of folklore, several plays and revues, and more than fifty short stories and essays over the next twenty years—making Hurston the most published black American woman up to that time.

For the next five years, through 1932, Hurston traveled between Harlem and the Deep South—going as far as the West

▲ Hurston on a folklore-collecting trip, late 1930s

Indies to research voodoo practices and listen to old folktales. She took pains to record the exact manner in which they were told and the characteristics of the storytellers themselves. After graduating from Barnard College in 1928, Hurston continued her studies in cultural anthropology at Columbia through 1935 and won a Guggenheim fellowship to do fieldwork in Haiti in 1936.

Aftermath

Misfortune. For the bulk of her life, Hurston, a poor black woman from the rural South, "was scaling the mountain of accomplishment, past barriers of race, sex, and poverty, destined for the heights" (Roses and Randolphe, p. 186). But it was not to remain that way. When the Great Depression struck, the Harlem Renaissance came to an abrupt end. World War II further drew money and attention away from the arts, and by 1950 Hurston was out of a job and unable to get a publisher for her work. She had been damaged not only by a bad economy but by a scandal concerning sexual contact with a young boy, which was proved to be totally false. Her reputation was further damaged by two failed marriages, due in part to her career demands—writing and traveling to uncover more stories. Still more damage was done by Hurston's fallout with some NAACP leaders over her refusal to wholeheartedly support their political agendas, and a rift with poet and one-time close friend Langston Hughes, who accused Hurston of plagiarizing, copying someone else's work and saying it was hers, in an opera they'd both worked on.

Mule Bone

An opera titled *Mule Bone* caused a permanent break between Hurston and Langston Hughes in 1931. The two, who were friends from Howard University and Harlem, were writing the opera based on an old folktale about two hunters who shoot at the same deer and then argue over who has killed it. In much the same way, Hurston and Hughes fought over the rights to the play and, unable to resolve the matter, shelved the project permanently—along with their friendship.

Final years. Hurston eventually found temporary employment with the Federal Theatre Project in Florida in 1951 and relocated there. She worked on and off for the next nine years, publishing stories when she could and serving as a maid when she could find no other employment. In failing health and unwilling to turn to family members or friends for help, Hurston entered a welfare home in St. Lucie, Florida, in October 1959, and died of heart disease three months later, on January 28, 1960. Friends collected the $400 to meet Hurston's funeral expenses, but at the services Reverend C. E. Bolen insisted that Hurston had not died poor:

> Zora Neale went about and didn't care too much about how she looked. Or what she said. Maybe people didn't think so much of that. But Zora Neale, every time she went about, she had something to offer. She didn't come to you empty.
>
> They said she couldn't become a writer recognized by the world. But she did it. The Miami paper said she died poor. But she died rich. She did something. (Hemenway, p. 348)

Hurston was a strong-willed, opinionated woman who refused to abide by social conventions. She wore what she wanted, did what she chose, and said what she felt. Her outspoken ways won her enemies, yet Hurston deeply affected her own generation and future generations. Later writers have acknowledged her tremendous influence on their lives and work. Writer Alice Walker considers Hurston's *Mules and Men* and *Their Eyes Were Watching God* two of the most important books ever written. In 1973 Walker helped preserve Hurston's memory by searching out her overgrown gravesite and putting up a proper gravestone, which says "A Genius of the South."

For More Information

Bloom, Harold. *Modern Critical Views: Zora Neale Hurston.* New York: Chelsea House Publishers, 1986.

Hemenway, Robert E. *Zora Neale Hurston.* London: Camden Press, 1986.

Hughes, Langston. *The Big Sea.* New York: Hill and Wang, 1963.

Hurston, Zora Neale. *Dust Tracks on a Road, An Autobiography.* Philadelphia: J. B. Lippencott Co., 1942.

Roses, Lorraine Elena, and Ruth Elizabeth Randolphe. *Harlem Renaissance and Beyond.* Boston: G. K. Hall & Co., 1990.

Women's Rights and Roles

1873

Comstock Law makes it illegal to even write about birth control devices.

1900-1904

Carrie Chapman Catt serves as president of the National American Woman Suffrage Association (NAWSA).

1910

Alice Paul returns to America from England, begins to apply English tactics to the American women's movement.

1912

Paul leads 5,000 women in a parade for the woman's vote the day before Woodrow Wilson is inaugrated as president.

1914

Paul breaks with NAWSA, forms separate group to press for an amendment to the Constitution on woman's vote.

1914

Margaret Sanger begins the magazine *Woman Rebel.*

1915

Catt becomes president of NAWSA for second term; launches her Winning Plan strategy for the vote. Sanger founds National Birth Control League (Planned Parenthood).

1916

Sanger opens birth control clinic in New York. Paul's group is renamed National Woman's Party.

1917

National Woman's Party starts using militant tactics.

1919

Senators pass the Nineteenth Amendment, which guarantees women the right to vote.

1920

States ratify the Nineteenth Amendment; it becomes law.

1936

Supreme Court strikes down Comstock Law; American Medical Association agrees to issue birth control devices.

WOMEN'S RIGHTS AND ROLES

In 1872 a group of citizens tried to prevent women from gaining the right to vote. Led by women of high social standing, such as Ellen Ewing Sherman, wife of the Civil War general William Tecumseh Sherman, they sent to Congress a petition with 1,000 signatures. Also opposed to women's suffrage were people against temperence, or the movement to outlaw the manufacture and sale of liquor in America.

After the Civil War temperance workers had joined forces with groups in favor of granting women the vote. Women organized two groups to work for the vote, the National Woman Suffrage Association and American Woman Suffrage Association. The two merged into one stronger group in 1890, forming the National American Woman Suffrage Association (NAWSA). Around the same time new women's leaders came onto the scene, who focused more expressly than ever before on a woman's right to vote. Reflecting a popular attitude of the day, social reformer Jane Addams pointed out that women, the moral caretakers of society, had a role to play in American cities. Given the vote, they could make sure that government provided pure water, police protection, and other services.

Male lawmakers were not convinced. Certainly they did not feel the federal government should dictate policy to the

CONGRESSIONAL UNION FOR WOMA
NATIONAL SUMMER HEADQUARTE
VOTES FOR WOMEN A SUCCESS
Congressional Union for Woman's Suffrage
National Summer Headquarters
128 Bellevue Ave. Newport R.I.

▲ **Members of the Congressional Union for Woman's Suffrage outside its National Summer Headquarters in Newport, Rhode Island**

states. Senator after senator held fast to the idea that each state was entitled to decide for itself if women could vote. Recognizing this mindset, **Carrie Chapman Catt** led the NAWSA in waging a state-by-state campaign. The idea of adding an amendment to the Constitution that guaranteed a woman the right to vote had been introduced by Susan B. Anthony and first presented to Congress in 1868. But interest in such an amendment faded before Alice Paul swept onto

▲ **Women marching for equal rights**

the scene in 1910. Paul, a Quaker, had visited England, where she joined feminists such as Emmeline Pankhurst in hunger strikes on behalf of women's gaining the vote there. Afterward, Paul's efforts in America turned the women's movement into a two-pronged attack. While the NAWSA waged a state-by-state campaign, Paul pressed for a Constitutional amendment. In 1912 she led 5,000 women on a parade the day before Woodrow Wilson was inaugurated as president, knowing full well that Washington would be chock-full of important visitors: "'The women,' said [a] newspaper story, 'had to fight their way from the start and took more than one hour in making the first ten blocks'" (Eleanor Flexner, *Century of Struggle,* [New York: Atheneum, 1974], p. 264). Paul developed a following. Her group splintered off from the NAWSA in February 1914 and then formed its own organization.

Meanwhile, **Margaret Sanger** engaged in a different struggle. Her years as a nurse had shown her women suffering miserable lives and deaths due to too many births and illegal abortions (operations to end their pregnancies). Sanger was convinced that the true cause of a woman's unequal position in society was her inability to plan the size of her family. She set out to educate the public on birth control, starting her own magazine, the *Woman Rebel,* in defiance of the Comstock Law, which made it illegal to write about birth control. She fled to Europe to escape prison, returning in 1915 after the charges against her were dropped. Undaunted by her brush with the law, she formed the organization known now as Planned Parenthood Federation of America and opened a birth control clinic, for which she was sent to jail.

Areas That Granted Women Partial or Full Voting Rights before 1920

1869	Wyoming
1893	Colorado
1896	Utah, Idaho
1910	Washington state
1911	California
1912	Arizona, Kansas, Oregon
1913	Alaska Territory, Illinois
1914	Nevada, Montana
1917	New York

The year 1915 was also pivotal in the campaign for the women's vote. After several years, Catt returned to the NAWSA, which had suffered greatly in her absence. She developed a plan, coordinating state campaigns with the work of a central group in Washington, D.C. The central group sent detailed information to the states on ways to pressure congressmen in local districts. The details were drawn from the group's files, which included facts on personal, political, business, and religious tastes of the congressmen. In 1915 NAWSA, like Paul's group, saw the wisdom of pushing for a federal amendment to guarantee a woman's right to vote and added this to their goals. Renowned for her ability to carry out her plans, Catt assigned every state a role in the struggle. If a state had already granted voting rights to the women who lived there, its NAWSA workers were charged with pressuring Congress for an amendment to the Constitution.

In 1917 Paul's group, called the National Woman's Party, resorted to militant tactics like those used in England. They picketed the White House, went on hunger strikes, started bonfires, and served time in jail. The National

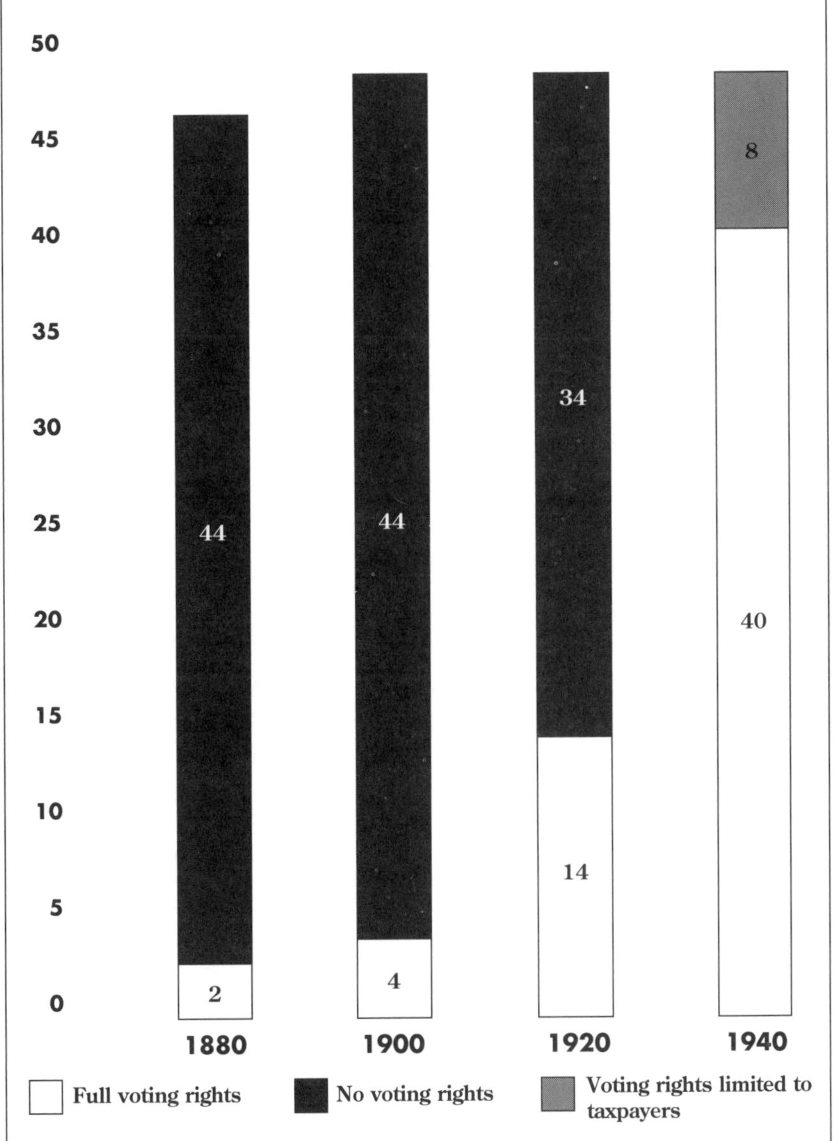

▲ **Number of states granting women's voting rights, 1880-1940**

Woman's Party came out against America's entering World War I, while Catt's NAWSA was in favor of it. Unlike women during the Civil War, however, Catt refused to put aside her crusade for the women's vote during World War I. She afterward confessed:

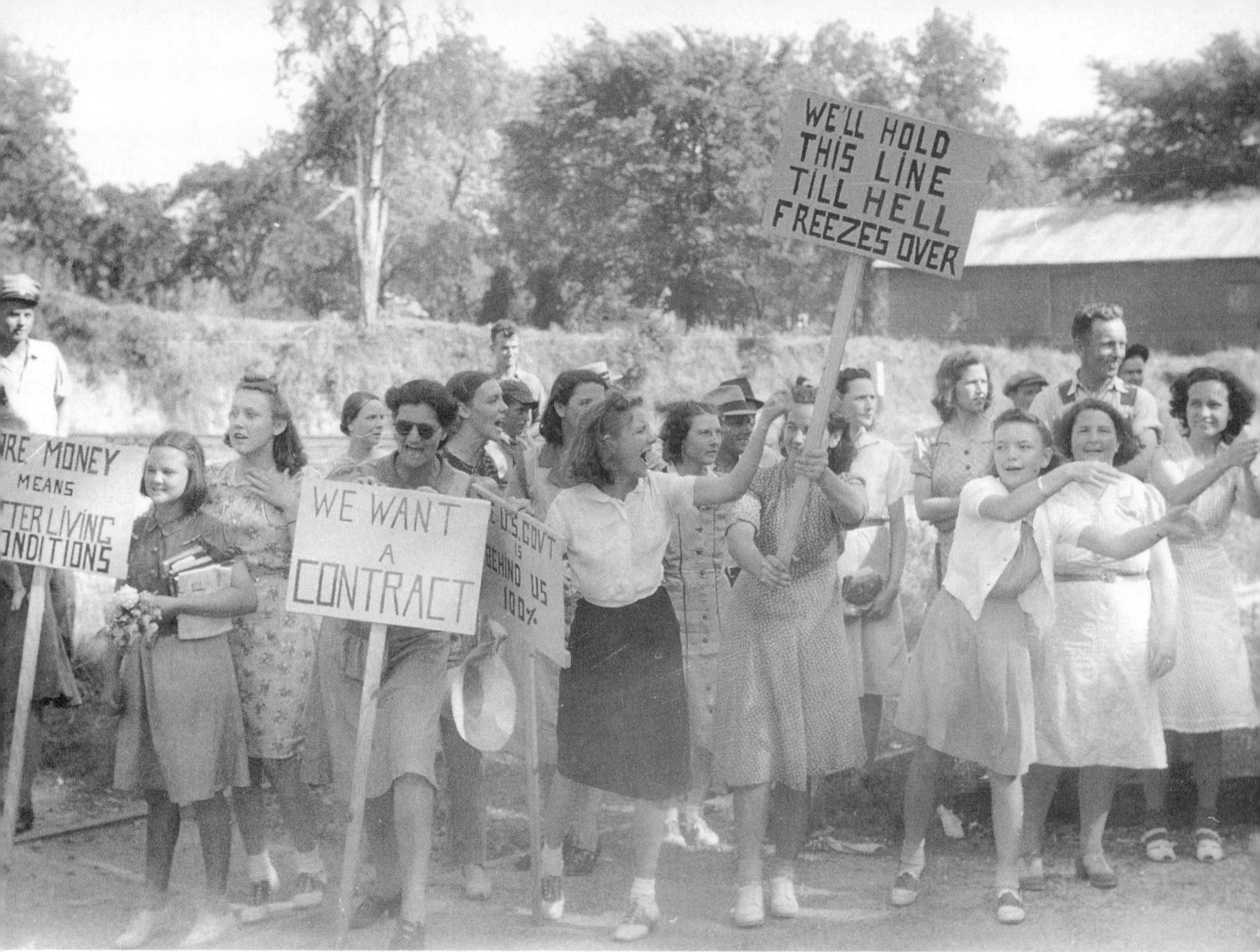
WE'LL HOLD
THIS LINE
TILL HELL
FREEZES OVER
MEANS
WE WANT
A
CONTRACT
US
100%

▲ **The fight for equal rights for women in all avenues of life still continues well into the twentieth century**

> The work of the past two years has been the most trying and difficult of my experience. All antisuffragists in the country did their utmost to make the public believe that suffragists were traitors to their country since they did not lay down their work when the U.S.A. went to war. (Flexner, p. 289)

Opponents formed the National Association Opposed to Woman Suffrage, and called supporters of the women's vote un-American. But Catt and her coworkers gained ground. They pressured President Wilson, and in 1918 he urged the Senate to pass an amendment guaranteeing a woman's right to vote as a war measure. Grateful for their help in World War I, Great Britain granted its women the right to vote in 1918, and the United States, champion of democracy, was lagging behind. Also, the United States had joined the war in part to help promote democracy, yet women in its own backyard were denied the right to vote. The contradiction was obvious. Wilson is credited with squeezing the last vote in Congress needed for the amendment from Senator William Harris of Georgia.

After a tough struggle, the Nineteenth Amendment was ratified in 1920. Women's winning the vote did not bring about the major, immediate changes in politics that many expected. But struggles continued on other levels. There were developments on the birth-control front, as Sanger continued to lobby Congress and the American Medical Association (AMA). The Supreme Court finally reversed the Comstock Law, and the AMA approved using birth control devices. Sixteen years after women gained the vote, Sanger too at last tasted success.

Carrie Chapman Catt

1859-1947

Personal Background

Parents. Carrie Chapman Catt was born Carrie Clinton Lane in February 1859 on a family farm in Ripon, Wisconsin. Her father, Lucius Lane, was a resourceful, adventurous, stubborn man who left the rush for California gold to develop his own farm. Maria Clinton Lane, Carrie's mother, was a bookish, quiet woman with whom Carrie shared a slightly strained relationship. Carrie inherited several traits from both parents: she was a studious, confident child who challenged the ways of the world from a very early age.

Carrie challenges conformity. A photograph of Carrie at age six shows the same determination, nonconformity, and sturdiness she would be known for later in her life. Dressed in an off-the-shoulder print dress, with hands adorned by fingerless black lace gloves, she was a portrait of innocent vanity and individuality at that age.

Around the same time she posed for the photograph, Carrie was discovering a world that was full of challenges for her as a girl. Once, after being scared away by her brother who sneaked up on her with a handful of snakes, she quickly came back at him with a handful of her own, which sent her brother running. She had reasoned that if handling the snakes couldn't hurt her brother, they certainly couldn't hurt her.

▲ Carrie Chapman Catt

Event: Women's suffrage.
Role: Carrie Chapman Catt worked for decades to help women gain the right to vote. She devoted her life to the cause of gaining equal rights for women.

Carrie seemed determined to stand up for other girls as well as herself. When a swarm of boys continually laughed at and teased one of her classmates whose hoopskirt had accidentally dropped to the ground during school recess, Carrie became enraged and slapped the leader of the taunting boys. She later remembered, "They had more respect for us girls after that!" (Catt in Van Voris, p. 5).

A memorable incident. At age thirteen, Carrie was faced with a discovery which changed her outlook on life. As her father prepared to go into town to vote in the presidential election of 1872, Carrie asked her mother why she wasn't getting dressed to go out, too. Her mother replied that she wasn't going, which prompted Carrie to ask, "Then how are you going to vote for Greeley?" (Catt in Van Voris, p. 6). Her question was received with laughter. Later she told a neighbor boy that she thought it was unfair that women were forbidden to vote. He laughed at her as well, and said that naturally women couldn't vote. She was shocked and angered that everyone around her seemed to accept the lower status of women and that nobody could properly explain why women were faced with this fate. Throughout her life, Carrie often referred to this incident as one that influenced her more than any other.

Early advances. As she later confessed, Carrie began following a voice she heard while she was out walking her dog one day. The voice said: "There is important work awaiting you in the future.... You have much to learn and you are wasting your time" (Fowler, p. 9). She began applying herself in school and, at the age of eighteen, enrolled at Iowa State Agricultural College. She worked as a teacher to pay for her tuition fees; her parents would not pay because they thought it was unnecessary for women to enroll in higher education.

While attending Iowa State, Carrie engaged in several struggles that resulted in advances for women there. She fought for and won the right for women to make speeches in the college's literary society (until then they had been limited to writing essays). Carrie also started the G (Girls) Company, whose members performed military drills with broomsticks in place of weapons, as a symbol for peace. In one of her first speeches, Carrie planted thoughts in listeners' minds about women's suffrage, asking, "How is it possible that a woman who is unfit to vote, should be the mother of, and bring up, a man who is?" (Catt in Van Voris, p. 8).

Her contributions to her college soon made Carrie a local topic of conversation. Her advances for women were reported in the local newspaper before her graduation in 1880; she was the only woman in her class to graduate.

Chapman, Catt, and the search for equality. After working as a teacher and superintendent of Iowa city schools for several years, Carrie met and married newspaper editor Leo Chapman in 1885. Their marriage was short-lived, for as Carrie prepared to join her husband in San Francisco, California, the next year, he died suddenly of typhoid there. The distraught widow still headed for San Francisco, in search of comfort and a new beginning.

Upon her arrival, Carrie took a job at a business newspaper office, where one evening a male associate made sexual advances toward her. When she refused his advances, he grabbed her. She managed to break free of him and left the office safely, but the incident, which occurred at a particularly delicate time in her life, only fueled a desire that had begun to burn within her for equal treatment for women everywhere.

Carrie eventually found the comfort she sought in San Francisco. She became reacquainted with an old schoolmate, now a bridge engineer, George Catt. Carrie cautiously fell in love with Catt, who pursued her immediately, and she married him a few years later, when she was thirty-one. Together they moved back to Iowa, where, with the generous financial and moral support of her new husband, Carrie Chapman Catt began her career as a full-time activist for women's rights.

The NAWSA and little victories. Women of the late 1800s formed suffrage groups, whose purpose was to gain the right for women to vote. In 1890 two women's suffrage groups combined forces to form the National American Woman Suffrage Association (NAWSA). Catt had joined other suffrage groups but became very interested in this one because it seemed more likely to effect change for women. Catt made her NAWSA debut by giving a speech at one of their conventions. It was well received, and with it Catt set herself on the track to becoming a powerful member.

Three years later, Catt successfully headed a widespread campaign for women's suffrage in Colorado. She had convinced dozens of male voters to allow women the right to vote at a time when it was difficult for women to achieve equal status with men. Her reputation began to soar, and she was asked to reorganize the structure of the NAWSA, a job she enthusiastically accepted. Almost immediately after Catt reorganized the group, there was a clear-cut victory. Utah reinstated the right to vote for women, a right which had been taken away nine years earlier. Catt was emerging as a champion for her cause.

Catt's presence in the group was becoming extremely important to founding members such as the acting president, Susan B. Anthony. The aging Anthony knew that the organization would soon need strong, new leadership to continue the fight for suffrage. With the turn of the century came a switch in power—Anthony stepped down and, with the support of most of the NAWSA, offered the presidency to Catt.

Participation: Women's Suffrage

The first term. Catt moved to New York with her husband to begin her job as successor to Anthony. She had several goals for the NAWSA at the start of her first term, a few of which would be realized, but not to the extent she desired. She hoped to further educate women, build up NAWSA membership, and get states to adopt women's suffrage so that the Constitution would someday be amended and women across the nation would have the voice they deserved. While memberships and convention attendance rose during Catt's first term (1900-1904), it was otherwise a relatively uneventful four years. Catt became frustrated and, because her husband's health was failing, she chose to step down as president, turning the job over to Anna Howard Shaw. The following year, her husband and most devoted supporter passed away, leaving Catt again a widow.

International suffrage. Catt was crushed by her husband's death and fell into a deep depression that did not allow her to perform her life's work for several months. She finally lifted herself out of the depression and, becoming reinspired, established the Inter-

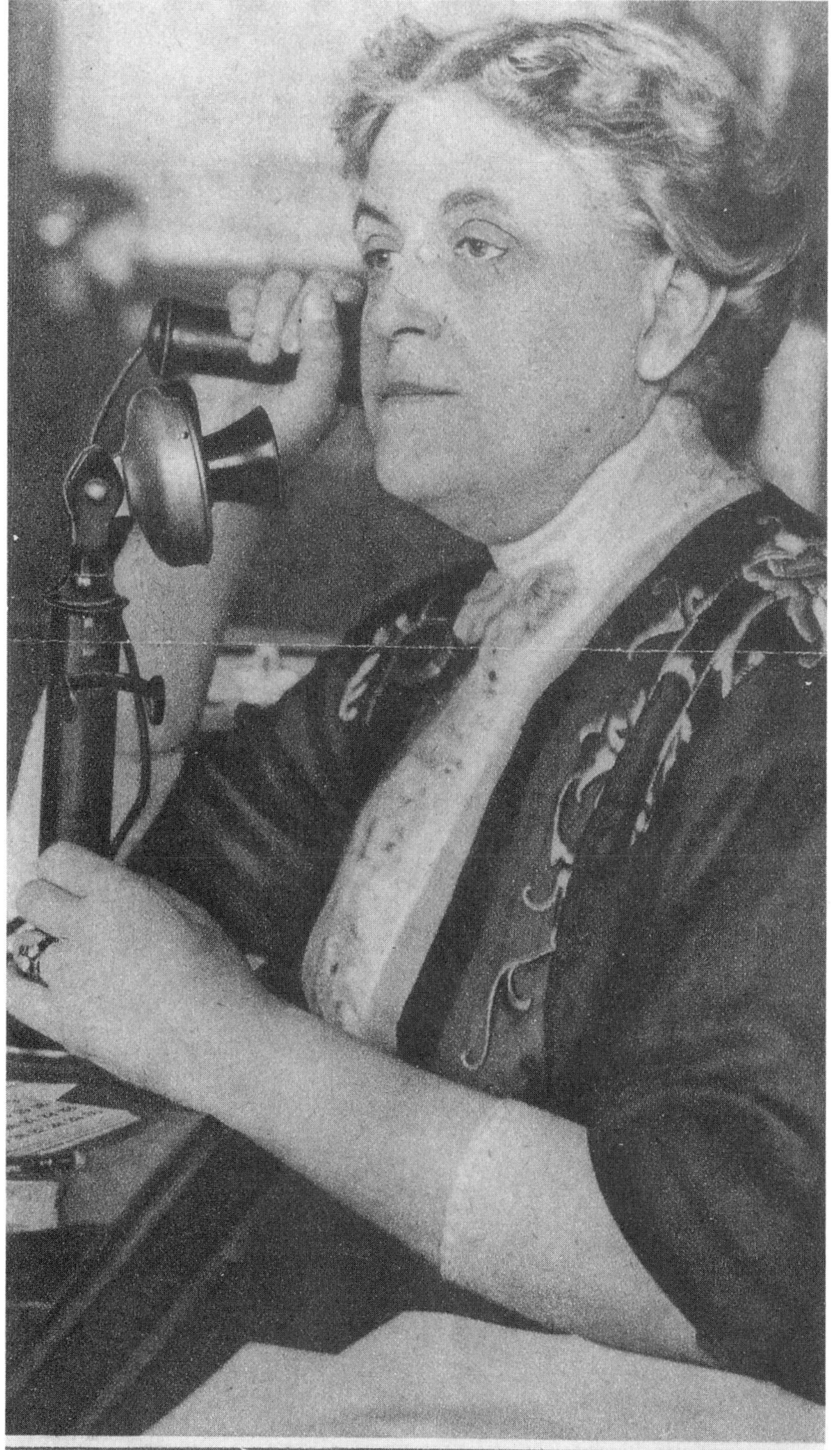

© UNDERWOOD & UNDERWOOD

SHE LEADS THE INTERNATIONAL SUFFRAGE MOVEMENT

Mrs. Carrie Chapman Catt, in Twelve Years of Executive Activity, Has Contributed Toward Victories in Tasmania, Queensland, Finland, Norway, Sweden, Denmark, Belgium, Iceland and at Home national Women's Suffrage Alliance (IWSA) to promote suffrage for women in countries around the world. As president, she traveled internationally for eleven years, gaining more momentum for the suffrage movement than the NAWSA ever had. She was making headlines everywhere and being asked to speak at more places than ever.

The Road to the Vote

Women's suffrage was achieved after a difficult struggle that lasted for over 100 years. Women took a great many steps to win the right to vote:

1848	Women organize and issue a formal demand for the right to vote.
1866	First post–Civil War women's rights convention.
1872	Susan B. Anthony illegally registers to vote. She is tried, convicted, and fined $100.
1890	Two strong suffrage groups join forces to become the NAWSA. Carrie Catt joins the new group.
1893	Male voters in Colorado allow suffrage for women. Catt is credited with the success of the campaign there.
1895	Catt is asked to reorganize the NAWSA. Utah reinstates women's right to vote.

The NAWSA had meanwhile fallen on hard times. After Shaw took over as president, the organization came to a virtual standstill—it was losing money and support across the country, and no significant victories had been made in over a decade. The job seemed to be too overwhelming for Shaw, and Catt appeared to be attracting all the attention given to the suffrage cause. In 1915 the NAWSA pleaded for her to return as president as a last attempt at realizing the goal of giving women the vote.

The second term and victory. By 1915 Catt had come home and entered the state campaign for the women's vote in New York. She was fifty-six when she reluctantly agreed to switch jobs and serve as NAWSA president for a second term. At the 1915 convention, in which she was sworn in as president, she praised Shaw's attempts and then told the crowd, "I am an unwilling victim and you all know it" (Catt in Fowler, p. 30). Yet Catt took a deep breath and stepped into action for the sake of women's suffrage.

In 1916 Catt addressed an assembly of state suffrage leaders, tired women who sat in a crowded, stuffy room with a map of the United States on the wall. Catt scolded them for the backbiting and personality clashes that had been recently getting in the way of progress. She demanded that they cooperate and dedicate themselves to gaining the vote in an organized fashion. She reminded them that if they really wanted to obtain the vote by making the right an amendment to the Constitution, at least thirty-six states must sign a compact to go after it with a will.

Catt further challenged the women to put her "Winning Plan" into effect. This was a secret strategy, and Catt would develop a corps of women lieutenants to help her carry it out. It was necessary that the women win a few more states—Iowa, South Dakota, North Dakota, Nebraska, New York, Maine, and any southern state—before the Federal Amendment reached the state legislatures for their rulings.

The Road to the Vote

1900	Catt succeeds Anthony as NAWSA president.
1904	Catt resigns as president, begins work for international suffrage for women.
1915	Catt resumes role as president of NAWSA.
1917	New York approves women's suffrage.
1918	President Woodrow Wilson declares his support for women's suffrage. Nineteenth Amendment passes House of Representatives.
1919	Suffragists set up a twenty-four-hour vigil near the entrance to the White House. Senate passes the Nineteenth Amendment.
1920	On August 26, the Nineteenth Amendment becomes law.

With Catt as president again, within two years the women's suffrage movement made major gains. Several states granted women the right to vote for a U.S. president. Thousands of Americans marched in a suffrage parade in New York City, the largest parade of any kind in that state's history. The House of Representatives voted for the first time on national suffrage for women, and the measure was defeated by only thirty votes. Women began picketing the White House, demanding to be recognized as equals. Finally New York, perhaps the most influential eastern state at the time, approved women's suffrage. Catt called it "the very greatest victory this movement has ever had" (Catt in Fowler, p. 30).

The victories did not stop there. In 1918 President Woodrow Wilson declared his support for the cause, the day before the House of Representatives voted on the national suffrage amendment. It passed the House by exactly a two-thirds majority. Catt and a group of the other suffrage supporters, after the exhausting, successful attempt at convincing the House to approve their amendment, marched out of the Capitol building singing, "Praise God, from whom all blessings flow" (Van Voris, p. 148).

▲ **Women marching for the vote**

Convincing the Senate to give women the right to vote did not come so easily. Two years in a row, the measure faced defeat by the narrowest margins—it failed by two votes in 1918 and by one vote in 1919. After the 1918 failure, Catt and her coworkers swung into action, trying to get antisuffrage senators defeated in 1918 campaigns for reelection. Though their efforts met with some success, the Senate still did not pass the suffrage amendment in 1919. Only after members of the NAWSA built a huge fire in an urn in front of the White House and kept it burning twenty-four hours a day did the Senate finally give in to the pressure and pass the measure on June 4, 1919. (The amendment had been written by Susan B. Anthony and originally introduced in 1878.) With the victory secured in the Senate, Catt was more enthusiastic than ever.

In order for the amendment to become a law, however, Catt and the NAWSA had to wait until thirty-six states—a two-thirds majority—would ratify it. This did not happen until August 1920, after a representative from Tennessee broke a tie and made it the thirty-sixth state to support women's suffrage. His mother had convinced him to support the amendment. Her behind-the-scenes argument was the climax of an intense struggle by other women workers, though. Two months earlier, suitcase in hand, Catt herself had arrived in the state to promote the amendment.

The day after the women's right to vote became a law, Catt traveled to New York for a victory celebration. She was greeted by thousands of cheering suffragists waving yellow ribbons in honor of their cause. Catt answered their cheers with a reminder about the meaning of the victory: "This is a glorious and wonderful day. Now that we have the vote let us remember we are ... free and equal citizens" (Catt in Van Voris, p. 162).

The League of Women Voters. Knowing that the NAWSA had successfully reached its goals, Catt decided to create the League of Women Voters (LWV), an organization with a new set of objectives. She described its goals to be "the education of women citizens, piloting them through the first years of political participation, and removing the relics of discrimination against women" (Catt in Van Voris, p. 154). Drawing on her past experience as a teacher, Catt set up political science classes all over the nation for women to attend. After the enormous victory of winning the vote, Catt was determined to press on and teach women how to use it.

The Nineteenth Amendment

The first two sections of the Nineteenth Amendment demand that women not be discriminated against in their constitutional right to vote:

Section I. The right of citizens of the United States to vote shall not be denied or abridged by the United States or by any State on account of sex.

Section II. Congress shall have power, by appropriate legislation, to enforce the provisions of this article. (Gluck, p. 272)

Aftermath

Continued action. Catt continued to keep a close watch on the LWV as Honorary Chairperson. Under her guidance, the organization became an effective way for women to be recognized in the political world and beyond. The LWV grew into a force that lobbied (tried to influence) lawmakers on women's issues, educated people on the need for more women in government, and sought reform in employment rights for women.

Catt's Greatest Gift

Described as women's most able organizer, Catt has been likened to Susan B. Anthony and Elizabeth Cady Stanton. Her greatest gift seems to have been her vision of a plan of action and her ability to put it into operation. Catt's direction led to conferences among state and national women's leaders, classes for the movement's organizers, ideas on fund-raising, and plans based on questionnaires filled out in every state.

In addition to being involved with the LWV, Catt spent many years trying to work toward another goal: world peace. "War is to me my greatest woe," she once remarked (Catt in Fowler, p. 30). At the age of sixty-one, Catt began traveling throughout the nation to plead for peace, disarmament, and the peaceful settlement of problems. She founded committees to educate people on peace and on explosive issues. In her small amount of spare time, she devoted herself to working toward supplying medical aid for pregnant women and establishing and enforcing laws prohibiting child labor.

A very private life. Although she stayed in the public eye for much of her life, Catt fought hard to remain anonymous and went to great lengths to do so. She burned all of the letters written between herself and both husbands as well as correspondence with friends and relatives. Toward the end of her life, her privacy became more important to Catt than anything else. She rebelled against recognition to the point of threatening those who wished to write about her. Of biographies based on her life she said, "whoever attempts it while I'm here, will try it over my dead body, and whoever tries it after I'm gone will be haunted by a ghost" (Catt in Fowler, p. xii). She wanted no credit for her action, just the results.

Catt's last years were filled with visits from adoring friends and fans. She finally settled in a New York home, complete with an enormous garden filled with another of her passions: flowers. She spent hours tending the garden for the sheer purpose of relaxation, even in her last days.

On the evening of March 9, 1947, Catt died after suffering a heart attack in her home. As she wished, the funeral arrangements were simple. Catt was buried in a New York cemetery under a monument she had prepared for herself. It spoke only of "constant service to a great cause" (Van Voris, p. 219).

Victories and Losses

In 1917 an amendment for the women's vote in Maine went down to defeat. Her eyes fixed on the future, Catt dismissed this defeat: "A battle has been lost. Forget it. Others lie ahead." (Catt in Flexner, p. 290)

For More Information

Flexner, Eleanor. *Century of Struggle.* New York: Atheneum, 1974.

Fowler, Robert Booth. *Carrie Catt: Feminist Politician.* Boston: Northeastern University Press, 1986.

Gluck, Sherna. *From Parlor to Prison.* New York: Vintage Books, 1976.

Van Voris, Jacqueline. *Carrie Chapman Catt: A Public Life.* New York: The Feminist Press, 1987.

Margaret Sanger

1879-1966

Personal Background

Home life. Margaret Higgins Sanger was born on September 11, 1879, in Corning, New York. The sixth of eleven children born to Anne Purcell and Michael Hennessey Higgins, Margaret grew up in a bustling household in the woods on the outskirts of town. While her mother took care of the large family, her father worked as a sculptor, chiseling headstones for local cemeteries. His work was unsteady, and with so many mouths to feed the family usually struggled to make ends meet.

Though poor themselves, the Higginses believed in helping others and taught Margaret to do the same. Her father often told her: "You have no right to material comforts without giving back to society the benefits of your honest experience" (Sanger, p. 23). Margaret greatly admired her father, who was known as somewhat of a rebel in town, and took his words to heart.

Rebel influence. A "freethinker" who was active in the cause of labor reform and social equality, Michael Higgins was no stranger to controversy. He often arranged for labor leaders and social reformers to speak in Corning and made his overcrowded house a center for political activity. His efforts were usually greeted with scorn from the townspeople, and as a result, Margaret and her siblings grew up being called "children of the devil" (Sanger, p. 21).

▲ **Margaret Sanger**

Event: Women's rights—birth control movement.

Role: Margaret Sanger dedicated her life to making birth control available to all women in the world and thereby increased the quality and length of women's and children's lives. Through a lifetime of tireless effort, she succeeded in opening New York's first birth control clinic. Sanger also was largely responsible for reshaping public opinion in favor of family planning and for changing the law to allow distribution of birth control devices in the United States.

But Margaret paid little attention to the name-calling. In fact, she rather liked being the daughter of a rebel and living amid controversy. The young girl developed a defiant spirit akin to her father's that would last a lifetime.

Education. Margaret attended public school through the eighth grade and then boarding school at the Claverick College and Hudson River Institute. (Her expenses were paid by two of her sisters.) Away from home for the first time in her life, Margaret flourished and began developing her leadership abilities. She became active in theater groups and for a time had an ambition to become a professional actress. However, when she learned that in order to get an acting job she would have to write down her leg measurements, she defiantly refused and "turned to other fields where something besides legs was to count" (Sanger, p. 38).

Awareness of the women's issue. The leg episode proved to be an important experience for Margaret. It alerted her to the ongoing debate about women's rights and illustrated for her the discrimination women faced. She developed a strong interest in women's rights and began studying the great female leaders in history. While researching women such as Helen of Troy, Ruth, Poppaea, and Cleopatra, Margaret became greatly inspired and wrote an essay on women's equality, which she read aloud to her class. She was filled with youthful optimism and wanted not only to help women, but to make the world a better place. Exactly how she could achieve this, she did not yet know.

Nursing sparks medical interest. After graduating from the Institute, Margaret worked as a teacher for a year and then was called home to take care of her mother, who was dying from tuberculosis. Her mother had been severely weakened by having so many children, and within a few months of Margaret's return home, she died.

Though it had been a sad time in her life, Margaret gained new direction from the experience of nursing her mother. She had always wanted to help society and she realized that working as a nurse was a way to do that. Shortly after her mother's death, she entered the nursing program at White Plains Hospital. She completed the year-long program then finished her training at the Man-

▲ To help support their ever-growing families, many children worked in factories from an early age

hattan Eye and Ear clinic in New York City in 1900 at the age of twenty-one.

Marriage. While working in New York, Margaret met a young architect, much like her father, named William Sanger. Sanger was politically active and had the same "artist's temperament" as Margaret's father. Her attraction to him led to their getting married shortly after Margaret's graduation from nursing school. They were soon expecting their first son, Stuart, who was followed by a second son, Grant, and a daughter, Peggy. Margaret quit nursing to be a full-time mother until after Peggy was born.

Sees connection between social ills and birth control. When Sanger returned to nursing, she worked as a visiting nurse in some of the worst slums in New York City. She most often was called upon to help deliver babies or nurse desperately weak mothers back to health. Some of these mothers suffered from bearing too many children. Others nearly bled to death because of unsafe abortions, operations that were performed on them to end their pregnancies. With each visit, the women, most of whom had more than ten children, desperately begged Sanger: "Tell me something to keep from having another baby. We cannot afford another yet" (Sanger, p. 87). But by law, Sanger was forbidden from teaching the knowledge they so eagerly sought.

Hearing the desperate cries for birth control on a daily basis, Sanger grew very depressed. Visions of weak and dying mothers—women who could never pull themselves from the depths of poverty because of their fragile health and burdens of their ever-growing families—haunted her sleep. "One by one worried, sad, pensive, and aging faces marshaled themselves before me in my dreams, sometimes appealingly, sometimes accusingly," Sanger said (Sanger, p. 89). She not only felt sad and angry about the condition of these masses of women but felt guilty because there was nothing she could do to help them. Finally, when a young mother who had begged Margaret months before for some means of birth control died from giving birth to yet another child, Sanger snapped. Convinced that the woman had only sought "the knowledge which was her right" and died from lack of that knowledge, Sanger vowed from that moment on "to do something to change the destiny of mothers whose miseries [are] as vast as the sky" (Sanger, p. 92). Sanger had found her cause and was ready to take on the world to fight for it.

Participation: Birth Control Movement

Sanger became convinced that the overall improvement of women's lives and society in general rested on controlling population growth. With this in mind, she quit nursing and spent the next year researching birth control at the library. Sanger then traveled with her family to Europe to learn family-planning techniques. She returned to New York in 1914, armed with knowledge and eager to pass it along to the mothers of New York.

Sanger was ready to take direct action, even if it meant breaking the laws she considered unconstitutional. She decided to take a three-pronged approach to promoting birth control in the United States: education, organization, and legislation. First she would educate the public on birth control using the information she had gathered. Then she would form a birth control organization that would help raise awareness and money for the cause. And finally she would seek to get the Comstock Law, which restricted the sending of birth control information through the mail, overturned. She would also lobby, or pressure, Congress for federal legislation allowing doctors to prescribe birth control devices.

At the time, it was illegal even for married couples to use most forms of birth control, except in the case of medical emergency. While most wealthy women could afford reliable—and illegal—forms of birth control or safe abortions, poor women could only continue to have children or risk death due to unsafe, illegal abortions. Sanger had seen enough women, including her own mother, die due to lack of birth control information and access, and she was determined to bring both to the poor women of the world.

Woman rebel. As the first step in that process, Sanger started her own magazine, the *Woman Rebel*. Working with friends who volunteered their services and funding it through subscriptions paid in advance, she produced and mailed the first issue of the *Woman Rebel* in March 1914 from her small New York City apartment.

A Personal Victory

When Sanger first took up the cause of birth control, her father was not wholly supportive. Though he was known as a rebel himself, making birth control legal seemed far too drastic, even for his liberal mind. Then, while visiting Sanger's apartment one day, federal authorities arrived to arrest her for sending family-planning information through the mail. As he sat in the next room, he listened to his daughter describe why women needed birth control information. She told of hundreds of thousands of families that were stuck in cycles of poverty due to lack of family planning. She described how thousands of women bled to death every year because of illegal abortions or too many births, and how as many children died of hunger or neglect because their families could not afford to properly care for them. As Sanger's father listened, he was so moved that he ran to his daughter, telling her that he now understood that birth control could have saved his own wife's life. Though the federal authorities did not drop their subpoena, Sanger won an important victory. She gained the support of her father.

As publisher, Sanger had complete control over the magazine's content. She wrote her articles for mothers and adolescent young women, announcing in the first issue that the goal was to "stimulate women to think for themselves and to build up a conscious fighting character" (Gray, p. 67). Further, she invited all readers to contribute articles on any subject and promised to back the idea of birth control and convey any knowledge that would help achieve that end.

Not one to back down from controversy, Sanger had a highly combative style, which both helped promote her cause and earned her many enemies. The Catholic Church, opposed to any form of birth control, became one of her fiercest opponents from the outset. Also, she made enemies of politicians and even among many women's groups who thought she should be focusing her attention on women's suffrage (right to vote) instead of family planning. But true to her family background and magazine title, Sanger was proud to be a "woman rebel" and never balked in the face of opposition.

Opposition. There was plenty of opposition. Under the Comstock Law, several issues of the *Woman Rebel* were banned by the U.S. Postal Service, which had sole authority to refuse the mailing of any material it termed "obscene." Rather than tone down her editorial content, however, Sanger wrote in capital letters on the front page of her next issue:

> THE WOMAN REBEL FEELS PROUD THAT THE POST OFFICE AUTHORITIES DID NOT APPROVE OF HER. SHE SHALL BLUSH WITH SHAME IF EVER SHE BE APPROVED BY OFFICIALISM OR "COMSTOCKISM." (Sanger in Gray, p. 69)

When the postal authorities realized they were not going to stop Sanger's efforts, the government stepped in and charged her with nine counts of breaking obscenity laws, which carried a maximum sentence of forty-five years in prison. As a result, Sanger was forced to flee to London for two years, leaving behind her children and husband.

Though the years apart from her home and family were trying for Sanger, she used the time to increase her knowledge and political connections. She gathered information both to strengthen her argument in favor of birth control and to mount a defense against the charges that faced her in the United States. She became familiar with the theory by Thomas Robert Malthus that advocated birth

▲ **Children born into large, poverty-stricken families had to work hard to survive**

control as a means of world stability and peace and with similar arguments by John Stuart Mill and other birth control advocates. Sanger began working such arguments, which were gaining popularity throughout Europe at the time, into her own philosophy.

Starts clinic. In 1915, after repeated attempts through her attorneys in the United States, Sanger was finally able to get the charges against her dropped. She returned to New York, reclaimed her children, and resumed her birth control fight where she had left off. Ready to mount the second and third phases of her plan, organization and legislation, Sanger founded the National Birth

Control League (now the Planned Parenthood Federation of America) and began lecturing across the country and gathering supporters and funds to aid her efforts. Having seen the successful operation of birth control clinics in the Netherlands, Sanger decided she must "challenge the law directly" in the United States and open a birth control clinic in New York City (Sanger, p. 211).

For Women's Well-Being

While men in Europe called for birth control because of economics and world peace, Sanger declared that birth control was necessary because of the personal tragedies of women. She argued that women were denied the right to fulfill themselves as human beings because they were often pregnant and died early deaths on account of too many pregnancies or illegal abortions. Also, children suffered from being born into large, poverty-stricken families. Sanger viewed birth control as basic to freedom: "no woman can call herself free until she can choose consciously whether she will or will not be a mother." (Sanger in Rossi, p. 533)

Clinic and jail. Sanger chose the poor Brownsville section of Brooklyn as the sight of the first birth control clinic in the United States because she knew it was the poor and middle class women who most needed birth control information. Run by three registered nurses—Sanger, her sister Ethel Higgins, and Fania Mindell—the clinic opened on October 16, 1916, and hundreds of women lined up for blocks to get inside. The nurses distributed to all the patients pamphlets printed in English, Yiddish, and Italian titled *What Every Girl Should Know.* The nurses also conducted general checkups, recording details about economic status and number of children to establish case histories. The histories would be used to prove the benefits of birth control on the physical, emotional, and economic well-being of women and their families.

The clinic proved overwhelmingly popular but, as expected, within a few weeks the police conducted a raid and shut it down. Sanger, Higgins, and Mindell were all arrested as hundreds of women poured into the streets of Brooklyn to protest. One woman, who had just arrived as Sanger was being led away by police, chased the police car for blocks and shouted: "Come back! Come back and save me!" (Rossi, p. 532). Sanger was so moved by this woman's plea for help that she became more determined than ever to fight for her clinic. The following day, when the judge told her he was willing to dismiss the charges if she agreed to respect the law and close her clinic, Sanger recalled the woman's desperate words and refused the judge's offer. "I cannot respect the law as it stands today," she said (Sanger, p. 237). She was sentenced to thirty days in a workhouse.

It's only just begun. Unmoved by her second brush with the law, Sanger reopened the clinic upon her release, but this time operated it out of her home. This second clinic employed a female doctor and was funded by an English contributor whom she had met while abroad. Though she was helping women in New York, Sanger felt the need for something to be done on a national level. So she began a national publication to advocate birth control and lectured throughout the country.

Sanger started *The Birth Control Review* in 1921, and during the first five years of publication she received more than one million letters from mothers throughout the nation. On a regular basis, the letters detailed personal horror stories of poverty, dying children, and mothers, sisters, and friends bleeding to death. Women described how they could never get an education or a decent job because they were continually pregnant. Many told of not being able to afford one child yet having ten or more simply because they were not allowed to legally plan the size of their families. Most of the women were poor and could not afford to deliver their babies at hospitals. All the women, no matter what their story, age, or income level, requested birth control information and pleaded for answers to their medical questions.

Hearing such an overwhelming national outcry for birth control, Sanger realized that if federal legislators could read these letters they would see the tremendous need for birth control on the part of the general population. With that in mind, Sanger assembled the best 500 letters into a book titled *Mothers in Bondage,* which she published in 1928. The book proved to be highly influential, and Sanger used it to rally her cause through the next decade.

A million projects. The 1920s and 1930s brought with them not only tremendous political turmoil but great personal turbulence for Sanger. In 1923 she divorced William Sanger and married an older man named Noah Slee. Her daughter, Peggy, died suddenly of tuberculosis, and her two sons entered college.

After Peggy's tragic death, Sanger buried herself in her work. She traveled throughout the world spreading her message of birth control but spent the bulk of her time in America lobbying legislators and the American Medical Association (AMA) in addition to lecturing and publishing her newspaper. She founded a lobbyist group in Washington, D.C., called the National Committee and set up the Clinical Research Bureau of the American Birth Control League to invent cheaper and more effective means of birth control. She organized the first national and international birth control conferences in the world and wrote extensively on the subject, publishing eleven books and pamphlets through 1938.

Sanger attacked birth control opponents on all fronts, and after numerous defeats of birth control legislation in Congress she focused her attention on persuading the AMA to allow doctors to distribute birth control devices. Finally in 1936, after the Supreme Court issued a decision permitting the mailing of birth control information (striking down the Comstock Law), the AMA reversed its position and decided that doctors had the right to distribute birth control devices to their patients. For Sanger, now fifty-seven, the victory could not have been sweeter. A lifetime of effort had finally paid off, and birth control in America became a reality.

Aftermath

Final years. After 1936 Sanger continued to work for affordable and efficient means of birth control and to push for worldwide acceptance of family planning. In 1943 her second husband died and she contracted leukemia. She moved to Tucson, Arizona, and died there on September 6, 1966, at age eighty-seven.

As her son, Grant, said at her death, Sanger was a dedicated woman who nearly single-handedly brought about the legalization of birth control in the United States:

> One thing about my mother that to me was most impressive was her utmost concentration on the [birth control] problem. From the time she started this business until she finished, she never deviated. (Coigney, p. 167)

Impact. Sanger did more than make birth control a reality in the United States. She demonstrated that dedication to a cause could be rewarded in one's lifetime and that there were several ways, from writing a magazine to lobbying Congress, that women in America could effect change.

For More Information

Coigney, Virginia. *Margaret Sanger: Rebel with a cause.* New York: Doubleday, 1969.

Douglas, Emily Taft. *Margaret Sanger: Pioneer of the Future.* New York: Holt, Rinehart and Winston, 1970.

Gray, Madeline. *Margaret Sanger: Champion of Birth Control.* New York: Richard Marek, 1979.

Rossi, Alice S., ed. *The Feminist Papers: From Adams to de Beauvoir.* New York: Columbia University Press, 1973.

Sanger, Margaret. *Margaret Sanger, An Autobiography.* New York: W. W. Norton & Co., 1938.

Bibliography

Adams, Mildred. *The Right to Be People.* Philadelphia/New York: J. B. Lippincott Company, 1966.

Allen, Leslie H., ed. *Bryan and Darrow at Dayton: The Record and Documents of the "Bible–Evolution Trial."* New York: A. Lee & Company, 1925.

Bailyn, Bernard, et al. *The Great Republic: A History of the American People.* Vol. 2. Lexington, Massachusetts: D. C. Heath and Company, 1992.

Bass, Herbert J., ed. *America's Entry into World War I: Submarines, Sentiment, or Security?* New York: Holt, Rinehart and Winston, 1964.

Bontemps, Arna Wendell, ed. *The Harlem Renaissance Remembered.* New York: Dodd, Mead, 1972.

Cashman, Sean Dennis. *America in the Age of the Titans: The Progressive Era and World War I.* New York: New York University Press, 1988.

Catt, Carrie Chapman. *Woman Suffrage and Politics: The Inner Story of the Suffrage Movement.* New York: Charles Scribner's Sons, 1923.

Chambers, John Whiteclay. *The Tyranny of Change: America in the Progressive Era, 1890–1920.* New York: St. Martin's Press, 1992.

Chesler, Ellen. *Woman of Valor: Margaret Sanger and the Birth Control Movement in America.* New York: Simon & Schuster, 1992.

Coigney, Virginia. *Margaret Sanger: Rebel with a Cause.* New York: Doubleday, 1969.

Cordasco, Francesco, ed. *Dictionary of American Immigration History.* Metuchen, New Jersey: Scarecrow Press, 1990.

Cronon, E. David. *Black Moses.* Madison: University of Wisconsin Press, 1969.

Davis, Allen F., and Mary Lynn McGree, eds. *Eighty Years at Hull-House.* Chicago: Quadrangle Books, 1969.

Dawson, Nelson L. *Brandeis and America.* Lexington: University of Kentucky Press, 1989.

Ehrmann, Herbert B. *The Case That Will Not Die.* Boston: Little, Brown and Company, 1969.

Frankel, Noralee, and Nancy S. Dye, eds. *Gender, Class, Race, and Reform in the Progressive Era.* Lexington: University Press of Kentucky, 1991.

Halsey, Francis Whiting. *The Literary Digest History of the World War,* 8 vols. New York: Funk & Wagnalls Co., 1919

Herndon, Booten. *Ford: An Unconventional Biography of the Men and Their Times.* New York: Weybright and Talley, 1969.

Hildebrand, Lorraine Barker. *Straw Hats, Sandals and Steel: The Chinese in Washington State.* Tacoma: Washington State American Revolution Bicentennial Commission, 1977.

Ions, Edmund. *Woodrow Wilson: The Politics of Peace and War.* New York: American Heritage, 1972.

Kennedy, David M. *Birth Control in America.* New Haven: Yale University Press, 1970.

Kramer, Victor A., ed. *The Harlem Renaissance Reexamined.* New York: AMS Press, 1987.

Kraus, Harry P. *The Settlement House Movement in New York City, 1886–1914.* New York: Arno Press, 1980.

Lewis, David. *The Public Image of Henry Ford.* Detroit, Michigan: Wayne State University Press, 1976.

Lewis, John Llewellyn. *The C.I.O. Crusade.* Washington, D.C.: Committee for Industrial Organization, 1937.

Lewty, Peter J. *To the Columbia Gateway: The Oregon Railway and the Northern Pacific, 1879–1884.* Pullman: Washington State University Press, 1987.

Marke, Julius J., ed. *The Holmes Reader.* New York: Oceana Publications, 1955.

May, George S. *A Most Unique Machine.* Grand Rapids, Iowa: William B. Eerdmans, 1975.

McKissack, Pat. *Zora Neale Hurston: Writer and Storyteller.* Hillside, New Jersey: Enslow Publishers, 1992.

Nash, Gary, et al. *The American People: Creating a Nation and a Society.* Vol. 2. New York: Harper and Row, 1986.

Rappaport, Doreen. *The Sacco–Vanzetti Trial.* New York: HarperCollins, 1992.

Rossi, Alice S., ed. *The Feminist Papers: From Adams to de Beauvoir.* New York: Columbia University Press, 1973.

Sacco, Nicola. *The Letters of Sacco and Vanzetti.* Edited by Marion D. Frankfurter and Gardner Jackson. London: Constable, 1929.

Sale, Roger. *Seattle, Past to Present.* Seattle: University of Washington Press, 1976.

Sanger, Margaret. *My Fight for Birth Control.* 1931. Reprinted, New York: Maxwell Reprint Company, 1969.

Schneider, Dorothy, and Carl J. Schneider. *American Women in the Progressive Era, 1900–1920.* New York: Facts on File, 1993.

Sinclair, Upton. *The Jungle.* New York: Grosset & Dunlap, 1906.

Strum, Philippa. *Brandeis: Beyond Progressivism.* Lawrence: University Press of Kansas, 1993.

Takaki, Ronald T., ed. *Strangers from a Different Shore: A History of Asian Americans.* Boston: Little, Brown & Company, 1989.

Urofsky, Melvin I. *A Mind of One Piece: Brandeis and American Reform.* New York: Charles Scribner's Sons, 1971.

Urofsky, Melvin I., and Levy, David W., eds. *"Half Brother Half Son": The Letters of Louis D. Brandeis to Felix Frankfurter.* Norman: University of Oklahoma Press, 1991.

Weinberg, Arthur, and Lila Weinberg. *The Muckrakers.* New York: Simon and Schuster, 1961.

Wise, Winifred. *Jane Addams of Hull House.* New York: Harcourt, Brace and Company, 1935.

Zieger, Robert H. *American Workers, American Unions, 1920–1985.* Baltimore, Maryland: Johns Hopkins University Press, 1986.

Zo, Kil Young. *Chinese Emigration into the United States, 1850–1880.* New York: Arno Press, 1978.

Index

Boldface indicates profiles.

C

D

E

F

G

H

M

N

U

V

W

Y

Z

Significant Events and the People Who Shaped Them

Volume 5: *Reconstruction to the Spanish-American War (1863-1898)*

Reconstruction
Andrew Johnson, Thaddeus Stevens
Indians and Government Policy
George Armstrong Custer, Carl Schurz, Chief Joseph
Labor Movement
George Pullman, Samuel Gompers, Mary "Mother" Jones
Struggle for Civil Rights
Ida B. Wells-Barnett, Booker T. Washington, W.E.B. Du Bois
Realism in American Literature
Mark Twain, Stephen Crane, Helen Hunt Jackson
Social Reform
Elizabeth Cady Stanton, Josephine Shaw Lowell, Frances Willard
Spanish American War
William McKinley, William Randolph Hearst, Theodore Roosevelt

Volume 6: *Immigration to Women's Rights and Roles (1880-1936)*

Immigration
Chin Gee-hee, Bartolomeo Vanzetti, Abraham Cahan
Social Welfare
Jane Addams, Herbert Croly, Louis Brandeis, Upton Sinclair, Ida Tarbell
World War I
Woodrow Wilson, John J. Pershing, Oliver Wendell Holmes
Industrial Growth
Henry Ford, John L. Lewis
Scopes Trial
Clarence Darrow, William Jennings Bryan
Harlem Renaissance
Marcus Garvey, James Weldon Johnson, Zora Neale Hurston
Women's Rights and Roles
Carrie Chapman Catt, Margaret Sanger